Poets in Their Time

Poets in Their Time

Essays on English poetry
from Donne to Larkin

BARBARA EVERETT

faber and faber

LONDON · BOSTON

First published in 1986 by
Faber and Faber Limited
3 Queen Square London WC1N 3AU

Photoset by Wilmaset Birkenhead Wirral
Printed in Great Britain by
Mackays of Chatham Ltd Lordswood Kent
All rights reserved

British Library Cataloguing in Publication Data

Everett, Barbara
Poets in their time: Essays on English poetry from
Donne to Larkin.
1. English poetry—History and criticism
I. Title
821'.009   PR502

ISBN 0-571-13978-7

Library of Congress Cataloging-in-Publication Data

Poets in their time.

1. English poetry—History and criticism. I. Everett,
Barbara.
PR403.P65 1986   821'.009   86-11594
ISBN 0-571-13978-7

Contents

Acknowledgements

The essays in this volume have previously appeared in the following publications:

'Donne: A London Poet', (Chatterton Lecture on an English Poet), *Proceedings of the British Academy*, 1972. Reprinted from *Selections from British Academy Chatterton Lectures* (OUP for the British Academy), by permission of the British Academy.

'The Shooting of the Bears: Poetry and Politics in Andrew Marvell', (Ferens Fine Art Lecture in the University of Hull), in *Andrew Marvell: Essays on the Tercentenary of his Death*, ed. R. L. Brett (OUP, 1979).

'The End of the Big Names: Milton's Epic Catalogues', in *English Renaissance Studies*, ed. John Carey (OUP, 1980).

'The Sense of Nothing', in *Spirit of Wit: Reconsiderations of Rochester*, ed. Jeremy Treglown (Basil Blackwell, 1982).

'Tibbles', in *London Review of Books*, 17 October 1985.

'Somebody Reading', in *London Review of Books*, 21 June 1984.

'Browning Versions', in *London Review of Books*, 4 August 1983.

'The New Style of Sweeney Agonistes', in *English Satire and the Satiric Tradition*, ed. Claude Rawson (Basil Blackwell, 1984).

'Auden Askew', in *London Review of Books*, 19 November 1981.

'Philip Larkin: After Symbolism', in *Essays in Criticism*, July, 1980.

'Larkin's Edens', in *English*, Spring 1982.

'Poetry and Soda', in *London Review of Books*, 5 February 1981.

Preface

Most of these essays were written in the last five or six years. But the first, on Donne as a London poet, dates back to the early 1970s. Few of Donne's readers can fail to be struck by the fact that, with all his abstraction, he gives a strangely strong sense of the world he lived in. Trying to define what I called his 'London' medium involved the bringing together of historical study with literary criticism. But it also made it seem false to regard the two things as separable: a process that sometimes leads historians to treat literature as a kind of modest footnote to history. History is after all just what we define it as. An invitation (a few years after the Donne essay) to write on 'Poetry and Politics in Andrew Marvell' took me into that world of the Civil Wars which forced Marvell's contemporaries to live out 'history' day by day. A large part of the reality that the seventeenth century has for us now is the creation of the greater writers of the time, those who were capable of translating events into meditated and conscious experience. Through their writings, history speaks with a fully human voice.

The interaction of the literary and the historical may be clearest in the work of these late Renaissance writers, caught up as they were in a moment of profound historical change. But any good poet can focus for us this vivid sense of the life of his own time. (Indeed, one of the reasons why poets appear to resist and resent attempts at biography may be their simple feeling that their own work is already biographical in essence.) A poet will, however, embody his time for us only if we read him as a poet and not as a crypto-historian – and give due attention to matters that can seem as contingent as Marvell's metres or Browning's syntax or Larkin's imagery. It is in such a belief that I have written these essays, necessarily varying the approach according to the very different circumstances and times of the poets in question. For giving me occasion to do so I am grateful to all those mentioned in the Acknowledgements. I owe especial thanks to Karl Miller, Editor of the *London Review of Books*, and to Craig Raine, Poetry Editor of Faber and Faber. Emrys Jones and Hester Everett Jones have helped most of all.

Donne: A London Poet

Donne's most recent biographer calls him 'a Londoner born and bred'.[1] Donne was born a few streets east of St Paul's, and it was in the environs of St Paul's and as its Dean that he died sixty years later. It is there too that his funeral effigy still stands, one of the very few to survive the Great Fire. The epitaph on it speaks of Donne looking eastward, towards 'eum cuius nomen est Oriens'. But Donne spent his youth and his prime looking westward – west towards the Court and towards those centres of power which had in his own lifetime finally established themselves in the capital. Donne was an ambitious man: he desired to be better than he was; and he did not lose his worldliness when he entered the Church – that Church whose Bishops had on the King's orders defended the depraved Countess of Essex the year before they ordained the poet. For Donne's life spans a period during which it was not possible, certainly not wise, to think with much simplicity about 'worldliness'; if it had been so, Shakespeare could not have written *Hamlet*. Or, to put the matter in terms of place rather than time, Donne was – despite the abstract habits of thought which might appear to dissociate him from place – a Londoner by nature as well as by birth and breeding, a man who (as Walton put it) 'could not leave his beloved London, to which place he had a natural inclination'. And he was a Londoner at that crucial phase in the city's history when it took on the character by which we recognize it now. For in Donne's lifetime London became a metropolis.

The emergence of London as a metropolis at the end of the sixteenth century – as one of the world's great cities, with a quarter of a million souls in it – is a fact on which historians of the period have recently much insisted, partly because the inordinate growth

[1] R. C. Bald, *John Donne: A Life* (Oxford, 1970), p. 19.

of London created such a crisis of awareness in Londoners
themselves. When Donne was a boy of eight, London's Lord
Mayor and Aldermen were already appealing to the Privy Council
for legislation whereby the alarming expansion and overcrowding
of 'this great metropolis' might be contained.[1] And the Proclama-
tion that answered this appeal was only the first move in four
centuries of struggle to meet the human problem posed by the
growth of the city. In the forty or so years since Henry VIII had
died, London had become a new Rome (and it was, apparently,
actually called 'Romeville' in the thieves' jargon of the time). The
sense of size is a relative thing: Donne's City and suburbs were
small in extent compared with Greater London today, but his
contemporaries had a notion of their city not by any means unlike
our own. '*Rome* was a *Metropolis*', wrote Thomas Heywood in
1612, 'a place whither all the nations knowne under the Sunne,
resorted: so is *London*.'[2] Or, to quote Professor Jordan, the
distinguished historian of London's charities: 'The London of 1600
was . . . a great urban complex. It was a metropolis in every sense
of the word, with an immense wealth and a size which compara-
tively made cities of the next rank seem no more than large
provincial towns.'[3] Some sense of what was happening to London
may be painlessly acquired if one contemplates for a few minutes
three of those map-pictures or long views of the City which have
survived from the sixteenth and seventeenth centuries. In the 1540s
Wyngaerde came to London and drew with economy and delicacy
the outline of an airy Tudor river-town that clustered round the
curve of the Thames. In about 1600 Visscher sent his traders' and
travellers' Thames in a straight line across seven feet of wall space,
and banked up behind it an incredible density of houses and towers
and spires and shops. The viewer stands in Southwark and looks
through the masts of great trading vessels into the City of 'profit
and loss' itself. When in the 1640s Wenceslas Hollar came, he drew
from above the grand prospect of a city that one now sees as almost
Restoration before the Fire and before Wren, so purely and widely
urban is the London he surveyed.

It was this astonishingly developing city, the 'national centre for
risk capital' as Jordan calls it, that produced John Donne; the son of

[1] See Norman G. Brett-James, *The Growth of Stuart London* (1935), pp. 67–8.
[2] *An Apologie for Actors* (1612), sig. C².
[3] W. K. Jordan, *The Charities of London 1480–1660* (1960), p. 16.

one of those rich London merchants who were as munificently and
independently philanthropic as they were mercenary, and who
played so large a part in giving their city its standing and its
character. Many of London's inhabitants came, made their fortune
(or lost it), and went home again. Donne was born there, lived there,
and died there. To appreciate this fact adds, I think, something to our
understanding of him as a writer. That there is some obvious and
simple sense in which Donne was a London poet may be perceived
by opening the *Songs and Sonnets* in the format of its first edition and
reflecting on the chaotic and formidable variety of available
experience that assails the reader there, as it might a country visitor
to the capital. The voices of the poems constitute a crowd; and in this
milieu to think, to discriminate, or to *be* at all with any individuality
it was necessary (so the poems seem to say) to withdraw to that
characteristic Donne place, the enclosed bedroom of lovers
overlooking a street from which arises all the perpetual noise of life.
The restless vitality of these poems, their arrogant expertise and
quick boredom, their amusement and anxiety and fatigue – these are
recognizably metropolitan qualities. But I should like to go on from
this superficial impression to explore some further senses in which
Donne might be called a London poet. Some of my definitions are
far removed from any literal or topographical meaning. Yet Donne's
own sense of London admits of the metaphorical: for him as for
anyone a familiar place was pre-eminently a fact of consciousness.
As he himself wrote: 'I do not make account that I am come to
London, when I get within the wall: that which makes it *London* is
the meeting of friends.'[1] Necessarily I am concerned here less with
the London of history than with 'that which made it London' to
Donne.

I

We can none the less meet in Donne a city evoked with that vitality
of social observation that was to characterize Donne's coeval
Jonson nearly a decade later. For Donne's most vivid evocation of
London comes in the first of his Satires, which must be the product
of his early twenties when he was still a student at Lincoln's Inn.

[1] *Letters to Severall Persons of Honour: written by John Donne Sometime Deane of St
Pauls London* (1651), p. 285.

This brilliant, original poem is mainly a monologue spoken by a
young scholar. He meditates on London – for he is being tempted
to forsake his bookish isolation and 'go on the town'. The tempter
is the poem's second voice, from whom we hear snatches, and of
whose person we catch glimpses, in its second half. He is the
antithesis of the scholar – Zany to his Pedant (if we think in terms
of the Zanni and Dottore of the *commedia dell'arte*):[1] a 'fondling
motley humorist' whose hunger to wander equals the other's
loyalty to a life that is for all its narrowness secure and sanctioned
by the wisdom of those dead philosophers, historians, and poets
who line the shelves of his grave-sized study: 'Let me lye / In
prison, and here be coffin'd, when I dye.' The dazzlingly animated
opening fifty lines disclose a prospect of crowded London streets
from which sharp details stand out: here the 'Captaine . . . / Bright
parcell gilt, with forty dead mens pay', there the silhouetted gesture
of salute by which the errant friend prices the passers-by: 'and to
that rate / So high or low, dost raise thy formall hat.' What Donne
is doing here, however, is very characteristic of him. This animated
scene is not (as we soon learn) the real thing – it is only the young
scholar's half-appalled and half-enchanted fantasy: for this prospect
of the London streets is only a reverie, entertained in anticipation,
and we have still to descend into the London of actuality. The point
at which we do so (hard to discern otherwise) is signalled by an
abrupt change of style. The addressed friend ceases to be *thou* and
becomes *he*; the reader ceases to stand in for that friend and
becomes an onlooker. The pair move into visible action before us:
we immerse in activity and are surrounded by crowd-like voices in
an acoustic effect almost stereophonic. And now the voices of the
two friends intertwine to the point at which their identities are
confused, despite the fact that their roles are in theory so far apart:

> Now leaps he upright, joggs me, 'and cryes, 'Do 'you see
> Yonder well favour'd youth?' 'Which?' 'Oh, 'tis hee
> That dances so divinely.' 'Oh', said I,
> 'Stand still, must you dance here for company?'
> Hee droop't, wee went . . .
>
> 'But Oh, God strengthen thee, why stoop'st thou so?'
> 'Why? He hath travail'd.' 'Long?' 'No, but to me'

[1]The pair recur a decade later as Morose and Truewit in Jonson's first London
comedy *Epicoene* (1609).

(Which understand none,) 'he doth seeme to be
Perfect French, and Italian.' I reply'd,
'So is the Poxe.'[1]

And then, the two young voices still casually running on, a third
change of style occurs, this time into rapid narrative, to record with
a negligent detachment the fate of the zany friend:

At last his Love he in a windowe spies,
And like light dew exhal'd, he flings from mee
Violently ravish'd to his lechery.
Many were there, he could command no more;
He quarrell'd, fought, bled; and turn'd out of dore
   Directly came to mee hanging the head,
   And constantly a while must keepe his bed.

So the poem ends.

This First Satire appears to drift aimlessly. Indeed its easy
rambling movement, as of a liberated self-abandonment to
whatever happens, is one of its chief charms. It flaunts a lordly
sprezzatura, as if its author isn't really trying. But in the modern
world a sense of the fortuitous may be a main route to the sense of
the real. Moreover the poem's structural peculiarity of vagrant
progress is reinforced by the topicality of reference: one can learn
things from it about the London of the early and mid-1590s as from
a newspaper – the rich heiresses, the thinking horse, the vogue for
black feathers. It seems clear that Donne has been taught by those
Roman satirists to whom he went to school, that satire must be, if
not urbane, at least urban; that it must focus itself on some central
civilized community. He borrows Horace's device of a saunter
through a peopled city in which there is much to entertain and
much to provoke derision; he takes over too the sophisticated
complication of Horace's dialogue formula. From Juvenal Donne
perhaps learned that a personal relation to a great city both loved
and detested was worth the expressing. In his third Satire (used
again by the Augustan Johnson in *his London*) Juvenal had created
one of the most brilliant crowd scenes in literature, and its powerful

[1]Quotations from Donne's Satires and Verse Letters are from the edition by W.
Milgate (Oxford, 1967); from the Elegies and Songs and Sonnets, that by Dame
Helen Gardner (Oxford, 1967); from the Divine Poems, that by Dame Helen
Gardner (Oxford, 1952); from The Anniversaries, that by Sir Herbert Grierson
(Oxford, 1912).

rendering of the feeling of physical immersion may have lingered in Donne's memory. Both these poets of Rome, Horace and Juvenal, helped Donne towards the half-casual re-creation of London in the image of Rome nearly a century before the English Augustans were to do it again. For it was in the last quarter of the sixteenth century, when London became a metropolis, that English poets were first able to make full imaginative use of the most metropolitan of the Roman poets.

There is a third debt to Roman poetry which must be accounted for. The dialogue between the young men which I have quoted takes its conventions neither from Horace's nor from Juvenal's more straightforward exchanges but from the mannered and knotted burst of conversation that opens the first Satire of Horace's younger imitator, Persius. Later in this satire Persius explains the principles of his dialogue: the second voice is, he says, merely an 'imaginary opponent'. I think it possible that Donne took a hint from Persius here in that his poem is as much an internalized debate as it is a piece of reporting. Of Donne's two young men, who are so closely involved with each other as to be at moments indistinguishable, one is a dominant, detached, and talkative scholar (the 'Pedant'), who loves the stability of theory, even though it may resemble the security of the prison and the grave. The other (the 'Zany') is an impulsive and susceptible clown, who wanders as the appetite for mere experience leads him – and it leads him finally to the 'stability' of the lecher's and brawler's sick-bed. It is not difficult to recognize the younger Donne in the learned and fanciful scholar. And though the 'grinning, smacking, shrugging' friend may seem a less familiar persona, it is relevant to recall that in an early verse letter romantically addressed to a young friend Donne refers to himself as 'Thy debtor, thy echo, thy foil, thy zany' – and there is much of the 'zany' that emerges in his poetry. Both young men, scholar and clown, may be twin aspects of the personality of which Walton was later to say: 'The melancholy and pleasant humour were in him so contempered, that each gave advantage to the other, and made his company one of the delights of mankind' (*pleasant* here meaning of course 'humorous' or 'amusing'). The zany friend of the First Satire, at any rate, is foolish mainly through his desire to be at the centre of things, a desire close to an impulse recurrent in Donne's writings and derisively captured in one of his Elegies:

> Although wee see celestiall bodies move
> Above tие earth, the earth we till and love:
> So we her ayres contemplate, words and hart
> And vertues; But we love the Centrique part.

We can in fact speak of the First Satire as less externalized commentary than internalized debate, a 'dialogue of one' in which London – though loved and hated as was Juvenal's Rome – becomes a setting more figurative than the Roman capital was to Juvenal. In Donne's scenic poems, 'The Storm' and 'The Calm', he was to portray a world of natural phenomena gone almost out of the mind's control. The London of the Satire has something of the chaotic violence of the Nature of these two poems – and the two young men are arguing about its value. Yet to say so much may have the effect of obscuring the poem's form, which expresses not debate but event. The two voices which become confused in the course of the dialogue suggest that what is happening concerns not two persons but change in one person. For all its realism, therefore, the anecdote is a fable suggestive of that natural and necessary passage, incessantly repeated in an individual's life, by which the mind's quietness gives way to the confusions of existence, and is exhilarated, and learns, and suffers loss. The movement here, that is to say, is closely related to that 'launching out' which Donne contemplates with a melancholy and humorous reluctance in *The Progresse of the Soule*:

> O let me not launch out, but let mee save
> Th'expense of braine and spirit; that my grave
> His right and due, a whole unwasted man may have.

This movement finds also a curious echo in the sentence with which Walton was reflectively to summarize Donne's situation some years after the writing of this satire, at the marriage that might have helped his rising fortunes but in fact ruined them:

> Mr Donne's estate was the greatest part spent in many and chargeable travels, books, and dear-bought experience: he out of all employment that might yield a support for himself and wife, who had been curiously and plentifully educated; both their natures generous, and accustomed to confer, and not to receive, courtesies.

The First Satire, one might say finally, is a poem about 'chargeable

travels' and 'dear-bought experience', a subject that goes deep into
what moved Donne as a poet throughout his career. There is an
implicit acceptance in Donne's writing that a man must go on his
travels and that one must make for the centre, the metropolis of
experience; it also accepts that the trip is likely to be dear-bought.
The scholar in the First Satire is without any real hesitation as he
descends into the streets, foretelling precisely what will happen –
'Come, let's go.' The lover of the Elegies never questions his sad
departures, but briskly 'bids farewell'. Among the *Songs and
Sonnets*, all Donne's tenderest poems are valedictions. And the
speaker in the magnificent, and magnificently worldly, late 'Hymn
to Christ' sets out without illusion on a journey that he knows will
wreck him:

> To see God only, I goe out of sight:
> And to scape stormy dayes, I chuse
> An Everlasting night.

II

Donne's Ovidian Elegies seem to have been written more or less
contemporaneously with the Satires, during the early and middle
years of the 1590s. The heroines of these love-poems (if one can call
them heroines, and if one can call it love) belong with those
'Daughters of London . . . / As gay as Flora, and as rich as Inde'
whom Donne salutes elsewhere. The sociological interest of these
Elegies, the sense in them of the historical London, does not extend
much further than that. These poems are uneven, perhaps only
intermittently focused, and not at all easy to be dogmatic about, yet
parts of them have power as well as wit. I would suggest that they
are most lively where we feel the friction of divided tones. For in
these Elegies Donne's creativity seems often to be a matter of
discovering situations and tones which reflect an ambiguous
response to experience – of giving voice once more to the Pedant
and the Zany, who find themselves this time in a more simply
amorous context. It is in this fashion that Donne is a London poet.

By means of this development of dramatically divided tones,
Donne re-works Ovid as radically and as originally as he reworked
Horace, Persius, and Juvenal in his figurative narrative. He seems
to be learning something both from the early comic Shakespeare

and from the brilliant Marlowe of the poems, as he creates here and
there an almost purely comical relation between the sober and
judicious voice of the narrator and the foolish presence of his own
zany desires, or of his mistress's body, or of any of the other
ludicrous appurtenances of a love intrigue:

> I taught my silkes, their whistling to forbeare,
> Even my opprest shoes, dumbe and speechlesse were.

So says the hero of the Fourth Elegy, 'The Perfume', who tells how a
secret affair was wrecked by his hapless choice of too pungent a
scent. The young lovers struggle to achieve the Roman pleasures of
an illicit *amour* while plunged up to the neck in the confusions of
English family life: threatening father, tired mother, hordes of
younger children making their way in and out of the bedroom all
night, and with all this the intimate betrayal by *things* – clothes,
shoes, the wrong perfume. The hero is in theory an ambitious, even
rather nasty, Ovidian seducer, but he finds himself committed to the
whole confounding and chaotic world of practical existence: things,
bodies, families, smells, London. And so, between intention and
performance, he stumbles, an exasperated, affectionate, and
would-be brutish dandy. In the Seventh Elegy, 'Tutelage' ('Nature's
lay Ideot, I taught thee to love'), we meet again this exasperated
dandy, patiently teaching 'the Alphabet of flowers' to one who is
clearly the dumbest of girls. Amusing as the image is, and fabricated
though it may be, it helps to offset that more prevalent image of
Donne as the lewd seducer that takes support from the more
apparently simply sensual of the Elegies. For even 'Love's Progress'
and 'Going to Bed' share the cool and amused element that one finds
in Shakespeare's comic–erotic Mannerist poem *Venus and Adonis* or
in Marlowe's more classical – but still funny – *Hero and Leander*.
Donne's two Elegies are surprisingly abstract pieces that play theme
and variations on what passes for a concrete procedure. 'Love's
Progress' wanders round the 'Centrique part' with a movement as
erratic as that of the two young men in the First Satire; and the more
the lines speak of the 'right true end' of love, the more the vagrancy
tells that the lover is both lunatic and poet, his desire indistinguish-
able from his fantasy. Similarly few first readers of 'Going to Bed'
have not, I imagine, been surprised to realize when the poem ends
that the proposed event has yet to begin, and that the speaker has so
far managed to undress no one but himself.

So much must be said of the ambiguous tone of the Elegies, the metropolitan wariness and humour with which they embark on erotic adventures. But these poems are far from satires, and it would be misleading to overstress their critical tone. To do so, we would have to ignore their 'zany' side, their capacity for total immersion in an experience, so that the most critical of readers is convinced so long as he reads. Even to call the Elegies anything as clear-cut as comedies would be a mistake, from another point of view. A comparison with the early Shakespeare would bring out how relatively unfocused mood and attitude are in these poems. Shakespeare has from the beginning a far firmer grip on his comic subject, the humour and pathos of man's dual nature in love; he achieves early and with little strain an almost classical generality of comic wisdom. But it is perhaps easier for a man to know what he thinks about love in Arcadia (or Navarre, or Athens) than in the City of London.

If one bears in mind such reservations as these, one may be in a better position to appreciate the degree and nature of Donne's success in the most striking of the Elegies, the sixteenth, 'On his Mistris'. He has in this poem invented a situation which, however odd it may seem, serves his needs perfectly. Much of the poem's power lies in the truthfulness of its mixed feelings. From the famous first line – 'By our first strange and fatall interview' – a voice speaks with tenderness, exasperation, pain, urgency, and humour. The curiously angular realism of the situation, by which a man persuades a woman *not* to accompany him in the disguise of a page, has been explained in terms of pure autobiography, but the poem's human warmth and poignancy have also prompted comparisons with *Romeo and Juliet*. Neither of these appeals to fact or fiction seems to me to get quite close enough to the actual substance of the Elegy. On the fictional side, Donne's sense of pain is not Shakespeare's; he lacks Shakespeare's *gravitas*, the tranquillity arising from a deep sense of the natural. Donne is much nearer in this Elegy to a work more internationally famous in the period than anything by Shakespeare: the Spanish prose classic *Celestina*. Rojas's long narrative presents the tragic fall of two young lovers and their nurse-bawd in a way that blends a piercing romanticism with a startlingly modern realism and harsh humour. One of the peculiarities of Rojas's powerful story is that though it contains great psychological accuracy in the telling, its tragedy is ultimately unexplained. The lovers take it for granted that they cannot marry and must meet furtively; but no reason is given why they cannot. This absence of primary motivation in no way impairs the work. Indeed its refusal to explain throws all the greater stress on the 'explanation' the reader makes for himself: he responds in terms of that profound fatalism of true romance that believes love to be unlucky and that expects a *Liebestod*. The strangeness of Donne's story – of a girl who wants to assume disguise – works, I suggest, in precisely the same way as *Celestina*. The element of the random, the chancy, projects us forward immediately into an excited anxiety whose cause is purely psychological. So too with the urgent repetitions of the Elegy's opening lines: they take us back by rhetoric to the plangent desolation of true romanticism, the authentic and brooding Petrarchan distress in which nothing lies ahead but *Laura in morte*.

If the Sixteenth Elegy relates in any way to real life, to 'fact', – and its anecdotal allusiveness awakes a sense of the real – then its facts are not biographical but psychological. The poem has a movement, circuitous but purposive, which is remarkably like that of the First Satire. Donne even uses the same device of a violently syncopated rhythm to give his sense of immersion in the world of the debauched Europeans –

> Men of France, changeable Camelions,
> Spittles of diseases, shops of fashions

– as he used when he described the London crowds. And the friend's rough fate in a brothel brawl ('quarrell'd, fought, bled') has its parallel – even a verbal echo ('taken, stabb'd, bleede') – in the imagined death of the lover. But in the Elegy the act of violence is given a finer form, in keeping with its more complex function: it here becomes – odd though the notion may seem – the climax of a nightmare which the lover warns his mistress *not* to give way to. The violence is thus deeply inset in a fiction within a fiction: fear (faced with sufficient bravado) becomes a controlled fantasy – is even, with luck, exorcized. The poem ends with the lover telling his mistress to

> walk in expectation, till from thence
> Our great King call thee into his presence.
> When I am gone, dreame mee some happinesse,
> Nor let thy lookes our long hid love confesse,

> Nor praise, nor dispraise mee, blesse, nor curse
> Openly loves force; nor in bed fright thy nurse
> With midnights startings, crying out, oh, oh
> Nurse, oh my love is slaine; I saw him goe
> Ore the white Alpes, alone; I saw him, I,
> Assayld, fight, taken, stabb'd, bleede, fall, and dye.
> Augure mee better chance, unless dreade Jove
> Think it enough for mee, to 'have had thy love.

In its psychological insight and its exquisite poise the close of the Sixteenth Elegy looks beyond anything in the First Satire.

At the end of this Elegy we hear for the first time a note that gives power to some of the best of the *Songs and Sonnets*. The poet's response blends longing and fear, attraction and recoil: from the tension between the two comes the nervous charge so characteristic of Donne's poetry – that almost electrical quality that energizes the reader and yet makes its harassing demands upon him. It is by virtue of this power that Donne earns the right to be called our first (perhaps our only) real master of the poetry of urban anxiety, the love poet of the 'national centre for risk capital'. In their ability to convert anxiety into an empowering force – to live on their nerves – any of Donne's lovers might ask

> what other way have wee,
> But to marke when, and where the darke eclipses bee?

One might take as representative of this conversion of apprehension into boldness and balance the archetypal hero and heroine of the 'Lecture upon the Shadow', pacing under the glare of the noonday sun and reflecting upon their condition:

> These three houres that we have spent,
> Walking here, two shadowes went
> Along with us, which we our selves produc'd;
> But, now the Sunne is just above our head,
> We doe those shadowes tread;
> And to brave clearenesse all things are reduc'd.

These instructive lovers, moving with the upright steadiness the level rhythm suggests, take with them a shadow ahead and shadow behind, one in space and one in time, one the suspicion of others and the other the doubt of themselves. Their very uprightness derives from the tension of being between shadow and shadow, and knowing it. And their dignity derives also from the dangerousness of the situation, in which love is defined only as some completely central noonday moment of feeling at which all is always crisis: 'And his first minute, after noone, is night.' The poem's sharp-edged brilliance consists in this exclusiveness. Indeed one of the most impressive things about it (as with so many of Donne's poems, but here to an extreme degree) is the amount of the natural which the poem finds expendable. It contains nothing but sun, shadow, lovers, nerves, and rhetoric. The tension that results is quite alien to that natural or pastoral wisdom which might teach its persons how to 'abide the change of time', as do the couples of Shakespearian romance. Donne's lovers belong to the great city, and they are powered by an anxiety as acute as it could be without sacrificing their lucidity. Their balance, and the 'brave clearness' of this whole abrupt and nervous poem, is a poise of alternatives reckoned with, an art of balancing upright on shadows.

III

Comparatively little has been said about Donne as a conscious stylist; not surprisingly, because a marked naturalism is so much a feature of his style. I now want to argue that he is in fact a London artist in another sense: a man who writes out of an extreme consciousness of himself as an artist and an equal consciousness of the 'understanders', that sophisticated audience for whom he writes, men and women likely to miss nothing. The naturalism of the style, that is to say, is in itself – like the apparently random structure of the First Satire and the Sixteenth Elegy – an effect of art. In the verse letters we meet, in place of the flawless *cantabile* of some of the *Songs and Sonnets*, a poet making himself master of that essentially English mode, the off-hand style. For Donne writes here as angularly to his friends as to those great ladies he was obliged to flatter. He likes to seem to be involved in a stumbling, stammering battle with language from which a cadence or a tenderness will suddenly float free, as though friendship or civility or writing at all were a matter of working against the grain of things until the miraculous happens:

> For 'twere in us ambition to write

> Soe, that because wee two, you two unite,
> Our letter should as you, bee infinite.

And at times he does this also, though more sweetly, in the lyrics of the *Songs and Sonnets*:

> These burning fits but meteors bee,
>   Whose matter in thee is soone spent.
> Thy beauty, 'and all parts, which are thee,
>   Are unchangeable firmament.

Donne distrusts the conventionally aesthetic, and often devotes his large verbal mastery to writing like an amateur: sometimes, as in the echoic and parodic Fourth Satire, with an effect of virtuoso clowning. There is possibly a clue here to two of his most famous stylisms, his rhythmic syncopation, and his use of conceits. He will with deliberation destroy the harmony of a lyric verse line; or withdraw from an emotional effect, by interposing a conceit that forces upon us the coolest intellectuality. He is a master of certain kinds of aesthetic or emotional spell, but like many artists of his time will repeatedly break that spell in order to assert the claims of life and reason.

The later sixteenth century was of course a great age of applied rhetoric; all the major arts of the time were public arts, arts for an audience. It is no accident that Donne, who was trained in the law, was in youth 'a great frequenter of plays', and later became a famous preacher. It throws some light on the peculiar artistry of the *Songs and Sonnets*, to recall that place in the letters where Donne speaks of the blessings and delights of good company, of family and friends, and then adds that he tends to be 'not the lesse alone, for being in the midst of them'.[1] Similarly, in his poems there is often a perfect equilibrium between their exact truth to mood and feeling and their acute awareness of an audience. Like an actor, he can give to any attitude, however complex and difficult, a splendidly full consciousness; he brings it, one might say, into full daylight. The reader of such poems finds a pleasure of concentration, of commitment, wittily involved with the pleasure of freedom: one thinks this because one chooses, not because one is compelled; and having thought it one may go on to think

[1] *Letters*, p. 45.

something else. This is the side of Donne that he himself described as a 'vertiginous giddiness', a ceaseless awareness of the mind's and will's alternatives. And in the libertine poems especially he shows himself to be (to quote him once again, this time from *Pseudo-Martyr*) a man who needed 'freedome and libertie, as in all other indifferent things, so in my studies also, not to betroth or enthral my self, to any one science, which should possesse or denominate me'.[1] So he writes

> Thus I reclaim'd my buzard love, to flye
> At what, and when, and how, and where I chuse;
>   Now negligent of sport I lye,
>   And now as other Fawkners use,
> I spring a mistresse, sweare, write, sigh and weepe;
> And the game kill'd, or lost, goe talke, and sleepe.

Many of the slighter of the *Songs and Sonnets* – and libertine poems like 'Loves Diet', which I have just quoted, are among them – have this special virtue of their own: their splendid surface lucidity gives pleasure in itself, but it also rides, or controls, considerable inward complexity, tonal or psychological or referential. If we look back at 'Loves Diet' we see that the man who speaks with such careless savagery of the 'game' does so in a tone whose chief effect is one of controlled purity. And it is clear from the rest of 'Loves Diet' that the speaker's libertinism has a good deal to do with failed or reluctant devotion, is an idealism *manqué*. Some of these libertine poems are complex in a different way. The title of 'The Indifferent', the phrase 'things indifferent' in 'Communitie', and possibly 'indifferent things' in the sentence I have just quoted from *Pseudo-Martyr* all (I would suggest) make glancing allusion to the important Reformation doctrine (associated mainly with rationalism and with the radical or Lutheran left-wing) of adiaphorism, or indifferentism – some things only are necessary to salvation, the rest are indifferent to it.[2] To meet such allusions is to be alerted to the breadth of range in which Donne's libertine poetry operates. It is focused on erotic experience but it resonates in a

[1] *Pseudo-Martyr* (1610), Preface, sig. B 2.
[2] See, for example, the brief discussions of adiaphorism in A. G. Dickens, *The English Reformation* (1964), pp. 78–9, 180.

wider area that is moral, intellectual, and theological.[1] This is very much poetry of the Elizabethan university graduate, setting to work his large but otherwise underemployed talents. We should not at any rate underestimate the degree of tonal complexity in even the lightest of these poems. 'Marke but this flea' opens a seduction poem with the prosy gravity of a sermonizing parson, a tone supported by theological allusion throughout; and the comparison throws an odd light on both preacher and seducer. The limpid directness of the moralist of 'Communitie' –

> Good wee must love and must hate ill,
> For ill is ill, and good good still

– leads, as it happens, straight into sexual anarchy. And the man who discovers, in 'The Indifferent', an uproarious promiscuity –

> I can love both faire and browne,
> Her whom abundance melts, and her whom want betraies

– is given by the liturgical rhythms of the piece all the modest pride of some well-brought-up lad just awarded the prize for universal charity. The presence of these bright tones is always a danger signal in Donne. Later in life, and hoping to make his way in the world, he preferred these worldly but provocative poems not to pass around too freely. They are not 'safe' poems: they have all the dangerousness of 'brave cleareness', the capacity to hold on to the logic of an idea until it emerges into an alarming daylight. Their 'free speech' has sometimes even a self-destructiveness in it, the power to undermine its own apparent premises. The preposterous comminator in 'The Curse' gets so involved in the artistry of his hatred as finally to lose interest in hating; the deserted lover in 'The Apparition' hates so hard that he finds out that he must be in love after all. This sharp paradoxicality occurs even in such things as the beautiful, pellucid opening of 'A Feaver':

> Oh doe not die, for I shall hate
>   All women so, when thou art gone,
> That thee I shall not celebrate,
>   When I remember, thou wast one

---

[1] William Empson discusses the theological bearing of some of Donne's love poems in 'Donne the Space Man', *Kenyon Review* (1957).

– where Donne comes very close to suggesting that for this beneficent lady to give up the ghost just then would be a foolish, or even a fatal, mistake as far as he is concerned. In all these poems conventional surfaces are both brilliantly displayed and yet dangerously undermined. This elusive 'dangerousness' makes one want to demur somewhat over that epithet most often applied to Donne: 'passionate'. The word is not unjust, since it takes account of what is most there to be noticed, the strange strength of the author's personality as it issues in a voice almost unnervingly close to the ear, and the candour and generosity with which that voice speaks. But in ordinary human and social terms, what one meets as often is not so much 'passion' as that amiable rancour, that wary civility, that distinguishes the tone of English social communication, but most particularly in the social centre, London itself. The real motto of the City that was already in Donne's day a great trade centre ought to be *Caveat Emptor*; and one of the most candid and generous sayings of the 'passionate' Donne is 'Take heed of loving me'.

It is not only in his slighter, merely libertine or complimentary poems that Donne works this kind of effect. One of the most haunting and tender of the *Songs and Sonnets*, the 'Valediction: forbidding Mourning', moves and convinces by the way it sets up an attitude or tone which is strongly threatened but which does not finally give way. In terms of subject the poem is a kind of perfect abstraction of that original experience so vividly present at the close of Elegy 16, but here refined almost out of sight. The situation of the 'Valediction', the parting of lovers, is introduced with an abruptness that gives it the raw immediacy of a street accident. Yet Donne handles it throughout with an extraordinarily sophisticated obliquity, almost with evasiveness, with secrecy. The poem opens with the removed conceit of the death of good men:

> As virtuous men passe mildly 'away,
>   And whisper to their soules, to goe,
> Whilst some of their sad friends doe say,
>   The breath goes now, and some say, no:
>
> So let us melt . . .

And it closes with the famous, even more abstract, three-stanza conceit of parting and re-joining compasses. Both images are at a remarkable distance from the world of 'yonge fressche folkes, he or she', and in that distance resides both the austerity and the reassurance of the poem. The tone of the 'Valediction' is less that of mere kindness than of a bracingly high style shared: we are involved in something halfway between the lightness of a courtier's *Coraggio!* and such cheerfully distracting games as might be played with a child in the face of a danger both great and imminent.

> Moving of th'earth brings harmes and feares,
>   Men reckon what it did and meant,
> But trepidation of the spheares,
>   Though greater farre, is innocent.

In the ambiguities of the word *innocent* here lies much of the power of the poem. The 'Valediction' has a note of experience, of the adult need to play games, deep enough to discount much belief in innocence; and yet the games themselves are innocent. Given all the freedom therefore of being necessarily half-ironical, or only half-believed, the whole poem carries a quality of light numinousness that comes to rest in its last conceit, that of the compasses, a suspended and spiralling image that never finally proves quite what it seems to.

In the 'Valediction', courage is a tone of voice, tenderness a high style. This tacit artistry, and a suggestion of the milieu it arises from, reappears at the climax of Ford's tragedy *The Broken Heart*, when the princess Calantha hears the news of the death of all those closest to her but continues impassively her formal dance, allowing herself to prepare to die of grief only when the music has ceased and the dance is over. Donne, who longed to break into the court circle but never succeeded, despite himself retained the independent humanity and undermining intelligence that could authenticate such marvellous gestures. Without these qualities we are left, as we are perhaps in Ford's case, with an art of surface, that second-generation art by which the radical revolution of Marlowe, Donne, and Jonson – their invention of an intellectual élitist culture – has quietly changed its terms and become a social élitism: the gentleman's art that governs seventeenth-century letters.[1]

---

[1] Cf. Grierson: 'There are no poets . . . whose style is so entirely that of an English gentleman of the best type'. (*Metaphysical Lyrics and Poems* (1921), p. xxxi).

IV

The obliquity of the 'Valediction: forbidding Mourning' is a part of its own special wit. Not many of the *Songs and Sonnets* work in this way, by an explicit art of indirection. They have that 'brave clearness' which gives the 'Lecture upon the Shadow' its strength and which is an essential characteristic of Donne's mind. Yet almost invariably the movement of feeling in these poems is subject to an opposing current: there are few statements which do not find the implied pressure of opposing counter-statements. To take one brief example of this: the poem in which most would agree that Donne's affirmation of the sense of security in love is at its height, 'The Anniversarie', magnificently celebrates a timeless love in lines whose movement is like that of a ship riding in deep water:

> Only our love hath no decay;
> This, no tomorrow hath, nor yesterday,
> Running it never runs from us away,
> But truly keepes his first, last, everlasting day.

But the whole of the rest of the poem is about 'yesterday' and 'tomorrow'; the deep water is, so to speak, fresh and flowing, a current that animates the poem. To make association between love and what must be (judging by the imagery that fills the last stanza of the poem) the Accession Day ceremonies of either an ageing Queen or an unageless King is to understand why those 'true and false feares' enter the poem. The monumental quality of 'The Anniversarie' lies in its affirmativeness; but its power to move derives from that truthful detachment that places Donne always outside the event, able to see a thing in its frailty as well as in its strength. The end of the poem converts a Catullan assertion into something far more touchingly English: an honest anticlimax, that in its precision takes the scale of the endeavour:

> Let us love nobly, 'and live, and adde againe
> Yeares and yeares unto yeares, till we attaine
> To write threescore: this is the second of our raigne.

It does not seem to me helpful to see this mixture of commitment and withdrawal as symptoms of some personal neurosis. The terms of 'The Anniversarie' (with its 'honors, beauties, wits') allow us to say that Donne is placing his love fairly and squarely in a capital

city. And this placing of love makes his language of feeling
perpetually vulnerable, arousing always, directly or by association,
echoes of the primary love-language of his time, that of courtly
Petrarchism – a language that had become open to corruption and
hence made the man who used it subject to considerable stresses.
The nature and uses of the Petrarchan love-language in the
sixteenth century is a large subject which, even if I had the
competence, I do not have time to explore. It can summarily be
said, however, that the formality of the courtly love-speech of the
period gave it always some qualities of a game. But it was a game
that could be played with intense seriousness and in various
contexts, some of them well outside the area of private feeling. A
literary scholar has recently reminded us of the 'Machiavellian' uses
made of the Petrarchan love-code by Queen Elizabeth, particularly
in the last decade of her reign when the waning of her personal
power made even greater political demands on the myth.[1]
Similarly a political historian has written of the fall of Essex in
terms that perhaps throw light on Donne's ambiguous relation to
this love-code – for whether or not he was in fact of the Essex party
Donne seems to have felt some degree of involvement with Essex's
fate when he spoke of himself as having died in that grey year when
the courtier fell and he himself married.[2] Professor Hurstfield says
of Elizabeth's court in the last years of her reign:

> Everything was in fact conducted on two levels: in the adorned
> language of amorous devotion, and beneath it in the sharp cut-
> and-thrust for office and power, in which the queen held the
> unbreached authority to decide . . . Essex made the fatal mistake
> of treating the façade as though it were the reality . . . He hoped
> that in gaining a peculiar place in the queen's affections, he would
> win a dominant voice in the queen's government. He broke the
> rules of the game.[3]

Any man who was of the world, or who hoped to be, played this

---

[1] Leonard Forster, *The Icy Fire* (1962). See chapter 4, 'The political petrarchism of
the Virgin Queen'.
[2] 'If at last, I must confess, that I dyed ten yeares ago, yet as the Primitive Church
admitted some of the *Jews* Ceremonies, not for perpetuall use, but because they
would bury the Synagogue honourably, though I dyed at a blow then when my
courses were diverted, yet it wil please me a little to have had a long funerall, and to
have kept myself so long above ground without putrefaction.' *Letters*, p. 122.
[3] Joel Hurstfield, *Elizabeth I and the Unity of England* (1963), p. 187.

game. We can observe Donne playing it by looking at the first letter in the volume which his son published after Donne's death. Unlike the reticent though often warmly friendly letters to men that fill so much of the volume this one, with all its exquisite hyperboles, is glacially cold:

> Madame, I could make some guesse whether souls that go to heaven, retain any memory of us that stay behinde, if I knew whether you ever thought of us, since you enjoyed your heaven, which is your self, at home. Your going away hath made *London* a dead carkasse. A Tearm, and a Court do a little spice and embalme it, and keep it from putrefaction, but the soul went away in you: and I think the onely reason why the plague is somewhat slackened, is, because the place is dead already, and nobody left worth the killing. Wheresoever you are, there is *London* enough.[1]

It scarcely needs arguing that this courtly medium has its place in the *Songs and Sonnets*, whether directly or in the commoner anti-Petrarchan forms. But it would be a mistake to go on from there and assume that Donne is too simply conditioned by this social and Petrarchan medium, that his poems are mere 'social gestures'.[2] True, Donne was a master of the urbane love-game, as of many games. But he was also a man – as all his writings surely make plain – for whom the notions of truth and sincerity were important.

It is relevant here that there are some lyrics in the *Songs and Sonnets* which leave us uncertain whether they were addressed to a beloved mistress (or wife) or to a patroness who was expected to pay the poet for the tributes he addressed to her. The great age of English love poetry was also, significantly enough, the time of the literary patroness – and Donne pursued the Countess of Bedford manfully. It was in fact in the relationship of poet to patroness that the problem of sincerity, of purity of motive in love and in art, confronted him in one of its most searching and explicit forms. Donne has been compared unfavourably with Samuel Daniel, on the ground that as a patronized poet he was over-subject to

---

[1] *Letters*, p. 1.
[2] Cf. 'His lyrics . . . do not define private sensations. Instead, they make public gestures, and produce social effects . . . Donne's Petrarchism shows his poems to be gestures made from social situations.' See Donald L. Guss, *John Donne, Petrarchist* (Detroit, 1966), pp. 108–11.

anxiety.[1] Yet there was clearly good cause for anxiety in his situation, as there was for the many hopeless suitors who peopled Elizabeth's court. Moreover, the patronized poet – if honest and intelligent enough – might find in his situation anxieties other than the simply material: namely the more abstract doubts and complexities of any thoroughly worldly love. A man can tell a truth when he writes of love for a person by whom he hopes to profit, and he can tell a truth too when he considers how fruitless his love has been; and to discover and express these truths without cynicism or self-pity demands a peculiar steadiness and clarity in the poet. This situation and these qualities unite two men otherwise so different, Donne and Ralegh. In Ralegh's splendid line, 'Twelve yeares intire I wasted in this warr', the courtly poet is love's fool but no other man's and certainly not his own; and this is the note – as of mere digested experience – that is heard in Donne's writing. Where Ralegh is tragic and retrospective, the more lucid (although more fantastic) Donne will present the game of worldly love as a wild farce in a strict form:

> Till then, Love, let my body raigne, and let
> Mee travell, sojourne, snatch, plot, have, forget,
> Resume my last yeares relict: thinke that yet
>   We 'had never met.

The same lucidity shows itself as Donne reflects in his Letters on his relation to his patroness. One kind of honesty appears in that letter in which he states his flat disappointment at the small sum at last paid to him by the Countess and regrets writing the elegy which had moved her compassionate interest (and so aroused his hopes).[2] Another kind of honesty, more anxious but not therefore inferior, appears in the letter in which he actually speaks of the problem of sincerity and truth, and of past and present experience, as it affects the relation with a patroness; and the language he uses carries a regretful and complicated echo of the Petrarchan sentiment itself:

> I should be loath that in any thing of mine, composed of her, she
> should not appear much better then some of those of whom I

---

[1]In 'The Literature of Patronage 1580–1630' by Patricia Thomson, *Essays in Criticism*, vol. 2 (1952).
[2]*Letters*, p. 219.

have written. And yet I cannot hope for better expressings then I
have given of them. So you see how much I should wrong her,
by making her but equall to others. I would I could be beleeved,
when I say that all that is written of them, is but prophecy of
her.[1]

A confusion of categories, or a heroic or merely brutish will to
unify them, broke the courtier Essex. Donne too 'broke' his
fortunes in the year of his disastrous and devoted marriage. But in
his poems the effort to unify, the note of 'I would I could be
beleeved', continues. This need to master and shape the disparities
of experience, and to write truthfully of a London love, takes one
of its simpler (even cruder) forms in 'The Blossome', a gay courtly
poem presumably addressed to a patroness but seeming to
commune with the poet's own 'naked thinking heart'. The 'heart' is
behaving somewhat over-romantically, and so, as a tart corrective,
Donne allows it a short spell longer with the *donna* before returning
to its proper place:

> Meet mee at London, then . . .
>   I would give you
> There, to another friend, whom wee shall finde
> As glad to have my body, as my minde.

The London of 'other friends', other times, other experiences,
always forms a ground of actuality even to the most high-flying of
Donne's poems, so that assertion is always a personal, sometimes
paradoxical, sometimes heroic, will to believe. It is only safe to
treat 'The Good-morrow', for instance, as confident assertion if
one notes that it opens with 'I wonder' and closes with an 'If' – that
the 'good morrow to our waking soules' takes place in a moment of
present time enclosed in a questionable past and a conditional
future, a London always outside the window. No poem is more
firmly located in the courtly London world than that exquisite and
remarkably cold romance 'Aire and Angels', which should perhaps
make its readers wonder more than they appear to whether its
nominal addressee was a mistress or a patroness – and wonder too
about the exact mode of the 'passionate' poet about whom this can
be said. It opens with the headiest of angelic compliments –

[1] *Letters*, p. 260.

Twice or thrice had I lov'd thee,
Before I knew thy face or name;
So in a voice, so in a shapeless flame,
Angells affect us oft, and worship'd bee . . .

– and it closes with a flatly depressed statement of the incompatibility of men and women. But the distance between beginning and end is not as great as it may at first seem; in one of his sermons Donne surprisingly refers to 'Angels and Arch Angels' in the same breath and with the same scepticism as he does to the 'Giants, Witches, Spirits, Wild Beasts' in the maps of the 'Old Cosmographers':[1] Angels are hypothetical creations. Love for an angelic mistress (or patroness) is an 'I would I could be beleeved' that suffers a certain attrition – or at least change of state – from the passage of time, and we are made to feel that passage in the poem's uncharacteristically loose, flaccid, paratactic narrative structure. As we read through the poem, from line to line, we seem to pass through a stylized accelerated version of real time, an effect reinforced by the odd but purposeful variations of tense. And much of the beautiful and slightly melancholy character of 'Aire and Angels' resides in the disjunction between this precise actuality and the soaring abstraction which is also its mode.

This whole aspect of Donne's mind is crystallized in 'The Canonization'. It is a poem that manages to define a heroic solitariness of love in terms of the city it excludes; and that takes much of its power and life from the life of that excluded city. It is important, I think, that the first two stanzas of this poem are based on Ovid's Defence of Poetry.[2] For 'The Canonization' is a formal Defence of Love in five stanzas, but its strategy is so paradoxical that its formal nature may not be recognized at once.[3] In stanzas one and two Donne rebuts the opposing claims of the busy world on the underminingly modest ground that his love is at least harmless; but his wit does little to diminish the real energy of the

---

[1]'A Sermon of the Commemoration of the Lady Danvers'; in *The Sermons of John Donne*, ed. Evelyn M. Simpson and George R. Potter, vol. viii, pp. 81–2.

[2]i.e. the fifteenth and last Elegy of the First Book of *Amores* – apparently a favourite poem with Elizabethan poets, translated by both Marlowe and Jonson, and the poem from which Shakespeare took his epigraph for *Venus and Adonis*.

[3]Though the device of opening and closing every stanza with the rhyme-word *love* neatly expresses Donne's firm but finite involvement with his subject: 'Love, love, nothing but love'.

world he rebuts. In stanza three he races through the conventional claims *for* love with a reductive airiness that displays taper and phoenix, eagle and dove as what they are in terms of real experience: emblems, no more. The point of rest for the poem, the fulcrum on which 'love's whole world doth wheel' in poetic terms, is the tired, terse line that opens the fourth stanza and that seems to proceed as by a peculiar inward logic from the incompatibilities of the first three:

We can dye by it, if not live by love.

The claim that follows in the fourth stanza is technically a paradox of self-reference: 'it will be fit for verse', said in verse. Thus Donne's last soaring stanza, the fifth, is something allied to a legal fiction; it has the lightness of pure levity, for nothing rational keeps it up, beyond the sheer self-referent wish that has driven the poem itself into being. The poem is a paradox, a worldly *Contra Mundum*, that defends love and poetry by 'ringing the bell backward'. It is entirely characteristic of 'The Canonization' that Donne's lovers in the 'hermitage' of the last stanza should speak with the tongues of 'Countries, towns', and 'courts'; and that the most lucid and moving definition of love Donne ever made, 'You to whom love was peace that now is rage', is here a notion about the past locked up in a mind imagined in the future by a poet existing in an all too paradoxical present.

V

I have been arguing that these poems, like so many in the *Songs and Sonnets*, are London poems in a double sense: first, because of their hold on the dense medium of actual experience, which qualifies all romantic abstracts; second, because of their author's selfconsciousness as an artist, his extreme awareness of himself in relation to a surrounding audience. I want to close by suggesting that this understanding of Donne as a metropolitan writer may be used to throw light on one of his more difficult and least apparently metropolitan poems, 'The Exstasie'. The difficulty of 'The Exstasie' does not, I think, lie in the abstruseness of its subject; it lies, rather, in the elusiveness of its treatment. The eloquence and power of the poem are undeniable, but its intention and even its tone are so disputable as to cause the sharpest disagreement as to its final meaning.

One way to approach 'The Exstasie' is to recall that there is a great deal of late Renaissance European art, in both its Mannerist and Baroque phases, in which the relation of the spectator to the art-work becomes a large part of the artist's subject. Many of such works demand a sceptical approach to their subject if one is not to ascend a staircase that ends in mid-air. Donne's relationship with this kind of work is suggested in 'The Exstasie' by a detachment which is, even for him (and considering the nature of the overt subject) unusually marked. Three features make this plain. The first is that, from the very beginning of the poem, the experience of the lovers is uncompromisingly set back in the past:

> Where, like a pillow on a bed,
>   A Pregnant banke swel'd up, to rest
> The violets reclining head,
>   Sat we two, one anothers best.

A man who can write (as Donne did in his *Devotions*) 'This minute I was well, and am ill, this minute', does not use a past tense unguardedly. And the problematical valuation of past experience is, as I have hoped to show, a subject to which Donne recurs. Indeed, one of the period's most constant themes is

> Poore cousened cousenor, *that* she, and *that* thou,
> Which did begin to love, are neither now;
> You are both fluid, chang'd since yesterday.

From the first stanza until the point – wherever it occurs – at which we are so possessed by the lovers' experience that it becomes our 'now', 'The Exstasie' is set in 'yesterday'.

Secondly, this peculiarity of time is reinforced by a peculiarity of place, which is manifested in terms of style. The opening is very oddly written, with a turgid, knotted abstractness that one would guess was meant to sound old-fashioned but which is hard to explain with any certainty: the twisted eye-beams and cemented hands, the reclining violet and sepulchral statues are presumably there by design and for a purpose. The lovers appear to be not merely in the past but in a semi-symbolic past: one might guess, in a state of nature. Wherever they are, they are clearly (at least at the opening) not where *we* are.

Hence Donne's third device of detachment: the invention of at least one intermediary (there may be more) in the middle distance between us and them:

> If any, so by love refin'd,
> That he soules language understood,
> And by good love were grown all minde,
>   Within convenient distance stood . . .

If it were not that the lovers are so very emblematic, a state of being
in a state of nature, it is true that one might be worried by these
intermediaries or lookers-on at a love-scene; and there are readers
of the poem who resent, and are even repelled by, their presence.
But few of those who visit the Church of Santa Maria della Vittoria
in Rome to see the most famous of Baroque sculptural groups can
fail to be startled by the fact that the on-stage ecstasy of Bernini's St
Teresa is being watched by modest stone cardinals in side-boxes.
They are there because the thing has, so to speak, to be seen to be
believed; they are sceptical reason embodied and sanctified, 'by
good love grown all minde'.

   These devices of detachment establish themselves strongly at the
start of the poem; they dominate it much as Donne's authorial
voice does in other poems. When we arrive at the ecstatic lovers,
therefore, we meet them with a certain preserved equilibrium. It is
not irony, of which there are only faint traces in the poem, and
even less is it a satirical impulse. What works on us in the opening
of the poem is something inherent in the mere movement of the
verse and the tone of voice we seem to hear through it. It is a
sophisticated mind which sees a grassy bank as 'pregnant' and two
young lovers as 'two equal armies', and it is an intelligent and
knowledgeable mind which places us so securely in possession of
the past. In the scepticism of this tone there is the essentially
metropolitan awareness that other experiences are always also
true.[1] As a result of this, when the lovers begin to talk – and by
definition they are persons for whom no other experience is as true
as this – they sound like elevated infants. For Donne invents for
them a reedy limpidity of diction such as the 'dead birds' of
Shakespeare's 'Phoenix and Turtle' might have used:

> This Exstasie doth unperplex
> (We said) and tell us what we love,

---

[1] Cf.: 'The effect of London is apparent; the author has become a critic of men,
surveying them from a consistent and developed point of view; he is more
formidable and disconcerting; in short, much more mature.' T. S. Eliot on Pound in
(the anonymous) *Ezra Pound* (New York, 1917), pp. 16–17.

> Wee see by this, it was not sexe,
> Wee see, we saw not what did move.

Ben Jonson's Young Shepherd was to use just such a diction some years later:

> Though I am young and cannot tell
> Either what death or love is, well . . .

and Marvell's Nymph Complaining, after him:

> The wanton troupers riding by
> Have shot my faun and it will die . . .

Donne is the earliest of these three sophisticated poets to register innocence by means of a child-like syntax and rhythm and a monosyllabic simplicity of diction. The impulse, however, is an impulse to register, not to deride. We may feel from outside the poem that the lovers' sentiments are, if scrutinized, turgid and even a little silly. But no poem is read from the outside: its truth must be read to be believed, for the reading is in itself a species of 'ecstasy'. It is important that Donne himself is quite as much interested in this kind of ecstasy as in any other. An ecstasy is to him a passion of human communication, outgoing the self, and the literary may well be more authentic than the amatory. So he will write to a friend, 'this writing of letters . . . is a kind of extasie',[1] and again, 'Sir, more then kisses, letters mingle Soules'. It is this 'ecstasy' of literary sympathy on the part of both poet and reader that makes our poem, where it succeeds, as elated as it is aloof. For when the lovers speak, all Donne's poetic energy gets inside these leaden quatrains and by sheer force of sympathy lifts them up until they float. The detached man falls silent, and the inset lovers give voice to a sense of glory.

But Donne cannot simply maintain these divided voices; for he is not a dramatist who can leave his persons unreconciled, but a poet thinking, and to some conclusion. The substance of the poem tempts us always to suppose that his 'thought' is a matter of the arguments produced. But the young people's intellectual contortions, like all the arguments in Donne's poems, remain that – mere

---

[1] *Letters*, p. 11. 'I make account that this writing of letters, when it is with any seriousness, is a kind of extasie, and a departure and secession and suspension of the soul, wch doth then communicate it self to two bodies.'

arguments: a gesture towards, rather than the real substance of that tough and thorough intellectuality which characterized the poet. His lovers here are troubled by the relation of soul and sense. But Donne has already introduced into the poem a person (that one 'grown all mind' who is his own and the reader's surrogate) who from his 'convenient distance' sees the lovers as souls talking sense; and 'mind' has the right to assume therefore that the essential mark of the love-ecstasy is the happy inability of soul and sense to be distinct. So much for the lovers' arguments. The poet's thinking (as apart from the lovers') goes into the shaping that obtains this effect; and, more, into the penumbra of intonations and associations that surrounds all that the lovers say. They talk about a timeless love for twelve steady stanzas, which comes to seem a remarkably long time; and while they talk, things begin to happen to them; or if not to them, then at least to that more time-bound mind which listens to them. For while he overhears with sympathy and even some awe their single-minded discourse, he has time to regain what he perhaps never lost, that scepticism with which he met them first. As a result, the arguments of innocence take on more and more of the complex and touching intonations of an imputed experience; and we begin to hear the familiar sound of 'I would I could be beleeved':

> But O alas, so long, so farre
> Our bodies why do wee forbeare?

'So long, so farre' is not the cadence of a child; and the listener hearing it may well echo with the beginnings of irony, 'O alas . . . our bodies'. And this note in the poem, as of a life lived, deepens with the categorical imperative of the stanza with which 'The Exstasie' begins to close:

> So must pure lovers soules descend
> T'affections, and to faculties,
> Which sense may reach and apprehend,
> Else a great Prince in prison lies.[1]

The resonances here move right outside the soul–sense debate, and it does not matter that the lovers' sentiments are at this point

---

[1] I do not adopt here Professor Gardner's controversial new reading of 'That' for 'Which'.

somewhat confused – indeed, it may be a necessary part of the effect that they are so. What we hear is the word *must*, and talk of a *descent* and of a *prison*; and the reader who – like the poet – has not the freedom to argue that fictive lovers enjoy but inhabits a prison of 'musts' thinks of the other descents which await the rapt speakers: from innocence into experience, from thought into action, from the past into the present and out of the poem. These last stanzas are involved in a curious, always perceptible melancholy, but also in a quickening of rhythm into a brisk decisiveness. Both moods meet in the magnificent image of the prince in prison, who seems so much greater than his immediate context needs him to be, and who brings into a knotted and self-analytical love-poem all the clarity and strength that Renaissance humanism could sometimes achieve. There are princes in prison in Sidney, Shakespeare, and Calderón, but the one most important to Donne here can be met in his own *Biathanatos*, where he writes of

> the search and discovery of truth, who else being the greatest Prince in the world, should have no progresse, but be straightned in a wretched corner.[1]

It may be said that 'The Exstasie' is in itself a 'progresse of truth'. What gives the poem its weight, in fact, is less the conclusion that the arguing lovers come to, than the conclusion they bring poet and readers to. And that conclusion is an ending, not a thing that can be stated as any theory of soul and sense in love. For the poet, and for the reader after him, poetic love in this otherwise curiously loveless though luminous poem is a raising up of a highly personal truth out of some 'wretched corner' of the mind into the daylight of a nobly common reason, where human confusions and contradictions exist in a clearer, more truthful equilibrium. And this is the daylight that poet and reader share, and where they may be said to meet in a rational ecstasy peculiarly their own. So Donne mingles the amatory and the literary in the last stanza of this highly self-conscious poem:

> And if some lover, such as wee,
>   Have heard this dialogue of one,
> Let him still marke us, he shall see
>   Small change, when we'are to bodies gone.

[1] *Biathanatos* (1609), p. 84

Using the *we* and *us* of lovers, Donne writes from within the now receding fictive love-situation.[1] But his authorial plural is directed at the poet's non-amatory partner, the reader – that person who is in the end his only audience. Donne is, I think, taking a hint here from Ovid's elegy in defence of poetry (which I earlier proposed as a 'source' for 'The Canonization'). Ovid ended his elegy by saying that he could endure contumely and unsuccess in this world in the thought of his posthumous fame: 'I will', he says, 'always be read by the careworn lover', 'I shall live, and the great part of me survive'.[2] Donne's last stanza, which has often been found difficult, holds perhaps an oblique echo of Ovid's resonant close. Like the Roman poet, the English poet and his lovers will surely survive their bodies. But these lines also contain a phrase – 'this dialogue of one' – that is wholly Donne's, and it serves to epitomize all the poem's different kinds of communication: those between lover and lover, between lover and poet, between poet and reader. For even here, in a poem as apparently private and self-communing as 'The Exstasie', Donne appeals to some human metropolis of letters, a London which is 'the meeting of friends'.

[1] The Renaissance device of breaking a convention before the close in order to establish another more apparently realistic takes various forms: e.g. the endings of Shakespeare's *Love's Labour's Lost* and *The Tempest*, Donne's own 'The Indifferent', and Milton's *Lycidas*.

[2] 'atque ita sollicito multus amante legar . . . vivam, parsque mei multa superstes erit.' Ovid, *Amores* 1. 15, ll. 38–42.

2

The Shooting of the Bears: Poetry and Politics in Andrew Marvell

Outside the universities, if a reading audience still exists there, Marvell is the author of one poem. 'To his Coy Mistress' is perhaps a surprising work to have kept alive the name of the reserved bachelor who wrote it. But this kind of mild surprise is frequent with Marvell. He is not at all an easy writer to see whole: the life and the reputation, the career and the work he left, have meant different things to different people. The man behind the lyrics is unusually elusive to us. Perhaps this is why Marvell has never really been a great poet to the general reader. For until about fifty years ago, the poems now regarded as some of our greatest lyrics were almost entirely neglected; and if Marvell is a great poet, then he is the only one we have who has stayed unread in this way for nearly two hundred years. Most great writers manage to survive, in one way or another. But Marvell did not – until half a century ago he emerged, rediscovered by poets and academics. He became what he remains, not the author of a single classic love poem, but something like the most admired of all 'critics' poets'. A decade or so ago, criticism began to take a new turn. The rediscovered poet had been the writer of the best lyrics. But Marvell in fact left behind him a much larger body of occasional work, most of it the outgrowth of his life in politics. When Marvell died, he was known – well known, and in some quarters much admired – as a public person, and the author of often combative and polemic literature. His lyrics stayed unpublished until several years after his death, and he seems rarely to have chosen to pass them around in manuscript – the usual custom of gentlemen of the period who did not wish for social reasons to publish their work. Marvell was known, instead, as the panegyrist of Cromwell and then the MP for Hull; the writer of brilliant satirical verses on the part of the 'Country' against the Court of Charles II, and of brave and successful prose defences of the Good Old Cause – in particular, of religious toleration. Criticism has begun to include in its appreciation some of the best of this large body of occasional writing, a good deal of which appeared anonymously in the first instance, thus raising lasting doubt as to its authorship. Even if it had not been anonymously published, the style of many of these verse satires, panegyrics, and commemorations of events, not to mention the works in prose, is different enough from that of the best lyrics to create real problems in discussing them. Despite these problems both of identification and of judgement, most of the major occasional poems – the salute to Cromwell on the First Anniversary of his Government, the elegy on his death, the satire called 'The Last Instructions to a Painter' – have all been studied recently with enthusiasm and interest.

This sharp rise of interest in the public poetry may well be an attempt, however little conscious, to come to terms with the strangeness that exists in Marvell's work, and in his career and reputation: to diminish the sense of fissure in it. A number of good critics have shown that a mind distinctly Marvellian is at work in the more authentic of the public poems.[1] But it is a thing that needs showing. Most ordinary, and – even now – most professional readers of Marvell are liable to be aware of the disjunctions in the work. The difference in kind and indeed in value between the best lyrics and the best occasional poems is enough to explain why Marvell has been systematized into a mythical chronology. There is no evidence for the dating of most of the best poems – that is to say, the lyrics; the occasional poems, almost by definition, are often written for a date. It is entirely customary, though the assumptions have not gone unchallenged, to take it that Marvell's lyrics are pre-Restoration, and that most of the public poetry is at least post-1650.[2] Marvell is assumed to have grown out of writing lyric poetry and into writing satire, a more mature even if a distinctly coarser style and vision. But this assumption is dangerous though

---

[1]See, for instance, Elsie Duncan-Jones's brilliant 'A Great Master of Words: Some Aspects of Marvell's Poems of Praise and Blame', (*Proceedings of the British Academy*, 1975).

[2]Joseph H. Summers gives some good reasons for scepticism about the generally accepted chronology of Marvell's poems in *The Heirs of Donne and Jonson* (O.U.P. New York, 1970), pp. 160–2. In the lecture already cited, Mrs Duncan-Jones suggests that the 'high palaces of kings' in 'Hortus' would, if taken literally, point to a time after Marvell frequented the palace of Westminster.

deeply based. It ignores the possibility that a writer of Marvell's studied brilliance and variety might have written very variously at various points of his life, and was capable of writing in or out of fashion when he was writing – after all – for no one but himself. It remains possible that Marvell wrote occasional poems and lyrics side by side throughout the whole of his writing life: and to assume otherwise may be to read into both kinds of poetic practice ideas about their different relation to truth and seriousness which are simply not justified. And the exact relation to truth of both 'private' and 'public' writing is a question which, I think, had some meaning for Marvell.

The sense of fragmentation in the poet's work is reflected in his peculiar career after death. For a while remembered as a distinctive public figure, he gradually lapsed into nearly two centuries of silence: before reviving, with immense acclaim, in our own time. Though this is a history rare among great poets, it is not rare among the lesser writers of Marvell's own period. Herrick waited years to publish his first volume; it came out in 1648 and met complete failure; he died without knowing success and moved into that 'great gap of time' which Marvell knew as well, until both began to be read again a little by poets in the early nineteenth century. The fate they both endured has a rhythm that can be recognized; it is part of the cultural history of the last four hundred years. By the 1680s writers of only two generations back had become the 'giant race before the Flood'. Most of the best minor poetry of the previous age, and even the shorter poems of several major figures, sank and almost drowned in the 'flood' which shaped the century. If we try to explain that great historic shift, then an aspect of what happened to Marvell may give a clue to it. For not all Marvell's work was lost – something survived. When the lyrics were published in 1681, they sank almost without trace. But the reputation of the public work survived. Marvell was remembered, not entirely accurately, as a kind of proto-Whig, a Protestant hero and a Republican poet: until the passing of time paradoxically destroyed what virtue the occasional nature of the work had seemed to hold. The poems that were lost first were those that were first recovered: the private poems.

It might be argued that all good verse is public, or public enough to communicate with good readers. But Renaissance poets proba-bly thought instinctively of the 'private' and 'public' realms as clearly divided: as clearly divided as was the personal life from what Marvell called 'our Lady State'. On the other hand, it is true that if the poetry written at the turn of the sixteenth century demands extreme respect, this is because of the way in which private and public matters are fused within it. The love poetry of Shakespeare, Donne, and Ralegh is heroic in scale, import, and intensity. Private poetry of this quality goes beyond a formal category; it sets an ethical standard. If, fifty years ago, poets and academics rediscovered seventeenth-century poetry, then it was probably private poetry they were discovering, rather than merely experiencing a taste for the Metaphysical; and what they were experiencing probably went beyond questions of mere taste at all. Donne and Marvell 'came back' because many intelligent individuals felt or thought they felt a severance from the civilization that both created and threatened them. Marvell rose into prominence, in the 1920s and 30s, as the creator of an acutely private art; and to read his brilliant, individual poems was perhaps like inheriting, at the end of a throttling civilization, a small landed estate to retreat to and to live in freely. If taste is turning now, as it seems to be, towards the occasional verse, then this probably says more about our own ever more publicly-orientated society – in many ways a second Restoration period – than it does about Marvell's poems.[1]

We perhaps now underrate the insistency – suggestive in terms of his own feeling, even if not literally true – of Marvell's own remark, in *The Rehearsal Transpros'd*, that 'I never had any, not the remotest relation to publick matters' before 1657, when he accepted a governmental appointment: reluctantly, so he said. Whenever they were written, the virtues of Marvell's best poems are those of a man who, from an unusual integrity and toughness of character, refused – or found himself unable – to abandon his privacy as a poet. A contrast might be made with his great predecessor, from whom he learned so much: Ben Jonson. Jonson's best work is high public art: but the private personality behind it is simple in the extreme; hence the real human limitations behind the poet's always beautifully used rhetoric. Marvell's lyrics inherit, gratefully, that lucid expository style which Jonson created and gave to the literature of his time, but the result is scarcely confusable with the

---

[1] On the subject of 'public' poetry in general, and Marvell's in particular, see, e.g., in addition to Summers, Patrick Cruttwell's *The Shakespearian Moment* (Columbia U.P., 1954) and L. C. Knights's *Public Voices* (Chatto, 1971).

work of the older poet. When Marvell actually brought Jonson in person into one of his poems, making him speak from the underworld in 'Tom May's Death', he invented for him – significantly – a high resonance of rhetoric that was then conceivable as years out of date, and simply inutile in the real complex circumstances of modern political life: life in the 1650s. Marvell's own 'true' lyrics possess something like the Jonsonian lucidity – but they inform it, ironically, with a private personality that is wholly different in kind: self-mocking, subtle, and permanently reserved. It is this private character which gives to Marvell's verse its chief endowment (after its obvious literary skills): a strikingly original sensibility. When we open an anthology we recognize Marvell at once. And we do so, not so much by the sound of a voice, as by the quality of a whole mind, a mind whose recesses it is not easy to exhaust. In a way, of course, it would be foolish first to notice the poet's peculiar individuality, and then to think of this as characteristic of an age. But there is little doubt that certain periods help to form (or to destroy) the selfhood of the persons within them; and that the first half of the seventeenth century produced an extraordinary number of talented poets, the least of whom is characterized by the flavour of individuality. Marvell's remarkably original sensibility, the degree to which he existed as a 'private' man, has to be seen against the background of change and development in the whole world of the later Renaissance. The Tudors had left England with a sense of its own greatness, and possessed, if not of wealth, at least of the tastes and expectations of the rich. The England of the 1620s, 30s and 40s where Marvell grew up – and while the rest of Europe was beginning to be torn by war – was in consequence experiencing a form of highly cultivated self-realization. Post-Tudor England saw the discovery of the formal private life, the projection on to the forms of society itself of the impulses of civilized inwardness. In the seventeenth century England becomes a country of high-walled gardens and collectors' cabinets. Its gentlemen hang their houses with muffling silk and with silencing Turkey carpets; its ladies read romances and write letters. Its finest aristocrats withdraw from the capital and make of their estates a 'college in a purer air'. The King himself is an amateur and a collector, who seeks to keep not only his Court but even his country as his private property, and leaves behind him in the chaos of the 1650s – when Marvell's career really begins – what might have been the best art-gallery in Europe. After the Civil Wars even the poor joined in, and began to level England, or so they hoped, towards a dreamed-of Fifth Monarchy of the mind.

One of Marvell's most distinguished scholars, Pierre Legouis, described his 'Bermudas' as a legend under crystal. Many of the best poems have something of this quality of enchanted self-enclosure; it is the source of their strength as well as of their charm. Marvell moved towards some of the devices of the self-consistent imagination discovered two hundred years later by the French Symbolists. Many of his poems have all Mallarmé's love of the small, the precious, and the innocent. But Marvell's mowers and glow-worms, children, flowers and fruit are, strictly speaking, collectors' pieces: cut, polished and set. His wonderfully subtle and disturbing 'The Mower against Gardens' makes of the collecting mind itself a kind of everlasting flower, or a coral preserved in the garden-cabinet of fallen time and space:

> The Pink grew then as double as his Mind;
> The nutriment did change the kind.

Those who celebrate Marvell primarily as a Nature poet are right to do so. But his landscapes are most frequently only moments of time in which the world's 'rarities' startlingly catch the light: like the dew-drop

> Dark beneath, but bright above

or like

> The hatching *Thrastles* shining Eye

that suddenly looks at us out of the lines of 'Appleton House'; or like that fruit of the Bermudas,

> the Orange bright,
> Like golden Lamps in a green Night.

Marvell's natural world exists to give back the profound shock of perception: a delighted-in limitation and circularity, which comes to the surface in the poet's fascination with eyes and tears – eyes rarely without their fruit of tears, tears reflecting like diamonds. The dew-drop, the thrush's eye and the lit-up orange tree are similarly so formal as to be almost in themselves Renaissance jewels, but jewels released into innocence by the poet's pervasive moral integrity: that tacit self-judgement and self-mockery which always destroys the garlands, opens up the galleries and dissolves the drop of dew, forbidding an over-valuing of what it has made.

If Marvell had been no more than a private poet in this sense, we should probably not be remembering the tercentenary of his death, but merely including him with that splendid gallery of Caroline connoisseurs who gave the age its elegance – a Lovelace who survived, a more eccentric Herrick. But Marvell is better than this, and bigger too. In the 'Horatian Ode' he wrote what may be the greatest political poem in English, a poem that stands like a landmark at the centre of the age: grave, weighty, and unshakeably judicious. But even in the poems that make no claims to public statement Marvell is much more than an artist in rarities. 'To his Coy Mistress' has a largeness, a substance, reflected in though not explained by the grandeur of all its dismissed fantasies – its Ganges and its rubies, its empires and its slow-growing love. It is this sense of largeness of scale in the best poems that suggests, perhaps, the chief critical problem of Marvell's work. The lyrics commit themselves willingly to the small, but they are not small poems. Great images inhabit them without any of that strain, that distortion or even perversity which might go with their use in Augustan verse. Moreover, if we ask how a poet so elusive, so drily content with the minor forms of the age, could leave behind him – unpublished – these great lyrics, it does not help to call in some concept of the 'great personality', as we might in the case of a Donne, a Milton, or even a Dryden. For, though both the writing and the career suggest that Marvell had a strong character, he does not appear to have had a personality at all, whether great or small. The public Marvell, the man whom the age saw, seems to be a blank. He rarely spoke in Parliament; Clarendon does not mention him. The handwriting in a letter to his constituency that survives in the British Museum is startlingly simple and regular, like the hand of a nineteenth-century office clerk; and this man of extraordinarily original sensibility seems to have maintained in his address to the world in general, to his acquaintances as to his constituency, just such an impersonal, flavourless rectitude. One of the most idiosyncratic poets in existence, called by Burnet 'the liveliest droll of the day'; a man who – so Aubrey suggests – loved his friends though he had no 'general acquaintance', Marvell also had no personality, at least in the public form which is an offshoot of egoism. This may be why he left behind him a handful of brilliant lyrics in all the manners of the time, but no artistic canon – no developing and datable body of work that preserves the laws of the psyche that produced it. This is also why, perhaps, even the very best of the occasional work, like the late satire 'The Last Instructions to a Painter', written in buoyant, brisk, and beautiful Restoration couplets, cannot compare in merit to the best satires of Dryden and Pope: whose attacking, far more egoistic energies subsume the minutiae of their time into a largely unjust but vital artistic harmony. Despite all his rhetorical skills, Marvell's very virtues – his essentially private decency and integrity, his strong loyalties, his amused attentive interest in the world around him – all the time seem to have prevented him from ever being an outstanding political poet: the crude mere 'occasion' dominates and disintegrates that patient artistic consciousness observing it. 'The Last Instructions' tells us something, and tells it brilliantly, about what it was like to live in the England of Charles II; it is still pleasurable and interesting to read, up to a point; but it is not a very good poem by Andrew Marvell.

The relative weakness of the occasional verse reflects the more credit on the man who tried to write it – who was not content to remain merely a private poet. And thereby it throws some light on the peculiar strength of the best lyrics. For the self-enclosure of Marvell's poems is not in fact as great as it seems to be, or as it dryly advertises itself to be. The difference in scale between Marvell and, say, Herrick – good as Herrick is – might be summarized as the greater *openness* of a Marvell lyric. It contains more of life; of the world; of its time; it matches the superior and secure finesse of its forms with a superior freedom in the elusion of its forms. But a poem by Marvell will be exceedingly difficult to relate directly to the life of his time. Many attempts have been made to hear the noise of the Civil Wars in the cadences of the lyrics, but such attempts seem often to go counter to the poems, instead of with them. The openness of these poems is not easy to define. In part, this remarkably beautiful 'cabinet' poetry goes beyond the standards it seems to set itself by virtue of the continual presence within it of irony; that highly intelligent irony which we hear everywhere in the lyrics without ever finding it easy to locate it convincingly. It may work as no more than a surprising absence of insistence, rare in an age of dogmatism: a sceptical 'Convince me then that this is true', an 'It is to be supposed they grieve'. Or it may take the form of a love of anti-climax, like the 'Let's in' that suddenly ends 'Appleton House', making of the whole rambling, ambitious work not so much a poem as a stroll around the garden, while the evening light fades. Such anti-climax works perpetually in small ways too, as in Marvell's pleasure in closing a forcible opening stanza concerning the 'forward youth' in war, with the derisive, difficult rhyme-word *languishing*. This irony may relate more directly outwards, as in the case of Marvell's curious titles. A private poem will be by its 'public' title mockingly associated with the world at large, as though overheard. Thus, 'To his Coy Mistress': which is *not*, in fact, a seduction poem, but something much lonelier; it tells, not woos, and what it tells is not encouraging. 'The Definition of Love' is *not* a definition, or not of love; but something much more silently subversive, said into the ear of the noisy opposing world, busy with definitions. 'The Nymph Complaining for the Death of her Faun', unlike its title, is *not* classical, *not* erotic; its lecherous 'faun' is merely a dying animal, its nymph is almost a child and startlingly close to us – she speaks the poem, not as well as the poet would; and whether all these facts make the whole more pathetic or more ridiculous is left unconcluded, though the poem is otherwise all conclusion. 'The Picture of little T. C. in a Prospect of Flowers' is nearly as long, as a title, as the poem it announces and rather grander than the little girl to whom the poem devotes itself; but the child has large hopes fixed on her, and perhaps also large ideas of her own dignity, which the poem kindly undermines. That most abstractly discussed of all Marvell's poems, 'The Garden', ends by making a reader wonder if *the* garden ever existed, outside those 'herbs and flowers . . . flowers and herbs' that help to pass the time away.

The mid-seventeenth century was a bad time to be a private poet. During the wars themselves, from about 1643 till about 1647, the young Marvell – perhaps symptomatically – went on a Grand Tour. Not long after he came home, in 1649, there occurred that event which shook the whole of Europe: the English nation cut off the head of its King. Marvell himself, the son of a fairly Calvinistical clergyman, had for a short spell as a young man inclined to the Roman church; a natural monarchist with a Royalist love of tradition, he had also a power of reason and sense of fact that moved him towards the Parliamentary position. The remaining forty years of his life would give him plenty of time to learn a poetic art that would confront the fissuring private and public worlds then coming into being: in 1650, the mid-point of the century.

Most of Marvell's public verse is now unread except by those with a professional interest in it. To appreciate it demands knowledge of the historical context which Marvell meets with such high adeptness of rhetorical skills. But there is one occasional poem which is an exception to this rule: the 'Horatian Ode upon Cromwell's Return from Ireland'. We can admire and praise this political poem, with its brilliantly adjudicated images of the condemned King and the living dictator-to-be, on the basis of a sense of history that may sometimes be founded, ironically enough, on the poem itself. It has that self-sufficiency of the true poem. Clearly, what makes it different from the other Cromwellian poems deserves to be isolated.

In the first place, the Ode poses a political conundrum. In the previous year Marvell had written three occasional poems: one addressed to Lovelace, the others lamenting the deaths of Villiers and Hastings. The sentiments of all three are to some degree or other Royalist; fiercely so in the Villiers poem, whose authorship has, however, been disputed. Some months after the 'Horatian Ode', whose date we do not know, but which is presumed to have been written in the summer of 1650, there appeared 'Tom May's Death', which certainly sounds Marvellian, and which satirized the case of a Royalist poetaster who had deserted and gone over to the Parliamentarians. A few months after this again, Marvell was living and working at Appleton House, as tutor to the daughter of Lord Fairfax, who had just resigned from the supreme command of the Parliamentary army. Given that the 'Horatian Ode' is often referred to as a 'panegyric of Cromwell', this sandwiching complication must prove suggestive. One of the things it should not suggest, probably, is merely political opportunism on Marvell's part. Both the poetry and the career suggest a habit of extreme tentativeness, succeeded and explained by a habit of extreme steadiness in commitment when once the commitment was undertaken. When once he had undertaken public appointment in the later 1650s Marvell stuck to the 'Good Old Cause' with a tenacity not very usual at that point in time. In any case, the political situation of the 1640s and 50s was so complicated as to make such terms as 'opportunism' unsuitable. It is not simple to change sides when there are no simple sides. This is not, therefore, a climate in which it will prove very easy to ascertain Marvell's attitudes in his 'Horatian Ode'; perhaps he wrote the poem to clarify them. For it must be said that in producing work that superficially at least belonged to the world of the public, Marvell was committing himself to something that demanded clear attitudes. This is why the greater part of the many critical essays on the poem are concerned with Marvell's attitudes, ever since the debate between Douglas Bush and Cleanth Brooks. Bush thought the poem a relatively clear and simple panegyric of Cromwell; Brooks found its attitudes more ambiguous, more critical. And since their dispute, many good articles have been written to prove that the poem's hero is Cromwell, or Charles, or both.

In a way any critic is right who tries, as Bush did, to keep a Marvell poem 'clear' in meaning. Brooks's reading, though far more sensitive and understanding, perhaps ends by getting the tone of the poem wrong: undervaluing the element in Marvell that associates him with Jonson and with the Augustan writers after him. Marvell seems to be always urging doubts outward, resolving ambiguities rather than causing them. But against Bush's conclusion, that the Ode is a simple panegyric of Cromwell, it must be said that Cromwell would have had to be a very *naïf* man to be thoroughly pleased with the poem – as pleased, for instance, as he presumably was by the 'First Anniversary of the Government under O. C.' which Marvell wrote five years later. And the most 'pleasing' of all these poems is the elegy which the poet wrote on Cromwell's death. Legouis has made the point that we learn much more about Cromwell from the elegy than we do from the Ode, and he values the elegy for this. What we learn is certainly different in the two poems. The 'First Anniversary', like the elegy, adorns a big man with big images:

> *Cromwell* alone with greater Vigour runs,
> (Sun-like) the Stages of succeeding Suns . . .

> *Cromwell* alone doth with new Lustre spring,
> And shines the Jewel of the yearly Ring . . .

Thou *Cromwell* falling, not a stupid Tree,
Or Rock so savage, but it mourn'd for thee.

These two panegyrical poems were written only five and eight years after the 'Horatian Ode', but their difference in tone and style is so great as to make them seem typically 'Restoration' in mode: the effort of idealizing draws out of them a rhetoric that seems necessarily touched by the factitious, a mere dishonest avoidance of the inevitable satiric note. This is perhaps why we hear, like an echo under these lines, derisive cadences written twenty years after, derisive in effect even if Dryden's connection with Marvell's verses is only accidental:

Shadwell alone my perfect image bears,
Mature in dullness from his tender years;
Shadwell alone of all my sons is he
Who stands confirmed in full stupidity.[1]

This peculiar note – of panegyric that is a near-miss to satire – is not heard in the 'Horatian Ode'. But the reason is not that the poem is satirical already: the perfection of its courtesy is well-known. The Ode is merely incontrovertible as the 'First Anniversary' and the 'Poem upon the Death of O. C.' are not. When the 'political' Marvell calls Cromwell 'Sun-like', or describes the natural world mourning for him, or even when he gives him the tenderer praise of the elegy, the result is simply less believable than when, for instance, the same poet elsewhere shows the Mower admiring the 'sun' of his rustic face in the bright curve of his scythe, or when he makes him crossly hack down the flowers and grass precisely because they will *not* mourn for him. This difference in credibility does not, I think, derive merely from modern cynicism. Heroic idealization is always believable if believed; it is a possible, even a necessary, human experience. But Marvell is writing panegyrics of the man who has 'cut off the king's head with the crown upon it' – of the dictator who committed himself to finishing the tyranny of myth. Clarendon was to quote of the dead king, 'I have heard him

---

[1] A. L. Korn argues that Dryden is here echoing the description of Abdon in *Davideis IV*: '*Mac Flecknoe* and Cowley's *Davideis*', *Essential Articles for the study of John Dryden*, ed. H. T. Swedenberg, Jr. (1966), pp. 170–200. It seems to me possible that there is some relationship between Cowley's lines and Marvell's in the 'First Anniversary', and that Dryden, whose lines are verbally closer to Marvell's, is here remembering both poets.

often say, that if he could not live a King then he would die a
Gentleman.' That Charles died a Gentleman, because he could not
find a way of living as a King, was a mixture of the beautiful and
the deeply discreditable – discreditable to himself first, to others
after. At all events, that transition from King to Gentleman was the
crux of England's political problems in the period. And it was the
problem, too, of Marvell, the panegyrist of the man who was
already called 'King Oliver': Marvell the political poet, whose
Cromwell is a man awkwardly draped with glory as with mist.

The 'Horatian Ode', by contrast, is believable as real poems are
believable. That it is so, suggests a distinction: though 'political', it
is not public as the other occasional poems are public. In this sense,
such debates as that of Bush and Brooks are permanently
unresolvable. This is not a poem in which personalities, or attitudes
to them, are primarily important; and the sense of greater freedom
in the poem is the mark of Marvell's not having had to care about
pleasing or displeasing this or that personality. The events of a year
or eighteen months presented a crisis, it must seem, or made a kind
of sense, that was beyond politics. The burden of opinionating
drops from Marvell, and a different kind of thinking takes over: the
Ode is beyond *attitudes*. The dropping of that burden in the
'Horatian Ode', written we must surely say as a private poem, is
revealed by a small point concerning its style: a point that seems to
me as important as its attitudes, though it has clearly been felt as
too trivial to figure much in criticism. Most of Marvell's genuinely
occasional verse is written in heroic couplets. The 'Horatian Ode' is
not. It is composed in an unusual pattern of pairs of rhymed four-
beat and then three-beat lines, the delicate monosyllables of the
second pair, the short lines, in effect undercutting the first pair,
changing the view, so that the stanzas seem to show the mind
altering itself, moving forward again and again. This remarkable
thinking metre begins with the poem's first phrases:

> The forward Youth that would appear
> Must now forsake his *Muses* dear,
>   Nor in the Shadows sing
>   His Numbers languishing.
> 'Tis time to leave the Books in dust,
> And oyl th' unused Armours rust:
>   Removing from the Wall

> The Corslet of the Hall.
> So restless *Cromwel* could not cease . . .

The five-stressed or heroic couplet is the emerging and dominant form of the 1640s and 50s; we celebrate men like Denham or Waller simply because they helped to bring forward its bright, balanced, and public mode. Its sound and style are already enough established in Marvell's time for the ear to hear the octosyllabic or four-stressed line which he loved, as apparently lacking something. Certainly, when it was used a decade or so later by a clear and external wit like Samuel Butler, this sound of something missing is felt as apt to its indecorous or playful function. But in Marvell's hands it does not precisely have this comic note, even when it occurs – as of course it does not here – in couplet form. The thought of the 'Horatian Ode' is hardly clear and external in the Samuel Butler way; the very first lines are compressed, even distorted. The opening line means, prosaically, 'The youth who would achieve fame'; but the lilting inversion (echoed in the slightly parodic '*Muses* dear' and 'Numbers languishing') is a departure from idiom that throws important stress on that word *appear*, which implies uncertainty, reservation, perhaps illusion, and so starts the involved machine of thought going within both poem and reader. The second line – itself poetry – advocates, or at least contemplates, an abandonment of poetry, in a tone – *forsake* and *dear* – which makes this seem regrettable as well as impossible. The rhythm of the next two lines ironically climaxes the swing of the stanza by a trailing and undercutting anti-climax, blurring off into darkness with an exquisitely uncertain rhyme-word, *languishing*. These are effects unimagined by a Samuel Butler, or even by an artist as great as Ben Jonson, who wrote some beautiful octosyllabics. And the tone they achieve is not one of omission, but of reserve. Marvell is using a metre for thinking aloud in.

This metrical effect is underlined by a different aspect of the style of the Ode, one bearing on its language and syntax. Its fourth, fifth, and sixth stanzas define the violence of 'restless' Cromwell, who

> like the three-fork'd Lightning, first
> Breaking the Clouds where it was nurst,
>   Did thorough his own Side
>   His fiery way divide.
> For 'tis all one to Courage high
> The Emulous or Enemy:

> And with such to inclose
> Is more then to oppose.
> Then burning through the Air he went,
> And Pallaces and Temples rent:
> And *Caesars* head at last
> Did through his Laurels blast.

The ambiguity of Marvell's language has been a well-treated theme; and it is well illustrated by the central stanza here, drily indicating the degree to which a man of power is indifferent to friend or enemy. But the three stanzas also reveal an aspect of the diction not so much noticed, one even more interesting than mere variability in attitude. It has often been noted that Marvell leaves *cruces*, like that of the double Caesar. Charles is, and Cromwell becomes, Caesar. But whose head, precisely, here bursts through whose laurels? The crux is in fact syntactical, and depends on the fact that *blast* in this last line may be either transitive or intransitive (as 'Caesars head' is either subject or object); and we have no time, such is the poem's steady if uninsistent progress, to stop and determine which – even if the laconic metre permitted, as it does not. In this short passage alone, a number of other words share this same grammatical uncertainty, with an active or passive implication: *his own side, divide, inclose, oppose, rent*. Marvell is describing a form of natural energy perfectly recognizable, and the passage cannot be said to be truly difficult: we know very clearly what it means, and even admire the strange elegance which the smooth movement of the verse gives to an extreme destructive violence. The transitive–intransitive uncertainty merely leaves a kind of chill, a shadow across some of the most potent words. The effect is striking enough to recall a poem far in time and mood from Marvell's, in which Coleridge was to describe the condition of nightmare as one of uncertainty

> Whether I suffered, or I did;
> For all seemed guilt, remorse or woe,
> My own or others, still the same
> Life-stifling fear, soul-stifling shame.

Marvell's world is not one of nightmare. It is the achievement of his poem, as indeed of his two leading characters in it, that they raise to heroism and even to a kind of gaiety, what could otherwise have been thought of as 'shame' and 'fear'. But that doubt of 'whether I suffered, or I did' is implicit in his syntax as in his metre. In this poem, action and suffering fuse; event becomes thought; the public becomes private. This dominating impression of the poem's style is supported by a trivial point concerning the possible origin of its metre. A poem probably by the young Sir Richard Fanshawe, and existing only in manuscript, uses this anglicized Horatian metre for an interesting subject: a decision to abandon verse in order to pursue a less time-wasting and impoverished career.[1] This seems too close to 'the forward youth who would appear' to be accidental. It was perhaps the personal theme of Fanshawe's modest imitation which caught Marvell's attention, and imprinted the Horatian form in his memory as the way to make personal, public matters. For Marvell's poem can be called 'personal', almost as Fanshawe's can. Its subject is politics, as expressed through the fate of its two persons, Cromwell and Charles; the triumph of Cromwell encloses, at its centre, the opposing triumph of Charles, the triumph of death within the triumph of life. But these persons are treated with a peculiar vividness of metaphorical transformation that has the effect of removing them out of history – Charles the hunted animal netted by Cromwell, Cromwell the fierce falcon held on the lure of the falconer. Powerful contemporary figures are in fact diminished, subordinated to a third person or subject stated at the beginning and repeated, in shadowy form, at the close:

> The Forward Youth that would appear
> Must now forsake his *Muses* dear . . .
> The same *Arts* that did *gain*
> A *Pow'r* must it *maintain*.

If the Ode has a hero, it is finally neither Charles nor Cromwell, but an invisible man; perhaps even the 'forward youth' himself, who would (like a published poet) 'appear'. Of its two Caesars, the King and the Dictator, the poem seems to say – at the political level – something profound but simple: that the King is beautiful in defeat only, and that the Dictator who defeats him will become a King – two Caesars in one wreath. But Charles and Cromwell are also symbols of different conditions. The Ode is certainly a brilliant

---

[1] William Simeone, 'A Probable Antecedent of Marvell's Horatian Ode', *Notes and Queries*, 197 (1952), pp. 316–18.

political poem; but the poet has extended his politics as far back as to the Rome of Lucan and Horace, and then further back still, to a time when life seems to consist only of the hunt, and the garden. And to take it that far is to take it almost out of history.

Marvell's poem has various literary sources. But there can be little doubt that its spirit is above all 'Horatian': that its style is indebted in a manner which Marvell's perfect imitation communicates as tacitly as fully. The opening two stanzas of the Ode pause at a brilliantly expressive gesture, like a gambit in chess, that of lifting armour down: an image reminiscent, though in reverse, of that which closes one of Horace's most familiar Odes, 'Quis multa gracilis' (i.v), (a poem much translated in Marvell's lifetime, by Milton and Cowley among others). The Roman poet there contemplates the thought of his sometime mistress Pyrrha's new lover, who is still held in the illusion that his delicious present moment will be his for always; and Horace then describes himself, by contrast, in the image of a man whose journey is forever ended on the sea of love, who has hung up his garments as an offering to the powerful god of the sea –

> suspendisse potenti
> vestimenta maris deo.

Whether Marvell in fact remembered this image is unimportant. His Ode is profoundly Horatian, with an artistry that has learned from many such images. Though critics have noted the Ode's Horatian context, it is usually the political attitudes which receive attention.[1] What is more striking is the effect of a whole mind and style; for it was in part the response to Horace that enabled an elsewhere intransigently 'English' and private sensibility to do what was on other terms often closed to it, to write a true poem that was also public. In another of his best-known Odes, 'Otium divos rogat' (ii.xvi), Horace defines peace or detachment as not merely order in the state, but lucidity and economy of mind, the art of being 'a mind happy in the here and now', *laetus in praesens animus*. This classic theme of the Roman poet recurs often in the Odes, and outside them in the Epistles, where Horace several times uses a phrase which defines Marvell's style almost more aptly than his own: *animus aequus*, 'a mind well-balanced'.

[1] The best study is John S. Coolidge's 'Marvell and Horace', *Modern Philology*, 63 (1965), pp. 111–20.

At the end of 11.xvi Horace refers to that 'small estate' where he lives, a place which becomes something like a symbol for the mind's house-in-order. If this symbol 'worked' in Horace's own poetry, and continued to haunt the imagination of Europe for many centuries, this was because the poet's verse continually made it real. What begins as a mere act of reference is confirmed by the peculiar organization and economy with which the entire poem is set in order. Horace's world is public, his tone urbane; if a sense of private personality infuses an Ode it will not be from the expression of Romantic ego, but from the pervasive, tight, and brilliant setting-in-order of objects and experiences, by which a mind is continually *laetus in praesens*, relating pasts and futures to its own steadily-advancing presentness. The impact of an Ode like 'Quis multa gracilis' comes from the dense collocation of a past and future existence which may hurt and threaten each other but which must co-exist. Indeed, the poet may be said to exist there, and with intensity, at the exact present point where the secure youth and the embittered man co-exist in one mind. Horace seems to have been perhaps the first in his language to prefer these highly original juxtapositions of words, images, and experiences, to more formal and logical sequences of thought: which is why his transitions are felt to be problematic, the subject of dispute. The art that results combines something like a maximum of the personal with a maximum of the impassive. It is not surprising to find an Ode like 1.xiv, 'O navis, referent' – which a reader might well take to be a classic, moving, and dry poem of ironic misery at the re-encroachment of love (and T. S. Eliot seems to have taken it as such, echoing it in his 'Marina') – firmly titled in the Loeb edition, 'To the Ship of State'.[1] Whether the Ode *is* addressed to the Ship of State, or to Horace's own battered and too-far-travelled heart is, beyond a certain point, immaterial: neither heart nor state now exist to argue about. But a poetic image has been released into history. The poem itself is a private place, a 'small estate', unshakeably individual though public in its clarity and realism. It maintains a poise that is responsible to experience, but that belongs to no one but the writer himself.

[1]E. Fraenkel argues that the Ode must be allegorical and that its Hellenic background, together with early interpretations of it, suggest that it refers to *res publica*; he adds, however: 'Horace preferred not to lift at any point the veil of the allegory' (*Horace*, Oxford 1957, pp. 154–6).

It is this quiet detachment which Marvell achieves in his 'Horatian Ode'. The poem has one direct connection with its artistic ancestor, which goes beyond its title and its metre and even the *animus aequus* always reflected in its language. Its most obvious feature is that startling poise or justice of mind that led a man writing what has been called 'a panegyric of Cromwell' to intersect the hero's victory with the king's defeat – to enclose the triumph of death within the triumph of life. The introduction of a third person, the forward youth present at the opening, permits both Cromwell and Charles to seem equidistant from us, and in a special way: the action of Charles belongs to the past, the action of Cromwell to the future. There is in Marvell's poem an organization of experience as exact and as personal as that of Horace's Odes, and this shaping is, moreover, that temporal procession of 'now, then, one day' – *nunc, antehunc, olim* – which will give an Ode by Horace its structure. Marvell's mind may here be *laetus in praesens* in a striking sense. In 1700, just half a century after the 'Horatian Ode', Dryden's *Secular Masque* would formally observe the end of an old age and the bringing-in of a new. It is possible that Marvell was in 1650 doing something very similar: that the unwonted depth and certainty of this political poem came from the unparalleled representativeness of the moment, in which a past and a future hold the human mind at a crisis reminiscent of the many human crises in time, in which losses will be as many as gains. For the execution of Charles, in the year preceding the Ode, had in fact – as we now recognize – marked the end of an era. The Middle Ages died with Charles; modernity came with the New Model Army. And the death of the King was also in some sense the end of ritual, of myth – it was the last Reformation, the final breaking of an icon: for the cult of Charles the Martyr, however long it lasted, took its intensity from its status as lost cause. The end of mythical history is an event which no poet, however rational and Protestant, can contemplate quite without disturbance. Marvell, who remained all his life a constitutional monarchist, records something of that distance in the great but confused images he gives to Cromwell, watching him,

> climbe
> To ruine the great work of Time,
> And cast the Kingdome old
> Into another Mold.

> Though Justice against Fate complain,
> And plead the antient Rights in vain:
> But those do hold or break
> As Men are strong or weak.

A poet elsewhere often cool as well as witty is recording here a degree of shock that goes well beyond what we usually mean by the political. It reduces to triviality any superficial approach as to what side the poet is on – where Marvell *is*; the poet is here, at the point of shock, between past and future. The syntax of the stanza concerning justice and fate is interestingly broken and involute, as though the thinking of the poem checked there in a knot before moving on again. It makes Marvell seem to be holding for a moment a perception which could not be clearly expressed in any of the technical languages of his time, neither theological nor philosophical, political nor scientific. For the peculiarity of the historical moment at which he writes is that in it, the very concepts themselves are changing – of history, of politics, and indeed of time itself. This is the stage of historiography at which time is ceasing to begin with the garden of Eden and end with Apocalypse; it is beginning to become the finally unending story of the State. And, where concepts of this scale are involved and – however obscurely – glimpsed by the poet, it is not surprising that 'antient Rights' should be pleaded 'in vain', and the stanza drops exhausted into the mere physical factuality of 'Men are strong or weak'. This is the Marvell who, twenty years later in his *Rehearsal Transpros'd*, was to say of the Civil Wars: 'Men may spare their pains when Nature is at work, and the world will not go faster for our driving.' Conflict resolves to the sense of process: Time, Nature, History move on and take Charles and Cromwell with them. The poem does not involve itself with the clash of Caesar and Caesar, as though one could choose between them: but with the achievement and cost of the transition in time from one to the other. It commits itself to neither, and the deep politeness it extends to both is a style for standing off.

Compared to even the best of the other occasional poems, the 'Horatian Ode' has the precision of a man whose probity comes from strict reference first to himself and to his own standards; it is in this sense a genuinely 'Protestant' poem, even a Commonwealth poem, which replaces Horace's Augustan style by the civilized

seventeenth-century conscience. Metre and diction alike become the
vehicle of this precision. Each stanza, though steady in its forward
insistence, at the same time narrows down to point after point of
delicate awareness:

> *He* nothing common did or mean
> Upon that memorable Scene:
> But with his keener Eye
> The Axes edge did try:
> Nor call'd the *Gods* with vulgar spight
> To vindicate his helpless Right,
> But bow'd his comely Head,
> Down as upon a Bed.

This whole famous passage sparkles with sharply dangerous words –
adorn, clap, bloody, mean, Scene, try, vulgar, helpless, comely, Bed – that
are nails in a coffin, though whose coffin, it is not at all easy to say.
Everything is beautiful, and something is betrayed. Rhythm under-
lines this uncommon aesthetic power in the diction. The incisive,
surprising rhymes that close the oblique and devious rhythms of the
'Roman' metre – a metre so alien to the colloquial, opinionative
strength of English, and therefore so accurate in undermining this
opinionativeness – end by making the tone finally reserved, almost
dreamlike. It may not be irrelevant that the only two really striking
poetic moments in 'The Last Instructions to a Painter' have this same
quality of dream-likeness. In one, the self-immolating hero 'brave
Douglas' lies down to die as one to sleep and dream –

> Round the transparent Fire about him glows,
> As the clear Amber on the Bee does close

– and in the second, Charles II encounters in 'the dead shade of
night' the ghost of England, or of Peace, and, observing her to be a
female, absent-mindedly reaches out for her,

> But soon shrunk back, chill'd with her touch so cold,
> And th'airy Picture vanisht from his hold.

The 'Horatian Ode' achieves this quality of reverie far more
consistently and more profoundly: but more tacitly too. There is
nothing superficially Romantic in the poem. The sense of removed
intensity perhaps depends initially on that oddly weighty *appear*
which closes the distorted first line:

The forward Youth that would appear.

The confused and – it may be – destructive involvement of life and literature, and of life and life, in the struggle to survive, is the subject delineated, with an extremely elegant negligence, in the poem's opening two stanzas: which drift quietly but steadily towards that critical gesture, the lifting down, for good and all, of the public armour, the defensive shell of a man. The poem begins with a submerged shock of paradox, an advised departure from the arts – art used not to conceal art but to betray it, a betrayal which is the price of that art of 'appearing'. Before Cromwell ever comes on the scene, the poem meditates on what this means, to 'appear': to live the public life. In the process substance and form are matched in a manner hardly found elsewhere in Marvell. The decorum of the Ode is peculiarly Roman, peculiarly public: hence the brilliant unity of the whole, as compared to a work like 'Appleton House', which pays its discreteness as the price of its Englishness. The Ode is a masque, almost a ballet, of pure action – of the appearance of events. We look steadily and with an unvarying equilibrium on the armour lifted down; on Cromwell not knowing friend from enemy, all alike 'inclosing' him, getting in his way; on Charles 'adorning' the scaffold, his death a mime applauded by the bloody hands of encircling soldiers – as in those theatre-deaths of criminals on the depraved late Roman stage, when life and art fused grossly into one show;[1] on the Roman 'Architects' of state running away; on the Irish 'seeing themselves tamed', like men reading their own history many years after in books or newspapers, their public commitment doing what their hearts never could – 'affirming the praises', 'confessing the virtues' of the man who has destroyed them. The whole poem is a pattern of related and yet terribly different actions, a 'dream of history', with gestures caught from past and present to suggest a future, actual, probable, or possible: the armour coming down from the wall, the falcon falling heavy from the sky; Charles bowing, the Pict 'shrinking'; Caesar's head blasted, the Roman head bleeding; the bloody hands clapping, Caesar's unseen hand keeping the sword erect; and last and most, the private arts forsaken at the beginning, the public arts gaining power at the end.

[1] As in Massinger's *Roman Actor* (1626).

These images of public life, of what we choose to call history, are all held in the scrutiny of the detached and private mind. That scrutiny reduces the conflict of the political elements to something much stiller, in which persons are 'united in the strife which divided them': so that within the poem Charles perpetually bows his head, Cromwell perpetually marches into the darkness of the future. The pattern of the whole reproduces in larger scale the continuing profundities of the simple six-syllable lines, which over and over again make the ruthless 'point' of the poem:

> those do hold or break
> As Men are strong or weak . . .
> And yet in that the *State*
> Foresaw it's happy Fate . . .
> How fit he is to sway
> That can so well obey . . .

Strength and weakness, success and fear, mastery and servitude circle on each other like a roundabout; and the images playing against each other are in their turn dominated by a greater counter-image, the heartless and yet beautiful flow of the poem's 'action', its circling, rhyming but steadily advancing passage through time. The poem unanswerably subordinates the arts of its beginning to the arts of its close. In this sense there is no doubt at all that the poem is 'about' Cromwell: for Cromwell is in it the fact that constitutes the future, and Marvell's is a mid-century, even a Restoration intelligence, for whom facts matter. But there is a fine artistry in the way the poem moves with full momentum towards that disturbing close: where Cromwell, himself now grown into Caesar, the now personally nameless as well as faceless 'son of War and Fortune', must march indefatigably on and on and on, like Time itself, into a future that is after all factless, unknown, and void:

> And for the last effect
> Still keep thy Sword erect:
> Besides the force it has to fright
> The Spirits of the shady Night,
> The same *Arts* that did *gain*
> A *Pow'r* must it *maintain*.

The pauses between 'fright' and 'The Spirits', between '*gain*' and 'A *Pow'r*', are like hesitations, difficult decisions; and the continuity between them, as the poem moves none the less on, is like a walk out into darkness on a raised high wire. These are 'effects', to use Marvell's own impassive word, which take the poem a long way beyond what we usually expect of political panegyric.

This best of Marvell's political poems takes its depth from its capacity to cut through the historic and to go down to a level which we do not usually intend when we name the 'political'. To some degree this can be thought of as the particular gift of Marvell, the obverse of what appears in other forms as an unsociable reserve and reticence, even eccentricity of mind; to some degree also it is the faculty of all real poetic intelligence to undercut the mundane in this way. But it is also an aspect of the historical moment when Marvell was writing. Writers of the mid-century were both privileged and burdened by living through a phase of history so critical as almost to seem archetypal. Political history in the penumbra of the Civil Wars, from about 1640 on to about 1690, can appear to be 'complete', as though statecraft were an experience as finite as chess, and as though everything that could possibly happen in political organization actually occurred then, once and for all. The most intelligent and conscious men of the time seem almost to have recognized this archetypal quality in their experience, partly voiced by Cowley's famous and bitter lament that a 'warlike, various and tragical age' was 'best to *write of*, but worst to *write in*': for the history of the time always, at its deepest, moves towards the dream-like, tragic, or mythical. The greatest case is of course *Paradise Lost*, which is – among other things – the history of Milton's own lifetime; but the same might be said of the more exalted of his own prose works, or of the quality of tragic fiction or heroic romance which lights up Clarendon's great *History*, and which still survives as a faint resonance of the sublime even in Dryden's mock-heroic treatments of his own age. At this point in time, the political was still fully open to the interpretations of it made by the whole man. Academic studies often assume that 'history' must mean constitutional history, and will be best assessed by the politically-minded in the modern sense. But this is itself historically questionable. History as a game of power, on a secular field free from religious sanctions, is a definition familiar only to a post-Machiavellian world; but Hobbes's *Leviathan* was not yet published when Marvell's Ode was written, and politics becomes

the modern rivalry of factions only with the Restoration. Marvell's
Ode seems even consciously transitional in this, as in so many other
ways: for this transformation of public life into an arena that could be
called political in a more narrow sense, seems to be a submerged
apprehension of Marvell's poem, one of the profoundly disturbing
transitions that will come with the returning Cromwell. For
Cromwell is the greatest of those 'forward youths' that would
'appear', killing the king and replacing ritual with power.

It is the strength of the Ode that the intensity of the moment's
crisis, as Marvell apprehended it, empowered him to cut down to a
level that most of the other political poems do not reach to. That the
age did not in general invite it, that the Muses *were* betrayed, is a fact
which the Ode both states and counteracts. Marvell can write
extremely distinguished political poetry only at a level of private
awareness that the public did not in general desire. But the reverse of
this is, oddly enough, operative. If we are content to allow our sense
of what may constitute the political to extend as widely as the time in
fact permitted for minds so inclined, then Marvell's most private
poems will over and over again throw light on the actual history of
the age. And it is here, I think, that the explanation lies of that
peculiar sense of scale in some of the poet's best lyrics. They cut deep
into their age. The ways in which they do so may be at once and
intuitively apprehended in the reading: for the reading mind may
make instant references and comparisons over an extremely wide
area, hardly aware that it does so, but acting by a huge system of
latent codes and brief hieroglyphics. To make this process articulate
and rational is not easy, and would take a quantity of time and space
that would prove neither possible nor – if possible – very interesting.
It might be better, therefore, to proceed simply by sketching in one
or two mere suggestions as to why and how it is that we find this
quality of historical depth in Marvell's lyrics.

Marvell's poetry is usually assumed to have been mostly written
in the 1650s. There is reason to question this as a matter of fact, but it
remains true that the 1640s and 50s are crucial to the poet's
experience: his mind was formed by them. This period, and that
longer age which contains it, are most often thought of as an age of
conflict – a century of revolution. Obviously there is sense in this.
But the people who lived through the period often seem to have felt
very differently. The most famous story to have survived the wars –
probably apocryphal, and the more suggestive for it – is that of

the peasant who, ordered off the field of battle at Edgehill, expressed some surprise and interest that the parties in question were engaged in arms. This lowly reaction is peculiarly reflected in one of the most insistent themes or myths of the more exalted Clarendon's *History of the Rebellion*, his stubborn recreation of the great golden peace of the Caroline period, so suddenly and so nightmarishly violated. Below the experience of rational conflict in the Civil War period is something much deeper and more humanly real: bewilderment, a sense of the violation of the natural, an attachment to a far longer historical past, in the perspective of which 'such things do not happen'. The experience of 'Though Justice against Fate complain' is perhaps not a sense of conflict, but its opposite – a bewilderment at the absence of clear issues, a tragi-comic sense of the withdrawal of the rational. The War itself had been 'this war without an enemy'. This is the phrase, now a famous one, which the Parliamentarian Sir William Waller used in a letter explaining to a great friend who was a Royalist that he could no longer meet him. Waller's sense of the irrationality – yet hardly meaninglessness – of the pressures that were driving them both emerges in his description of the Wars as both 'this tragedy', and yet *Opus Domini*, the work of the Lord.

Waller's image of the Wars is representative of the feeling of all the moderates of his time – which means the greater number of sane and conscientious English gentlemen. They felt themselves held in an impasse, a tragedy that was none the less fated, necessary, godly: and they felt it similarly whether they were nominally of the Parliamentarians or the Royalists. But the time was governed by men who were not moderate. Marvell in his Ode confronts, as though face to face with each other, the two men who almost certainly never met, Charles and Cromwell. It could be said that the vocation of Charles, like the instincts of most of the Stuarts, was so absolutely to define the nature of Kingship as to make most of his subjects have to choose between betraying themselves and betraying their country. And the vocation of Cromwell was absolutely to stop him doing it: to 'cut off the king's head with the crown upon it'. Since the age could scarcely manage without a king, the process was also to some degree self-betraying, even in the case of King Charles and King Oliver. In April 1646, Charles escaped from Oxford disguised as a servant: the Royalist poet Cleveland commemorated the event with his *Kings Disguise*,

whose dozens of conceits make over and over again the one simple
embittered point:

> Oh for a State-distinction to arraigne
> *Charles* of high Treason 'gainst my Soveraigne.

This process of self-betrayal, enforced by the historical milieu, is
generic to all the greater literature of the age. It affects Milton's
Adam as deeply as it does that little group of aristocrats who gather
at Great Tew in the Royalist Clarendon's *History of the Rebellion*;
cultivated, rational, and peace-loving individuals fighting off the
knowledge of evil in the world outside, and becoming, in the
writer's hands, almost an image of the betrayal by History of the
innocent intellect itself. Many of Clarendon's heroes rode into
battle despairing; some died unarmed. The pattern of Royalist
death in the Civil Wars is epitomized in Clarendon's account of the
fall of the King's standard-bearer, Sir Edmund Verney, who rode
into battle at Edgehill unarmed and undefended, because he was
fighting for a king whose cause he did not respect:

> I do not like the quarrel, and do heartily wish that the King
> would yield and consent to what they desire; so that my
> conscience is only concerned in Honour and Gratitude to follow
> my Master.

In terms of 'cause' and 'conflict', Verney died defending bishops
whose rights he did not believe in. But not only Royalists died
bewildered. The best of the surviving Parliamentarians had only to
wait a few years to feel equally betrayed by the execution of their
King, whose powers – diminished and reformed – many had
believed themselves to be fighting for. (It was Lady Fairfax, the
wife of the great Parliamentarian leader who was also Marvell's
'patron', who shouted out in rage from the public gallery as the
King was sentenced at his trial.) And after ten years more, they
could feel equally betrayed by the King's Restoration; for the reign
of Charles II not only undid what the religious principles of the
Commonwealth achieved, but even abandoned the patriarchal
habits of the Caroline period before it.

The mid-seventeenth century called into being, in response to
historical changes going back many generations, all-or-nothing
intensities which the actual politics of the time could do little but
betray. Marvell himself, in his *Rehearsal Transpros'd*, speaks of 'that

imaginary absolute government, upon which rock we all ruined'.
To put it another way, it was the age of Paradise Lost: an age in
which Paradise was never more clearly perceived than at the exact
moment at which it ceased to be believed in. In political terms,
Eikon Basilike – the holy image of the King – appeared almost as
soon as the King was executed (as Marvell's Cromwell is called
'Caesar'); and the image of Charles in the famous frontispiece of
that work of hagiography brings together at once all the time's
impossibilities, reverently haloing an exquisite monarch whose
eyes are directed upwards to an air-borne crown. It has been
noticed that Charles looked sad long before he had good reason to;
that the portraits fashioned by Van Dyck throughout the 1630s
gave the King a lustrous melancholy owing perhaps less to
spirituality than to the high style of aristocratic and indeed imperial
portraiture from which they derived.[1] And even the idealizing
court masques of the time are gestures of royal power. It is hard
now not to find the 'mask' of the King in the *Eikon Basilike* simply
too high-bred, too sophisticated, too late in time for a holy image:
Charles can merely *act* it, with a grace that is only just not
condescension, and that Marvell in his Ode catches with a perfect
dryness:

> *He* nothing common did or mean
> Upon that memorable Scene.

Much later in time, at the end of the 1660s, Marvell comes to write
about Charles's eldest son, in his satire on 'our Lady State', 'The
Last Instructions to a Painter': and his Eikon of the son is as clear-
eyed as that of the father. Having failed to seduce the ghost of
England, Charles II bustles off to meet his chosen associates:

> To her own Husband, *Castlemain*, untrue.
> False to his Master *Bristol*, *Arlington*;
> And *Coventry*, falser than any one,
> Who to the Brother, Brother would betray;
> Nor therefore trusts himself to such as they.

That betrayal which Shakespeare's stage kings, his Richard or his
Lear, had experienced as a sin of the private heart, becomes at last in
Marvell's Restoration satires a rule of the political game.

[1] Roy Strong, *Van Dyck's 'Charles I on Horseback'* (1972).

Marvell's best poems lie within a territory that charts out the transition from one field to the other. The Elizabethan sense of tragic involvement has ebbed; the Restoration sense of comic ruthlessness has hardly yet developed. Marvell writes within a period of time in which political events are still only a shadow of other experiences. The bewilderment of the age seems unconsciously to have reflected the modern recognition that the English Wars were, in fact, only the surface symptom of a temporal transition beginning generations earlier, and not to be categorized into any single one *casus belli*, ecclesiastical, economic, or sociological. The Wars were merely the temporal focus of the meeting of new and old. Sir William Waller, caught up in the 'war without an enemy', living through a tragedy which is none the less *Opus Domini*, sees, as it were, through and behind the War itself, a deeper war intrinsic to the mere passage of time. The appalling sense of unreality which came to many men like him may explain curious incidents like the ghost-battles in the night-sky after Edgehill, when all the sounds of battle were re-enacted for shepherds and passers-by.[1] The War itself was a kind of ghost, hardly believed in even by the combatants who died in it: a momentary nightmare, in which past and future were caught together as in Hobbes's evocation of the ghostly present moment:

> the prognostics of time to come . . . are naturally but conjectures upon experience of time past.

In this context it is striking that Marvell should have opened the major political poem which succeeds the 'Horatian Ode', the 'First Anniversary', with an image that extends the milieu of his benevolent dictator, Cromwell, across a natural field both enormous and generically destructive:

> Like the vain Curlings of the Watry maze,
> Which in smooth streams a sinking Weight does raise;
> So Man, declining always, disappears
> In the weak Circles of increasing Years;
> And his short Tumults of themselves Compose,
> While flowing Time above his Head does close.

The fault of the 'First Anniversary' is that Cromwell's actual

---

[1]See, e.g., Peter Young, *Edgehill 1642* (1967), pp. 162–6.

activities never give Marvell a chance, imaginatively, to impose the dictator's image upon that tremendous field glimpsed at first: Cromwell the Ruler refuses to 'go down' humanly, without convincing us that he 'stays up' superhumanly, and the poem, therefore, never sounds true. But its opening affords an instance of what would, for Marvell, constitute a truth – political or otherwise – to which he could respond with imaginative certainty. His image of the destructive 'Watry maze' brings to mind the fact that 'politics' are only one aspect of that larger disturbance which troubled the whole century, and changed the dimensions of the past behind it and the future before it. The fatalism of these lines reminds us that many of Marvell's contemporaries believed deeply that the world was drawing to an end, running down in self-disintegrating exhaustion. And since the old Renaissance Europe was crumbling around them, they were in a way right. It is difficult to read much in later Renaissance literature without coming to share this sense of a culture that is gradually, like our own, dying on its feet. But a new more scientific culture was emerging as the old faded. If we translate this double sense of threshold and collapse into an outward-looking, classical image of Nature as a whole, then we arrive at the image of the stream of 'flowing' Time, in the 'First Anniversary': a Time that is always beginning as it ends, as the metre of the 'Horatian Ode' flows on from conclusive rhyme to rhyme, and ends with the word *maintain*.

Marvell's lifetime was a meeting of old and new in a sense more specific than this. It was the destructive wars themselves that helped to create new studies. A historian of the Society of Antiquaries tells us that

> soldiers on the King's side of the warring armies used their enforced travels to take antiquarian notes. Richard Symonds's *Diary of the Marches of the Royal Army During the Great Civil War* includes many notes on churches, chiefly heraldic.[1]

It is easy to imagine Charles's lace-collared knights carefully annotating the ruins as Cromwell's leather-jacketed forward-looking colonels everywhere added to them. Other new studies and techniques originated in the Civil Wars: the Royal Society began from wartime meetings of refugee scholars; the lively accounts of

[1] Joan Evans, *A History of the Society of Antiquaries* (Oxford, 1956), p. 21.

military events in wartime Cavalier journalism helped to generate both the characteristic style of Restoration comedy and the prose fiction of men like Defoe.[1] But it is antiquarianism in general which most reflects that involvement of old and new characterizing the period, a delighted power of insight brought about directly by the crumbling of a betrayed past. The best prose writer in this new antiquarianism, death and new life oddly blending in his work, is of course Sir Thomas Browne: 'Time hath endless rarities' in the remarkable last chapter of his *Urn Burial*. But Browne's mosaic vision is endemic, in much simpler form, to the whole mid- and later-seventeenth century. The antiquarian, historian, and biographer John Aubrey can be found writing a note on the ruins of Malmesbury Abbey, which absorbs politics into history and history into one great green landscape:

> Where the Choir was, now grass grows, where anciently were buried Kings and great men.[2]

And towards the end of the century the traveller Celia Fiennes was moved to an unaccustomed poetry by what she saw:

> Grass grows now where Winchelsea was, as was once said of Troy.[3]

Andrew Marvell is a special kind of antiquarian poet. He has a peculiar attentiveness to the whole literary life of the age, borrowing here and there with an absorbed eclecticism, and seeming to throw off a perfected specimen of every form that offered. It is noticeable, however, that Marvell is a 'finisher', that his beautiful lyrics produce the effect of making every form seem incapable of further development: each is the last in its line. What Marvell does to it, sets it in amber. But other poets than Marvell were antiquarian. Herrick and Lovelace are equally men enchanted by the small, preservers of the minutiae of cultural history, with

---

[1]Cf. C. V. Wedgwood, *Seventeenth-Century English Literature* (Oxford, 1950), pp. 96–8; also P. W. Thomas, *Sir John Berkenhead* (Oxford, 1969), pp. 127–8: 'Royalists' literary activities, far from being crushed in the Interregnum, were stimulated by the changed conditions. The *esprit de corps* built up in the years of warfare was not dissipated but in some respects consolidated. . . . Indeed, what they saw as the triumph of anarchy and iconoclasm made them more than ever conscious of their destiny as guardians of all things precious and noble in the world of letters.'

[2]John Aubrey, *Wiltshire: The Topographical Collections*, ed. J. E. Jackson, (1862), p. 255.

[3]*The Journeys of Celia Fiennes*, ed. Christopher Morris (1949), p. 138.

their anciently-traditioned Anacreontic poems on the Grasshopper, the Fly, the Ant, the Snail –

> Compendious Snayl! Thou seem'st to me
> Large Euclid's strict epitome.

If Marvell, with all his concentration on the small, is nevertheless obscurely larger than even such excellent fellow-miniaturists as Herrick and Lovelace, this is because his imagination sustains such antiquarianism more consistently and more profoundly. His poems, which may be seen as a virtuoso's elegy for a whole past tradition that is crumbling into fragments, are at the same time faithful to a new vision of that Nature which, like Time, flows overhead as Man goes down. 'Grass grows now where Winchelsea was': so Marvell takes his visitor down into the meadows beyond the historic Appleton house, where the grasshoppers laugh down on men:

> They, in there squeking Laugh, contemn
> Us as we walk more low then them:
> And, from the Precipices tall
> Of the green spir's, to us do call.

Such lines as these give Marvell at his best: a man private, idiosyncratic, strange. But these private qualities at the same time seem to render the real life of the age quite as truly as do the lucid externalities of the 'Horatian Ode'. The meadows in question after all belonged to Lord Fairfax, sometime head of the Parliamentary army, a man of equal public and private honour: who had retired to his estate – into *his* 'privateness' and 'strangeness' – because he could not face that invasion of Scotland which Marvell in his Ode so impassively recommends to Fairfax's some-time second-in-command. Fairfax found that he had reached, as it were, his personal maximum of betrayal, and elected as a result to step for the time being out of 'history'. Marvell's green world appears to be at the opposite pole, in its playful quasi-pastoralism, from the urgent world of affairs; but it intersects just as well the inward consciousness of the time, the divergent creative mind that drove men then – as much as now – to do what they did.

In his 'First Anniversary', a public enough poem, Marvell described history as the waters closing over a man's head. The meadows of Lord Fairfax's house are the place where we go down:

To see Men through this Meadow Dive,
We wonder how they rise alive.
As, under Water, none does know
Whether he fall through it or go.
But, as the Marriners that sound,
And show upon their Lead the Ground,
They bring up Flow'rs so to be seen,
And prove they've at the Bottom been.

It is hard not to read into these lines an almost Symbolist image of poetry as the reward of the death in life. Perhaps Marvell meant that; or perhaps his imagination was affected by something closer to his own time, a new archaeologizing, antiquarian spirit that was developing startlingly far and fast. Aubrey has a note that seems a brilliant prevision of Victorian geology, visualizing the world under an Ocean that ebbed to leave the earth exposed and fishy:[1] there is something of this in Marvell's flooded meadow; and his image of meadow-flowers at the bottom of the sea makes one wonder if he had seen North Sea fishermen bringing up land-flowers from the sea-bed. The Humber, near which he had spent much of his youth, and which had drowned his father, is an extremely ancient river, that flowed before the North Sea covered the land. However small the chosen areas of Marvell's poems, they often turn out to be surprisingly extensive in this way. Where they don't go wide, they go deep: like Lord Fairfax's mowers, who step into a meadow, and drown in the sea of time, or of history, or merely of the mind. The poet's green world is charged with that new intuition which made Aubrey insist that 'the World is much older than is commonly supposed', that 'these Antiquities are so exceeding old that no Bookes do reach them'.[2] But where Aubrey was a scholar and even a scientist, Marvell was an artist; and it is not the visible world alone, that 'Pomegranat full of cavernes' as Aubrey called it, which holds the poet's attention. It is the depths of the mind, a world within and yet beyond the dying culture of his time, which become Marvell's subject: a green world always extending like an abyss within the formal enclosures of the age, its intuitions of a 'wild and fragrant innocence' coming to rebuke the high-walled garden.

[1]John Aubrey, *Three Prose Works*, ed. John Buchanan-Brown (1972), p. 317.
[2]Aubrey, *Wiltshire*, p. 318.

In February 1656, late in the Interregnum, a minor but interesting event occurred in London. A company of soldiers under orders from Colonel Pride, the High Sheriff of Surrey, came to the Hope Theatre (once used for both plays and bear-baiting but long abandoned by the actors), led out all the bears, and shot them dead. A diarist of the time records that the troopers left alive only 'one white innocent cub'.[1] Such incidents must have been frequent during the war period: Aubrey tells a tragi-comic anecdote of soldiers shooting an old man's pet gander, which was exactly the same age as the man himself. But the wartime stories, usually involving Royalist troops, suggest no more than the ordinary brutality of their military context. The incident of the bears has some further resonance that makes it stay in the mind, seeming to communicate an oddly acute sense of life as it actually was in the empty squares and market-places of Commonwealth London. This is because the event holds in itself, as so much pre-Restoration history does, the lineaments of the psychological meaning the whole period has taken on for us. It embodies, in a small symbol at once savage and grotesque, all the time's impossibility. Which is better or worse: to bait bears or to shoot them? The decisive gesture proved futile: both bear-baiting and play-acting came back with the Restoration. But not to the empty Hope Theatre, which was turned into tenements. Time had after all moved on.

Just as this crude event of the bears can in itself appear to symbolize so much that was actual in the political choices or impossibilities of the period, so Marvell's tender and ironically beautiful poems can be reminiscent of a whole historical past. His 'Nymph complaining for the death of her Faun' is itself a historical event (it figured in a lifetime) that goes one stage further in its power to reflect the world around it. It is an invention, not a happening; it says more, and more truthfully. Marvell makes his poem catch its heroine in a moment of real time, which he deliberately relates to the public life of the age:

> The wanton Troopers riding by
> Have shot my Faun and it will dye.

Everything that happens in this poem takes place between the past

[1] See J. Q. Adams, *Shakespearean Playhouses* (1920), p. 337; Leslie Hotson, *Commonwealth and Restoration Stage* (1928), pp. 59–70 ('Bear Gardens and Bear-Baiting').

of 'Have shot' and the future of 'will dye'. And this acute temporality is echoed in a fact that accounts of the poem sometimes scarcely bother to notice. The 'Nymph Complaining' is a masterpiece of travesty on the part of a tough, highly literate Yorkshireman, the present or future MP for Hull and satirist of Charles II's government. The poet completely disappears into the precise voice of a girl, its bad grammar, its baby syntax: all the bravely quavering chant of a well-brought-up young innocent, now robbed of her innocence, but doing what she can with what is left. To recognize the travesty is to measure the distance – which is also a closeness – between the poet and the child, which is also, in its turn, a way of knowing from the beginning that something is finished. The nymph is done for as much as her fawn. The girl is childish, the fawn after all a spoiled pet, chewing up the roses and trampling the garden; no wonder Sylvio got tired and went. All the same the lines are an exquisite elegy as well as a comedy, and the white statue of the fawn is almost an icon: a fragile icon, but not yet quite broken.

A poem like 'The Nymph complaining for the death of her Faun' seems to hold together for a moment, late in time, some of the fragmenting private and public feelings that mattered most in the seventeeth century: and it does it the more intensely for its own triviality. A small thing may symbolize more adequately than a large, given the right reticence and absence of egoism in the artist; it commits itself to the imagination of a reader. Marvell may be said, in the end, to represent or commemorate his age, not by such traces of 'conflict' as may be found in his work, but by these reconciling, elusive (perhaps treacherous) symbols. The importance of conflict in his work can be greatly overstated; Marvell is the least dramatic of poets, and always has difficulty in either animating or concluding his dialogue poems. It is not debate or revolution which really interest or disturb him, but the necessity of compromise and reconciliation, the habit of loyalty and the nature of tradition. He seeks to find images that will express coherently the fusions and confusions of existence in history, with the self always hopeful, always betraying and betrayed:

> fetter'd . . .
> In Feet; and manacled in Hands.
> Here blinded with an Eye; and there
> Deaf with the drumming of an Ear . . .

> So Architects do square and hew,
> Green Trees that in the Forest grew.

Marvell may be said, therefore, to be most himself, *and* most capable of mediating a truth of his time, through images and poems whose relation to their time is only that oblique relation of the house or the church to the green tree in the forest. As a poet, he throws light – if this is the kind of light we want from a poet – on the constitutional history of his time, and the massive changes in the development of bureaucracy, by effects as reticent as (for instance) his transformation of pastoral. 'The second temple was not like the first': Marvell brought new life to pastoral by the mocking energy with which he killed it off. What appear to be his early love-pastorals, though few are datable, give the impression of having been written, with great brilliance of style, one day after their conventions of language and feeling finally ceased to be tolerable. The shepherd and shepherdess Thyrsis and Dorinda, being converted to Christianity, blissfully depart to commit suicide by opium; Daphnis abandons his agonized suit to Chloë at the moment when she begins to relent, and takes up a career of promiscuity. Like his Petrarchan love poems, 'The Gallery' and 'The Unfortunate Lover', these pastorals can make the conventions they use seem dated beyond belief, and yet these same conventions still exert power over the mind: as though Marvell's characters were trapped, with one foot in the past, one in the future. The grotesquerie of all these works – which are brilliant, but uncomfortable – is resolved in the creation of the Mower, Marvell's highly original invention. The Mower is less a character than an elusive new convention who voices some of Marvell's most individual apprehensions. As strong as a peasant, as polite as a courtier and as vulnerable as a child, the Mower may well be Marvell-the-poet as seen by Marvell-the-politician. All the old pastoral props have been diminished and then naturalized into that world of small creatures that fill the Mower poems: the hot grasshoppers, the green frog wading in the brook, the nightingale reading music all the summer night long, the 'darling Daffadils' and thrusting grass itself. It is a brilliant toy world that reflects, as in a glass, the reflecting consciousness, perhaps equally small, of the Mower in love, labouring, philosophizing, grieving, scolding, chopping himself down with his own scythe, and always singing as he does it. If

Milton's 'Lycidas' shows how powerfully an artist may use the pastoral conventions of the late Renaissance, then Marvell's 'Mower to the Glo-worms' shows how quietly such conventions may be undercut.

To recall Marvell's great contemporary, a colleague and friend who also learned how to transform politics into poetry, is to sharpen the sense of what is individual to the author of the Mower poems. Milton too can be the most ravishing of verbal artists; but his genius needed space. Full as it is of detailed brilliance, *Paradise Lost* needs all its twelve books to make its point: it is not finished until all its massive length has arrived at that final 'solitary way'. Marvell was at home in small poems. 'The Mower to the Glo-worms' imparts a sense of a lost paradise – irretrievably, if in the end lightly lost – not qualitatively less deep than any comparable moment in Milton. Marvell can even do this with a single word. It would be fanciful to say that the poet compacts most of what was important in the history of his time into the way he uses the word *green*, but such a claim would not be meaningless. The longest of his unsatirical poems, 'Appleton House', tends to rely for its form and mass on conventions and circumstances now not too easy to retrieve from their past moment, but we continue to make the attempt because of the life that floods the poem once the poet moves to the meadows, where the water has ebbed from the cut grass:

> For now the Waves are fal'n and dry'd,
> And now the Meadows fresher dy'd;
> Whose Grass, with moister colour dasht
> Seems as green Silks but newly washed.

To call 'green silks' – like 'green thought' – a Metaphysical image, is only to gesture at the degree of power some poets managed to get into certain conjunctions of words at a given moment of history: conjunctions that, without exception, reflect shock, disjunction, reconciliation.[1] Marvell's 'green' is always the colour of a concept, almost an act of faith in some possibility of the natural that transcends and outgoes the most destructive sense-experience, as the grass, mown, for a moment is green silk. To conceptualize in this way Marvell will empty out his lines around the word *green*, or

---

[1] Marvell's phrase perhaps recalls Milton's line in *Comus*: 'That in their green shops weave the smooth-haired silk' (l. 715).

associate green with grass, or with glitter, or with brook- or sea-water, or will abstract his *green* or *grass* by comparing it to hope, or to miracle, or by calling grass *green* only as days may be called *golden*. In the mowing of the meadows, which fugitively and at deliberate distance reflects the history of its period – so that a dead king diminishes, impossibly, to a small slashed bird – the mind, or the soul, or Time, or Nature, or merely grass, gets itself resurrected as *green silks*: an image that exquisitely radiates all the fastidious connoisseurship of the period, like a rarity that catches the light a long way away and a long time ago.

The single poem which has most of this quality is the haunting but elusive 'Bermudas'. Part icon, part ironic or even comic elegy, this is in some ways Marvell's most perfect poem, though less popular now than among the Victorians, who probably responded to its charm without letting its deep irony disturb their reading. In the early 1650s Marvell lodged with one John Oxenbridge, who had in 1634 been turned out of his Oxford college for Puritan practices and had gone to the Bermudas, ending his long if interrupted spell there by becoming governor of the Islands. Marvell's poem is likely to have some connection with Oxenbridge's experience of the Islands, which was troubled by disruption and not idyllic; the same detached connection, perhaps, as the poem seems to have with a longish poem by Waller on the Islands, a piece of more or less mock-heroic description in heroic couplets. Marvell's relationship with any apparent sources is likely to be of an extreme detachment, just as the poem may have been written, I think, many years after the early 1650s. Like 'The Nymph Complaining' and 'The Garden', 'Bermudas' has a philosophical quality that suggests middle-age, not youth. It is the most detached, dissociated of poems, though its central experience is tenderly involved. The chief part of the poem is a hymn of praise and thanks that comes from a small boat; and this boat is discovered caught in a mysterious and tropical calm, which in effect divides the singing from us as if by glass. The opening quatrain builds a frame or barrier containing, and cutting off from us, the poem's lyric substance:

> Where the remote *Bermudas* ride
> In th' Oceans bosome unespy'd,
> From a small Boat, that row'd along,
> The listning Winds receiv'd this Song.

If the Bermudas are *remote* we are not near them; if they or the ocean's bosom are *unespied* we do not see them; if the *listning Winds receive* the song we do not hear it; if there are individual persons in the boat we are not told of them. The boat moves, it is unclear where, and the song rises, it is unclear from whom or to whom – indeed, it seems unclear to the singers themselves, whoever they are, for they throw their thanks up at

> Heavens Vault,
> Which thence (perhaps) rebounding, may
> Eccho beyond the *Mexique Bay*.

As the song ends, the boat moves away, in no stated direction but –so it seems – that of the clock:

> Thus sung they, in the *English* boat,
> An holy and a chearful note,
> And all the way, to guide their Chime,
> With falling Oars they kept the time.

The first line of this last quatrain, 'Thus sung they, in the *English* boat', always brings a faint and reassuring shock in the reading, late in the poem: it seems to be one of Marvell's beloved anti-climactic climaxes. There *is* someone in the boat after all: and the boat is, of all things – considering the exotic circumstances – an *English* boat; and the vision they have sung about is not only *holy*, it is *chearful*. The effect is rather as though Ariel had turned out to be a practising Methodist. With a transition as profound as a change of key in music, the last quatrain roots a dream in reality. For the singers are without doubt involved in a vision of Paradise. They may be going to or from the Bermudas, but it is Paradise that they see:

> He hangs in shades the Orange bright,
> Like golden Lamps in a green Night,
> And does in the Pomgranates close,
> Jewels more rich than *Ormus* show's.
> He makes the Figs our mouths to meet;
> And throws the Melons at our feet,
> But Apples plants of such a price,
> No Tree could ever bear them twice.

Waller's descriptive couplets had praised without convincing. Marvell's abbreviated medium transforms the other poet's images by dramatizing them into the monosyllables of innocence. The gratitude sounds childish – Paradise is a heavenly garden-fête, hung with paper lanterns, shining late at night. But the sophistication and control of the recording mind, Marvell's unerring instinct for the central unsatisfied delight, converts that childishness into an intense wistfulness permanently human, a longing from which the habitual scepticism is almost withheld, except, it may be, in the dryness of 'such a price'. So long as they sing and row, those in the small boat are in the presence of, if not Paradise, then at least an image of it. But that 'so long as' is bounded, as the song itself is framed, by the mysterious void all around. The poem catches the small boat and holds it for a moment out at sea, locked in this silence of the unheard, the unseen: a silence that allows to lapse into a real doubt the rhetorical question with which the singers begin:

> What should we do but sing his Praise
> That led us through the watry Maze,
> Unto an Isle so long unknown,
> And yet far kinder than our own?

In his 'First Anniversary' it is Time that Marvell calls a 'watry Maze'. A moment of time, of history, holds his singers where they are. With such a context, the outcome could always have been different – could always *be* different, in so far as the poem is present and alive. Paradise exists, then, only in the singers' marvellous, doubtful image of it.

In the 'Bermudas', Marvell takes a green world somewhere far out of sight, and finds it at the centre; he writes a hymn so private as to be essentially inaudible, and it echoes 'beyond the *Mexique Bay*'. This public art of the private dream is a reversal of that impulse by which in the 'Horatian Ode' Marvell made a private legend out of public events and persons. His Bermudan singers praise God for turning oranges into 'golden Lamps in a green Night'. The phrase will do very well for the creative transformations of Marvell's own poetry.

3

The End of the Big Names: Milton's Epic Catalogues

Argument is carried on oftener and more firmly
by name than by notation.
(*A Fuller Institution of the Art of Logic*, Columbia
Milton, xi. 225)

If . . . any name whatever can be so pleasing to God,
why has he exhibited himself to us in the gospel
without any proper name at all?
(*Christian Doctrine*, Columbia Milton, xiv. 295)

When a good poet writes adversely of another, his object may be not the other man's work but what Bacon might have called an *idol* of it. Ben Jonson's 'Would he had blotted a thousand', and 'For not keeping of accent he deserved hanging' do not sound like serious criticisms of Shakespeare and Donne; they are loaded sentences aimed at current misconceptions of what the two men's genius really consisted in. The other Johnson's 'dull in a new way' and 'easy, vulgar and therefore disgusting' appear to take as their target an illusion in the reader more than the malpractice of the writer. What Gray and Milton had written would stay written; but readers' minds can always be cleared of cant. No writer seems more strongly to provoke others into this attempt to destroy *idols* (or more to create the idols) than does Milton – an interesting fact, in view of his career. And equally interesting is the fact that F. R. Leavis chose the world 'dislodgement' to describe Milton's case as he saw it, nearly fifty years ago now: for dislodgement is a thing that happens to idols. Leavis took as his point of reference certain of T. S. Eliot's poems, together with the occasional word that Eliot had let fall critically concerning Milton's 'magniloquence'. A few years later, in 1936, Eliot himself wrote the essay later reprinted as *Milton I*. It is often assumed that this is an attack to which the later *Milton II* provides a treacherous or reassuring counterpart of defence; but *Milton I* does something more useful than attack. Taking pains to advise the reader that criticism is neither 'iconoclasm' nor 'hoodlumism', the writer defines a current *idol* and does what he can about demolishing it. He does so through that style of all-but-formal irony which brings Eliot's criticism closest to his own later verse. For in this essay he considers the nature of Milton's greatness while stating explicitly (and always assuming implicitly) that it is at least as important for poetry to be *good* as it is for it to be *great*. Milton becomes the case of the 'great poet', all too attractive to a reader whose love of a good poem is replaced by the need for a great poem; who hungers for the *classic* in a bad sense, for the established, the authoritative. For such a reader, Milton is a mind whose function it is to emit large, oracular, and handy public statements.

Near the end of his essay Eliot displays the brilliant knack he had of nailing his theses to particular local points. He brings up the question of Milton's name-dropping: usually practised to gain 'the effect of magnificence', but now and again (Eliot suggests) so intemperate, so grotesque as to bring to the fore a real weakness in Milton's art. He quotes, as example, from that long catalogue in Book XI of *Paradise Lost*, which lists all the places revealed to Adam in his vision of future time, from

> Cambalu, seat of Cathaian khan,
> And Samarchand by Oxus, Temir's throne,
> To Pachin of Sinaean kings, and thence
> To Agra and Lahor of great mogul . . .

and all the way round the 'hemisphere of earth', ending with *El Dorado*. The list is long, the names impassive, the action static. We assume, says Eliot, that Milton really did want what we clearly want him to want: to be a very great, a very important public poet, a mouthpiece of philosophical and theological statement – a man, as we say, of weight. Therefore everything in his work that does not succeed in these aims, or even appear to attempt them, must be the equivalent to nonsense – mere style, mere 'music'. The conclusion that Eliot comes to is that *Cambalu* and the rest, being evidently not weighty, must be the alternative: 'mere levity . . . not serious poetry, not poetry fully occupied about its business, but rather a solemn game'.

Eliot's distinctive gift as a critic was economy of means in achieving largeness of ends: turning rapidly – however obliquely – to the most important issues and surrounding them with question-marks. For on to the smaller question of Milton's 'great names' he is here focusing, and wholly justifiably, the whole larger question of the poet's Grand Style: what he did with it, what we make of it. And meanwhile under this argument there are all the time moving even larger issues. By lightly and provocatively questioning the Grand Style as a self-justifying value, Eliot is also asking: Should we think a writer *good* because he is *great*? And (in any case) should we think a writer *great* because he is *grand*? And (in any case) should we call Milton *grand* because he merely names grand names? He raises the possibility that Milton is culpable of having first enforced these divisions of 'great' and 'good', 'meaning' and 'music'; and culpable too because a passage like the Book XI catalogue encourages us to connive with the poet in confusing a high-falutin meaninglessness with poetry.

Any reader who appreciates Milton's verse should be able to answer Eliot: to say why he finds this Book XI catalogue *good*, without having recourse to the word 'music', or its equivalent. And yet, despite the apparent increase in the sophisticated analysis of poetic language since Eliot published his essay, Milton's roll-calls still seem to induce a lapse of thought. In 1977 A. L. Rowse's *Milton the Puritan*, for instance, stated firmly:

> Really, it is a baroque poem, gorgeous in its magnificence when it chooses to be. . . . There . . . follows a roll-call of reverberating names, a regular feature contributing crystal and chalcedony and chrysoprase to the poetry. (If one may have such baroque splendour in verse, why not in church? But Milton was visually defective here, inhibited by his Puritanism).

There is curiously little distance between this and a work that one can take as characteristic of the whole late-Victorian approach to Miltonic style, Mackail's seventy-year-old (and not insensitive) *Springs of Helicon*, which lamented that old age, fatigue, and disillusionment should so have malformed the writing of Book X of *Paradise Lost*, and much after it: 'This is not the organ-music that we knew. What's become of all the gold? Has the golden oil ceased to flow into the lamp now that night is so deep? . . .' Mackail's tone was compassionate. Rowse perhaps does rather worse in imputing to the poet's whole career what must be either stupidity or dishonesty – Milton was 'inhibited by his Puritanism'. Rowse is using the word 'Puritanism' here in its common sense of 'hatred of the arts' – a usage that cannot be wisely applied to a man as signally aesthetic as Milton shows himself to be; but the error, and the illogic (or worse) imputed to Milton are both entailed by thinking of poetic style as semi-precious lumps of applied adornment. Similarly, Mackail's regret that *Paradise Regained* shows something like a stylistic death of the spirit depends on the assumption that the earlier writing was 'organ-music' – it was lovely, it was public, and it worked by starts and stops.

Eliot's grave allusions to Milton's *music* are a deference to and a provocation of that part of our mind and of the poet's audience at large that looks to his work for this kind of too-easy pleasure. The poet who on another occasion referred ironically to his own verse as 'a mug's game' (and who in Section III of *East Coker* was to imitate Milton at his darkest and most unworldly) called the Book XI catalogue a 'solemn game'. The challenge was clearly for someone to describe it better. But it is less clear that anyone has ever answered the challenge on Eliot's own terms, and made poetic *sense* of Milton's long, cold rigmarole. Eliot's point was taken up, only a few years after he wrote, by Sir Maurice Bowra's study of the literary epic, *From Virgil to Milton*. This stated that the Book XI catalogue could not possibly be a solemn game because Milton was there practising a formal device of epic: he was in this particular case indebted to the vision of the future in the tenth book of Camoens's *Lusiads*. But Bowra's scholarly point is less potent as a critical argument; for it is open to anyone to answer that an epic device is only an even solemner game. The argument hardly advances beyond a more sedate form of Rowse's 'It's-naughty-but-it's-nice' aestheticism. This distinction may seem in itself a mere game of words and terms. But it has to be remembered that Milton's epic was written at just that moment in time when mock-heroic was emerging as the new form: and some very nice literary points were turning on the fact that differences could be greater than resemblances. Milton's *Cambalu* passage has an individual quality that makes it quite different from the vision of the future in Camoens. It differs, probably, from most other epic catalogues; and certainly enough from (say) Homer's Catalogue of the Ships to have almost, though not quite, an ironic relationship with it. This personal quality, this differentiating predominance of what it is necessary to call style (though it is also dangerous to isolate that quality of style from substance) – this is so positive a factor as to undermine the idea that there can be a general style which we call 'epic form', and which can explain Milton's poetry.

Bowra turns, having dealt with Eliot, to examine another epic device, the simile: in particular, Milton's Book I comparison of fallen angels to autumn leaves in Vallombrosa. In doing so, he throws some incidental light on the use the poet makes of these 'great names'; for the cluster of names here both resembles and differs from the Book XI catalogue. Bowra finds in the image a *topos* which he traces back, very interestingly, through Marlowe and Tasso and Dante and Virgil to Bacchylides, a Greek poet of the fifth century BC, who imagined:

> the ghosts
> Of unlucky men by Cocytus' streams
> Like leaves that the wind flutters
> On Ida's glittering headlands
> Where the flocks graze.

Bowra concludes: Milton's 'Vallombrosa is exact as Bacchylides' Ida and has the immediacy of Greek poetry.' Again, the search for a classic ideal is clouding the difference between two poets. It is relevant, I think, that Bowra quotes of Milton only two and a half lines, which may seem to bring the later image closer to the lucidity of the far-distant Greek source; but the truncation radically alters Milton's image:

> His legions, angel forms, who lay entranced
> Thick as autumnal leaves that strew the brooks
> In Vallombrosa, where the Etrurian shades
> High overarched embower; or scattered sedge
> Afloat, when with fierce winds Orion armed
> Hath vexed the Red Sea coast, whose waves o'erthrew
> Busiris and his Memphian chivalry . . .

It is often difficult to tell where to start or finish a quotation from *Paradise Lost*, where every phrase, sentence, and paragraph can seem to intertwine within a great mesh of currents of energy that hold the whole poem from beginning to end. It is because *Vallombrosa* has its place on that great mesh or map of energy that it is *not* 'exact and immediate' and *not* like the Ida of Bacchylides – or any other place, in or out of any other poem. *Vallombrosa* is not a place, but an aspect of its own brilliant context, a shadowy meeting-place for legions, angels, leaves, winds, waves, and chivalry, for Hell and Heaven and the whole of Milton's poem. In this sense the name is what it declares, an actual 'Valley of Shadows'; and it is this aesthetic self-consciousness, perhaps, which most measures the distance between Milton and his Greek predecessor.

If such formalist descriptions as 'epic device' give only a limited insight into what Milton does with names, the same must be said of any scholarly treatment of the poem's substance which separates that from form. The forty-odd years since Eliot wrote his essay have seen a great expansion in theological and philosophical, and more recently historical and political, work on Milton: an interest reflected also in the concern for relevance to be found in the glosses of a good modern edition, or in the discussion of particular stylistic points. A critic will attempt to relate this or that epic simile with some grammatical firmness to this or that vehicle, or will display the local appropriateness of a given great name. This is a gain in clarity, common sense, and information. But the method often meets suggestive difficulties. It may be impossible to be convinced that (say) 'Jacob's ladder' or 'the careful ploughman' really does refer decidedly to this *or* that poetic actor, *or* would make better sense or better poetry if it did refer so decidedly. A similar problem arises when the names are considered as cases of the informational. In his Longman's edition of *Paradise Lost*, a splendid mine of information in its own right, Alastair Fowler tackles *Fontarabbia* and is driven very close to admitting that strictly speaking it almost doesn't exist:

> . . . all who since, baptized or infidel,
> Jousted in Aspramont or Montalban,
> Damasco or Marocco or Trebisond,
> Or whom Biserta sent from Afric shore
> When Charlemagne with all his peerage fell
> By Fontarabbia . . .

The problems of *Fontarabbia* Professor Fowler sets out in a note which tells us that Fuenterrabbia was forty miles distant from Roncesvalles, where Roland fell; that though one Spanish author, Mariana, put the defeat of the French at Fuenterrabbia itself, '*There was no version in which Charlemagne fell*'; and wonders whether Milton may be contrasting the greater Charles with his own later monarch, who went to Fuenterrabbia in 1659 to engage in some ignoble diplomacy. This speculation of Fowler's provides a genuinely fascinating context for *Fontarabbia*; but it is a context which (like all scholarly contexts) defines the field of Milton's poem as shadow does light. That field can only be crossed by going to Fontarabbia through Milton's own directions. The meaning of the name is not in history or geography or other nations' myths or other men's poems; but in the repetitions and iterations and monotony of splendour. The lines have their climax in the dying fall of Charlemagne, followed by the greatness and the smallness of mockingly alliterated Fontarabbia: a good name for the romantic place, recalled with tenderness and harsh irony, where a battle was not fought for a king who did not die there. The context is the arrogant, dreaming mind of Satan, as he desperately calls up his legions to send them against a God bound to defeat them: a heroic gesture – as the names are beautiful – but with a heroism that always moves on the rapid current of the godly poem towards its proper end, the expulsion from Innocence. Thus, the echoing high polysyllables, Aspramont and Montalban (the dark mountain and the bright mountain), baptized or infidel, by recurrence converge to the purity and monotony of trumpet-blast, a note that by its emptiness holds enormous power of connotation: all courage, all romance, all arrogance, all delusion – the pastness of the dead past recalled in a voice of brass: *Fontarabbia*.

These effects are not best called 'musical': for the reason that we do not praise the B Minor Mass or *Così fan tutte* by calling them 'very musical'. Verbal art resembles music only in the purity with which it isolates and concentrates to obtain meaning, not in its absence of any meaning; and the music and the meaning of Milton's verse should only separate themselves out if we choose to define either term in a manner perversely contradictory of the other. That the will to affect the opinion of others ('meaning') and the need to enjoy private aesthetic pleasures ('music') are both of them intensely strong in Milton's mind, and perhaps so self-defining as to exist, each in some dislocation from the other – this is the possibility that Eliot raises; and it is clear that Milton does provoke in readers reactions that seem to be alternatives, to comment on the context *or* to enjoy the 'gorgeousness' *or* to do both, alternately. It can only be said in answer, if we consider the 'great names', that the Fontarabbia passage manifests an intense awareness of the possibilities of language that places Milton among the greatest verbal artists; but it is an awareness that goes well beyond the Tennysonian. It is perhaps an aftermath of the Victorian disease of mind that makes us call artists like Milton and Marvell 'Puritan', meaning 'haters of the arts', because they disbelieved in rule by bishop, and then makes us find them self-contradictory: when in fact their principles infuse and shape their art. Milton's *Vallombrosa* and *Fontarabbia* have an extreme beauty of form and association: each is like Othello's image of the world, 'one entire and perfect chrysolite'. But (like that same image) they carry with them always the distinctness of detachment: their elegant consistency is a self-judging quality. It is to the point that, though always described as of a Tennysonian musicality, occurring as a random and inevitable stylism, these great names in fact come in quite local clusters. To put the matter as briefly as possible, they come densely in the First Book, then with less frequency in the Second, Third, and Fourth; they disappear until the Ninth, when they return to describe the charms of the serpent; then disappear again until their 'positively last appearance' in the great catalogue of the Eleventh Book, where they reveal the fallen world to Adam. Where they occur, they have marked literary effect. Their *absence* from God's speech at the beginning of Book III, and from the Eden of Book IV, has an effect of an almost audible and visible simplification, even of purification; they re-enter only with Satan's re-entry into these books; and it is under the aegis of Satan's surveying consciousness that they colour our developing reaction to Paradise with that profounder, sadder, and therefore more penetrating complexity of nostalgia and doubt which 'Not that fair field / Of Enna . . .' and the rest so classically voices.

If we look briefly outside *Paradise Lost* there appears the same effect of artistic purposiveness in the use of these great names. Milton's first public poem in English, the 'Vacation Exercise', introduces

> kings and queens and heroes old
> Such as the wise Demodocus once told
> In solemn songs at King Alcinous' feast,
> While sad Ulysses' soul and all the rest
> Are held with his melodious harmony
> In willing chains and sweet captivity . . .

The traditional heroic art which the names attend seems to involve the hypnotic capacity to enslave: a 'sweet captivity'. If we turn to Milton's last works, *Samson Agonistes* has Dalila thinking with some complacency of becoming one of the 'famousest of women'; in *Paradise Regained*, the great names primarily grace the devil's temptations, though they also describe the disciples' bewilderment when they have lost Christ: so that they could be said finally to constitute that whole established 'public' culture, whose power to authorize Christ formally denies.

Though there is clearly artistic consciousness here, it is not necessary to ascribe to Milton some kind of special symbolic cleverness over names; for what is perceptible in his art is to some degree generic throughout the seventeenth century, which was a period that saw a great wearing-out – or casting-aside – of the great names. A moment's reflection on the functions of the Proper Name will not be irrelevant, particularly since Milton himself considers the topic theologically and philosophically in his prose writings. A name's virtue is its specificity. Like Dryden's style in Eliot's definition of it, it may not suggest much but 'it states immensely'. When an age or an individual loses the sense of distinction between proper names and common nouns, and personifies too much – like the late Augustans, say, or W. H. Auden – there is always a consequent sense of being culturally lost. But the reverse process can happen too, and any proper name may be appropriated into use as a common noun, or its specific knowledge may be borrowed for uncommon purposes. This is what is happening when Milton replaces Fuenterabbia by *Fontarabbia*, or when he removes *Vallombrosa* into a context that dissolves it into its valley and its shadows ('Shades/High overarched embower . . .'). Milton's use of names continually converts the denotative into the connotative. This might seem evidence of his egoism, that digests everything into the great private dream of his epic style, that 'sweet captivity'. If it is so, then all civilization shows traces of such egoism, continually converting names into History, and History into Myth. But in the course of time myths wear out or their uses grow corrupt; great names are found to be too far from any meaning they once had, or ought to have; the power retained by name or myth will seem tyrannical, irrational. The process is beautifully summarized in Shelley's sonnet 'Ozymandias' – the big name, the broken statue, the empty threat, the wide desert: 'My name is Ozymandias . . .

Nothing beside remains.' During the seventeenth century a comparable process of thought produced the Civil Wars; in his *First Defence* Milton angrily orders his audience to stop thinking about 'the State of Grammar – of Words, to wit' and start thinking about the State of England; forget the name of King 'and for the future know that words are subordinate to things'. In more literary terms one could say that the decade which saw Charles capable of endowing one Captain Smith with the medieval order of 'Banneret' for retrieving his captured standard at Edgehill also saw Milton giving up his project of writing an *Arthuriad*. The name had died on him. A few decades later, Augustanism invents derisive games with names – 'This *Flecknoe* found'; and even more cruelly, Pope will reduce names to noise – 'Noise and Norton, brangling and Breval'.

It is not surprising that Milton, who lived through the major power struggles of his time, should show in his verse continual reflection concerning the meaning and value of the 'great names', what one might call the 'words of power'. Few poets have displayed a more direct instinct to inherit the great names of their culture, its powers and its traditions; or a more rational and principled decision to reject them. Something of the changes and developments in Milton's style throughout his career seems to depend on this inheritance and this rejection: from – one could say – the appropriative heroics at their most magnificent in the early books of *Paradise Lost* to the potent abstentions of the closing books, most mysteriously beautiful in *Paradise Regained*. It is within this process of development that one should perhaps see the oddities of the Book XI catalogue of names in *Paradise Lost*. For the qualities which made Eliot find in it something like 'levity . . . a solemn game' surely do exist there, and need explaining: a coolness, a dryness, an impassivity; almost, one could say, a striking tone of tonelessness. The passage has a quality of unaccidental absence: absence of glamour, absence of energy, absence of commitment of any kind. And yet it is not 'bad': while we read it, it means a great deal. All these attributes, I think, derive in part from its context, and from its mixture of similarity and dissimilarity to the great names that occur earlier in *Paradise Lost*. To these it bears that relationship of near-irony always emerging in Milton's use of epic devices. The poetic use of names in Book I and after needs therefore to be momentarily recalled.

The invocation of Book I of *Paradise Lost* contains a scattering of lucid and quiet 'holy names'. But the real 'great names' begin where the action of the poem begins, after the colloquy of Satan and Beelzebub. After their speeches the vision of the poem moves backward in an almost cinematic panning to reveal the arch-fiend objectively, replacing the sympathetic inwardness of near-monologue with the cold externality of the physical. Seen thus Satan looms in a great cluster, indeed a sardonic overplus of nouns and epithets of scale, *long, large, many a rood, huge, monstrous, hugest*; and this gigantism flowers effortlessly into an excrescence of great names –

> As whom the fables name of monstrous size,
> Titanian, or Earth-born, that warred on Jove,
> Briareos and Typhon, whom the den
> By ancient Tarsus held, or that sea-beast
> Leviathan . . .

The virtue of the poem's insistent style – idiosyncratic from the beginning – is to create an isolating medium of the 'aesthetic' within which, in fact, ethical and even political points make their effect instantly. It could be said that, within the first two hundred lines of the poem, the great names form a code which converts the holy into the great, and the great into the big: from God to Leviathan in two easy lessons. *Scale* is the devil's spirit, a shining linguistic 'bad eminence'. This impression derives not merely from vocabulary, but from rhythm and syntax as well. For the big names enter to a significant rhythm, a paratactic sprawl towards simile: and that simile is the vexing story of the whale. Just as the poem's first great names are those of mere size, the giants on the earth (as its last great names are,

> whose great city Geryon's sons
> Call El Dorado

– the replacement of Paradise, a Golden City, named by a giant's sons) – so does its first great epic simile involve a whale, and concern delusion and bewilderment: it is the grotesque *size* of the whale, its 'unnatural' nature, which tricks and may destroy the unwary sailor. It is not insignificant, either, that the exact grammatical function of the simile creates dispute among commentators. For there begins here that splendidly energetic, large and licentious movement that characterizes the style of Milton's Hell – never precisely random, but always tending towards randomness. So original is the movement, so elusive the decorum that divides 'narrator' from 'actor' and 'actor' from 'poem' that these entities continually interpenetrate. Within that all-dominating Grand Style of the poem the meditative and yet heightened statements of commentary are scarcely distinguishable from the proud rhetoric of fallen angels. Thus, the great names do not merely succeed the description of the 'head uplift above the waves', they positively appear to emanate from it. To put the matter loosely: so closely does the aggrandizing fantasy of the images approach the nobly sick consciousness of Satan, it appears a form of it; the big names are 'Satan's dream'.

While we read, it is always possible to feel the opposite of that impression of sickness: to feel that the names introduce a disturbing but wonderfully refreshing breath of the real world elsewhere, as the whale-simile brings in a deeply touching memory of the absurd but living littleness of the real, the natural. But it is presumably this very response, this precise hunger for the 'real', which tugs Satan irresistibly towards the fourth book, to find created Paradise: to offer, 'Hell shall unfold / To entertain you two, her widest gates'. Just as the import of the whale-simile is that things are not remotely what they seem, so the great names, which seem to interrupt Hell with the real, can also seem a means whereby Hell reaches out and dissolves history and geography into the shadows of Satan's imagination. For the most imaginatively dazzling aspect of Milton's Hell is its voracious instability, instability that often undermines through the delusion of great names:

> His ponderous shield . . .
> Hung on his shoulders like the moon, whose orb
> Through optic glass the Tuscan artist views
> At evening from the top of Fesole . . .
> His spear, to equal which the tallest pine
> Hewn on Norwegian hills, to be the mast
> On some great ammiral, were but a wand . . .

The immense shield diminishes into the distant moon which shines close to the eye in Galileo's glass before retracting into Hell to join the spear, which extends to a pine which is hewn into a mast which is really a wand. Milton knows all the games of relativity which the Augustan Swift will later on play in *Gulliver's Travels*: no wonder

Satan's steps are 'uneasy'. Tuscany and Norway, which seem to promise the security of the known – they are proper names – are appropriated into epithets and used for mere name-dropping, little more than footholds in the vertigo of 'greatness'. The poet does something similarly astonishing in the beautiful narrative of Mulciber's fortunate fall, accompanying him rhythmically on a shining descent through space and time – then dropping backwards out of it into a quite different dimension of truth:

> like a falling star
> On Lemnos, the Aegean isle: thus they relate,
> Erring.

The softness of the names is soporific, and the bald word *Erring* wakes us.

Mulciber is the architect of Pandaemonium, the palace of sound or the 'State of Grammar', and the remarkable description of its raising is in effect oddly close to the poet's own use of great names, the 'words of power':

> Anon out of the earth a fabric huge
> Rose like an exhalation, with the sound
> Of dulcet symphonies and voices sweet,
> Built like a temple . . .

Something with the apparent solidity of the world itself – physical, material, *real* – goes up like a meteor and dissolves into breath ('exhalation' includes these meanings); though built like a temple and accompanied by sweet sound, all it has is a spooky simulation of the holy. At the heart of its raising is a dreamy evocation of names that call up all the bad grandeur of history:

> Not Babilon,
> Nor great Alcairo such magnificence . . .

The description of Pandaemonium could be said to be somewhere between intoxication and nightmare. In this, it summarizes the first two books of *Paradise Lost*; and the great names have a vital part to play in this.

All the more striking is the contrast when Book III takes us out and up, through rapidly thinning names, to a nameless empyrean where God sits and speaks. The book's invocation shows something not unlike a negative way, a state where 'the bird / Sings

darkling', and the true seer is blind. There is perhaps faintly
adumbrated here that divine negation which emerges as a gover-
ning principle through Milton's later work, whereby goodness is
'*not* to have sinn'd, *not* to have disobey'd', and to be '*un*wearied,
*un*obnoxious to be pain'd': a denial of the world felt as intensely
dramatic, from a mind so naturally physical. There is something of
this divine negation in the first appearance of God. His first long
speech has had few admirers. What appears here is not, perhaps,
Milton's God but Milton's poem's God: for whom morality is a
matter of what can be done with words. Eliot himself had
something to say about Heaven's unfurnished apartments; but it is
also true that this very emptiness, relatively, of God's mind has a
distinctly healthful and astringent effect when it immediately
succeeds the overcrowded, dizzying, and name-dropping cons-
ciousness of Milton's Hell:

> So will fall
> He and his faithless progeny: whose fault?
> Whose but his own?

Milton's God is not much worse than logical. His long and icy
speech may be thought legalistic, and is so; but it is the pride of
English common law to be independent of persons, including kings
and other big names. By comparison with the fierce lawlessness of
Hell, legalism takes on the white light of justice.

It is also, and very obviously, true, however, that that rich
lawlessness has already undermined – and makes us feel that it has –
our capacity to respond with full feeling to mere justice, in a failure
that foreshadows the complex experience of fall. Milton scarcely
meant his Heaven to be disappointing: but his inability to
communicate it, or Paradise either, except through fallen language
(*not* this, *not* that) is a motif of the poem. The sense of loss, by
contrast, of the *price* of experience, is intrinsic to the pattern, as to
the meaning, of his poem, and gives it its title. The whole epic is a
lapse towards that grey, luminous daylight of the real into which
Adam and Eve step in its last lines; the poem is, on its tragic side –
and its origins are with tragedy – an enormous elegy. In a poem
that depends as massively as does Milton's on sequentiality, on
what becomes of things in time, Heaven is the reality that survives
Satan's intoxicating illusions. This relation of the Third to the First
and Second Books has some light to throw on the relation of the

Book XI catalogue to what comes before it. Intrinsic to the great names of the first books of the poem, there is a perpetual excitement, a hope and promise of experience. By the end, this has been transmuted into disillusioning fact. Something of the blank hardness of the Book XI catalogue derives from the presence in this part of the poem of the sense of reality, conjunct with the sense of loss. Even the great world as yet undiscovered, the cities as yet unfounded, and the history as yet unwritten, are lost: fallen from the beginning. And we feel this all the more as we hear, in the great names, the unexpressive irony of the trumpet-calls, still sounding:

> His eye might there command wherever stood
> City of old and modern fame, the seat
> Of mightiest empire, from the destined walls
> Of Cambalu, seat of Cathaian khan,
> Or Samarchand by Oxus, Temir's throne,
> To Pachin of Sinaean kings . . .

The limits of Adam's vision here, while Michael shows him in dream and as from a high mountain all the world there is, lie at *El Dorado*: the illusory Golden City of the future, which will replace Eden, the innocence of the past. For it is at the end of this sequence of the poem that we have the extraordinary, painful, and yet magnificent vision of Paradise itself wrecking, going

> Down the great river to the opening gulf

to become only a bare island out at sea, echoing with the inarticulate cries of animals and birds.

The wreck of Paradise comes as the climax of that vision of History which is given to Adam. The landscape before him transmutes into a sequence, static but greyly luminous, of moments of time: the world as site of fratricide, as sick-bay, as battlefield, as ocean. These scenes from Old Testament history have a curious characteristic which the Longman's editor has pointed out: they entirely lack proper names – even Cain and Abel are nameless. This partly intensifies their timelessness. History, though a sequence of moments, is also something in perpetuity; civilization is no more and no less than the consciousness of falling, and the world is a landscape whose future is always frozen under the grey dawn of its past. But the absence of names has another effect. The vision from the mountain was all names, nothing but names – the scenes on the plain below are nameless; the two sequences take on a relationship, as of an antithetical pairing. The catalogue becomes almost the index to a book, and *explains* what follows; and Michael's role as a Presenter increases this suggestion that the catalogue is explanatory prelude. As a result, Adam's objective scanning changes its nature and becomes a root act of conquest by knowledge – 'His eye might there command'. Even the contemplative life is not free of the sins of the active. From this primal act of possession, however unwilled and dream-like, this instinct for what the catalogue names as 'glory', 'command', 'fame', there descend directly those horrors of fratricide, disease, and warfare that drown the world.

Adam's dream in effect revives Satan's dream; and it does so through the continuity of the great names. They are assisted by the peculiar time-scheme of the poem, that circling and spiralling timelessness-within-time which results from Milton's having subordinated his materials to an epic structure (and a grand style) in an act of possessive discipline like Adam's: so that we have the continual sensation of being *in mediis rebus*. In a way, nothing has happened since the beginning of the enormous poem: and the very bareness of the format of this late catalogue makes lines like

Mombaza, and Quiloa, and Melind . . .

seem to be saying, 'Not again!' to be answered –

(Morocco and Algiers and Tremisen) –

'again and again'. The difference lies in that bareness of format, that 'solemn game', whose very abstentions and withdrawals are signs of knowledge, of consciousness. At the end of the list, Michael tells Adam, 'Now ope thine eyes', but the names are open-eyed already. Being so, they have lost their power either to seduce or threaten. All the same, Adam's degree of guilt makes sense of the Quaker Ellwood's protest to Milton that he had shown in this poem only *Paradise lost*, not *Paradise found*. Only in his last poem does Milton conclude his struggle with the inherited powers of history, and outstand – as does his Christ – the end of the big names.

4
Rochester: The Sense of Nothing

Rochester's general character as a poet is evident to any reader. He is a realist, his world bounded by the limits of King Charles II's court and the London that lay immediately beyond. If this makes his field seem narrow, then so it is – compared at any rate with the greater of his contemporaries: Milton, Dryden, even Bunyan, all live and write in a wider, larger world. But if, in turn, the relative thinness of Rochester's work is noticed as little as it is by any enjoying reader, this is because of the poet's compensating skills: the casual certainty that makes the elegance of his style, the extremity with which he goes to the limits of his vision.

It is from the balance of these opposing elements that Rochester's work gets its peculiar character. On the one hand there is the accepted commonplaceness of its content and milieu, the lack of preliminary with which the poet takes his place ('Well, sir, 'tis granted I said' – this or that) among the 'merry gang' as Marvell called them, Dryden's 'men of pleasant conversation . . . ambitious to distinguish themselves from the herd of gentlemen', or Pope's more lethal 'mob of gentlemen who wrote with ease'. Precisely because he so takes his place, there remains a border area of his work where editors still argue about who wrote what; and about how much, precisely, can be thought to function ironically – irony in itself being an index of that social commitment. But, on the other hand, the best of Rochester's poems could have been written by no one else; just as it is a fact that he was clearly not just *one* of the 'mob of gentlemen' but himself a social legend in his own time and for at least a century after. The particular nature of Rochester's involvement in the social life of his time is perhaps a matter on which biography has never placed the right kind of stress, or from which it has never drawn conclusions useful enough for the poetry. Those of the events in his life which we know something about suggest how necessary it was to Rochester not merely to be in the fashion but to excel in it, to transcend it almost – to do a thing so well that the mode itself broke under him, unrepeatable. It is impossible to draw any other conclusion from the Alexander Bendo incident, in which the poet impersonated a quack with high success. The affair is usually treated as evidence of his obsessive acting talents. What is not mentioned is that the trick had been played at least twice before: once by Buckingham, then more recently by Rochester's own friend Sedley. Acting a quack was in fact a fashion among the Wits.[1]

What distinguished Rochester was the strange intensity of his need not only to follow the fashion but to follow it to breaking point – the *extremity*, one might say, of his worldliness. That he had been (in youth) drunk for five years on end is something he was eager to tell Burnet on his repentant death-bed; and it is a fact that his final collapse followed on a sick man's ride back home to Somerset from London where he had returned with the King after insisting on attending the races at Newmarket. It is this quality of extremity that distinguishes Rochester's poems, balancing their realism and elegance. Or perhaps, in the end, bringing about the *im*balance that an original genius must consist in. For a work of art is recognized by its incapacity to be absorbed wholly by the society which produces it, and which it represents so admirably. Rochester's most social poems are very odd products indeed, but with an oddity that has nothing to do with eccentricity. This oddity – the oddity of art, not of social or psychological idiosyncrasy – is less easy to define than it is to illustrate, and I should like to illustrate it, as it were, from the life, taking an incident and using it as a kind of metaphor for Rochester's poetry; but the life I want to use is not, as it happens, Rochester's own, but his father's.

The elder Lord Wilmot, a general in Charles I's army and an adviser of the young King Charles II, is said to have been a brave

---

[1]See V. de Sola Pinto. *Sir Charles Sedley 1639–1701* (1927), pp. 62–3; also p. 62, note 5: 'The idea of masquerading as an itinerant quack always had a fascination for the Restoration gallants.' Anne Barton suggests to me that Ben Jonson's story of his own disguise forms a possible precedent: 'he with ye consent of a friend Cousened a lady, with whom he had made ane apointment to meet ane old Astrologer jn the suburbs, which she Keeped & it was himself disguysed jn a Longe Gowne & a whyte beard at the light of <a> Dimm burning Candle up jn a litle Cabjnet reached unto by a Ledder.' (*Conversations with Drummond*, in *Ben Jonson*, ed.C. H. Herford and P. and E. Simpson (1925–52), I, 141.)

man and a wit – as a companion of the King probably needed to be. He was made Earl of Rochester, the title his son inherited when he was only ten, for helping the King escape after the defeat at Worcester in 1651. At least, 'helping' is (again) what the history books say he did. Clearly the award of an earldom suggests that he did *something* for it: but the King himself almost implies, in the account of the flight which he dictated to Pepys thirty years later, in 1680, that it was *he* who helped *Wilmot* to escape after the battle, and this is a view not unsupported by contemporary witnesses. For it is clear that Wilmot complicated the flight in one particular way. Charles says: 'I could never get my Lord Wilmot to put on any disguise, he saying that he should look frightfully in it, and therefore did never put on any'.[1] This is one of the King's own footnotes to his account, as though he found it an importantly lingering memory, even if he could not entirely fathom it. And the refusal of disguise certainly did affect the flight, enforcing Wilmot's travelling separately, either in front or well behind, keeping his court silks and laces well away from the strenuously walnut-stained and ostler-coated King, whose menial state of dress the recording Pepys – describing it in immense and awed detail – nearly faints to think about. Wilmot, on the other hand, condescended to one compromise only: he carried a hawk on his fist. He must have been, one cannot help reflecting, glad to see the back of it, when after six long weeks they reached the coast and embarked for the continent: where Wilmot was to die in exile seven years later, during the Interregnum, leaving his title to his ten-year-old son. But Rochester may have inherited from that necessarily little-known father more than the title and the estate, quite as much as he had from his mother, a powerfully dominating and able Puritan lady: and what precisely he inherited is reflected somewhere, perhaps, in that curious event which the King recorded.

Probably Wilmot was being funny – certainly his remark *is* funny, when one considers that to look 'frightfully', or at least to look unlike one's normal courtly self, is the whole purpose of disguise, especially when one is running for one's life pursued by troopers across the boggy English woodlands. And Charles's evident happiness in all the play-acting of this marvellous adventure

[1] *The Boscobel Tracts.* ed. J. Hughes (1830), p. 151. See also Richard Ollard, *The Escape of Charles II* (1966).

– which he harked back to, wistfully, for over thirty years afterwards – might well have aroused an acerbic wit in a more battle-scarred companion. But the humour remains conjectural. What shines principally in Wilmot's remark is its quality of sheer 'face', its highly independent disobliging *panache* that yet operates within a narrow social context that gives that mocking word 'frightfully' its peculiar character. ('One would not, sure, be frightful when one's dead.') It is the very impassivity of the general's remark, our difficulty in knowing what precisely Wilmot was at (though there is no difficulty in seeing that he did what he wanted, in his easy way) that suggests its special social function. This is an occurrence of that highly English social phenomenon, the use of *manners* to get away with almost anything: for heroism, folly, intelligence, guile, whimsy or sheer blankness of mind may lurk beneath that recorded turn of phrase.

A sense, perhaps unconscious, of what social tone may serve for must have come quite naturally to the Cavalier courtier. But when the same sense occurs in the far more conscious Restoration wit of the son, it forms the great originality of his verse. For it is Rochester, perhaps, who invents *vers de société* in English. The act of translation places a radically new stress, it might be said, on the mere proposition, so that the poem is now written 'about' rather than 'from' society, with a new kind of inside-outness that helps to explain why Rochester should be also perhaps the first user of pure irony in English after Chaucer. The complexities latent in writing English *vers de société* are nicely suggested in a recent poem by Philip Larkin which takes the actual phrase for its title; one of his most undermining poems, what is undermined in it is basically the '*société*', and yet it is, for all that, a brilliantly 'social' piece of verse.

Another and more explicit case of this highly ambiguous social fidelity can be observed through the letters of Henry James, from the moment at which the young American writer sends back home, in the late 1870s, his impressions of the English social scene –

> The people of this world seem to me for the most part nothing but *surface*, and sometimes – oh ye gods! – such desperately poor surface!

– to that, some twenty years later, at which James struggles patiently to explain to a correspondent less sympathetic than his family just what he had meant by the extraordinary art with which

he had recently (in *The Awkward Age*) dealt in that world of
'surface':

> I had in view a certain special social (highly 'modern' and actual)
> London group and type and tone, which seemed to me to se
> prêter à merveille to an ironic – lightly and simply ironic! –
> treatment . . . with no going behind, no *telling about* the figures
> save by their own appearance and action and with explanations
> reduced to the explanation of everything by all the other things *in*
> the picture . . .[1]

Rochester himself would not have been caught making such
'explanations' at all: he was even further ensconced behind that
social 'surface', that world of appearance and action which there
was 'no *telling about*'. He inhabited, he half invented, that English
social world where James was never much more than a wonderful
lifelong tourist; which is why, perhaps, Rochester needed those
compensating retreats to his country estates which were his
equivalents to James's American nationality, his family background
and his Puritan inheritance.

It is because of this very immersion and silence on Rochester's
part that, despite all the differences of temperament and period and
nationality, James's more self-conscious and detached reflections
can be useful in suggesting some of the peculiarly ambiguous,
confining conditions of a social art like Rochester's. There is an odd
parallel, perhaps, between that famous Max Beerbohm cartoon
which makes some sort of cool comment on the way in which the
James of the *Sacred Fount* period did and did not 'belong',
representing him as stooping to examine with horrified concern the
mixed sexes of the pairs of shoes left to be cleaned overnight
outside the bedroom doors of some hotel or house party – and a
hostile aside on Rochester by a Victorian critic. Alluding to the
anecdote of Rochester's having posted a footman in a sentinel's red
coat and with a musket outside the doors of court ladies to watch
the goings-on, the critic glosses it by saying that the poet 'for no
earthly reason you can think of, set detectives to note him the
indiscretions of the Court'.[2] Criticism ought perhaps to be better
than this at thinking of earthly reasons.

[1] *The Letters of Henry James*, ed. Percy Lubbock (1920), I, 67, 341.
[2] G. S. Street, *Miniatures and Moods* (1893), p. 27; quoted in *Rochester: The Critical Heritage*, ed. David Farley-Hills (1972), p. 254.

For, if Rochester's verse transcends its own representativeness, this is by virtue of the way in which it goes, one might say, to the end of the road; the way in which his commitment to social forms was a manner of breaking those social forms. The story of his drunken destruction of the King's upward-pointing chronometer, and the apparent prudery of his for centuries unprintable reason for breaking it, is one of the best-known anecdotes that have survived him – and in the same way, even his most elegant verse often resounds with the crash of breaking glass; or where there is no crash, a startled reader will find himself glimpsing a void beneath the bright surface, a vacancy beneath the brilliant style.

As an example of this method of transcending the temporal mode, it is worth considering what happens to a Hobbesian idea of time in one of Rochester's best-known poems. In another of these often-repeated jottings that compose the legend of Rochester's life, Anthony à Wood remarks – thinking, perhaps, of the sensitive and well-read seventeen-year-old who first arrived at court with a tendency not only to blush but to stammer – that 'the Court . . . not only debauched him but made him a perfect *Hobbist*'.[1] Hobbes, whose *Elements of Law* include the laws that

> Continually to be outgone is misery.
> Continually to outgo the next before is felicity.
> And to forsake the course is to die . . .

was certainly the philosopher of Charles's court, as he had himself been the tutor of the King – as he was, in fact, the most popular philosopher of the age in some cultural sense: we are told that in the year after Rochester died 'the folly and nonsense of meer mechanism' had passed to the very craftsmen, even the labourers of the time, who were 'able to demonstrate out of *Leviathan* . . . that all things come to pass by an eternal Chain of natural Causes', and that human nature was a mere machine.[2]

It is hardly surprising that Rochester committed himself to this most fashionable system, which was also the most imaginatively challenging of his time, having a hard self-consistency not easy to refute. All the more striking is the transmutation of these ideas within the medium of Rochester's verse: within, for instance, his

[1] Anthony à Wood, *Athenae Oxonienses* (1691), II, 489.
[2] Edward N. Hooker, 'Dryden and the Atoms of Epicurus', in *Essential Articles for the study of John Dryden*, ed. H. T. Swedenberg Jr. (1966), p. 241.

'Love and Life'. This incorporates the materialist and mechanistic doctrine of Hobbes that the only *real* time is time present: 'The *present* only has a being in Nature, things *past* have a being in the memory only, but things *to come* have no being at all . . .'[1] But in Rochester's lyric these ideas are *not* incorporated, but rather disembodied, attenuated, made to float lightly in the emptiness of the 'flying hours':

> All my past Life is mine no more,
>   The flying hours are gone
> The Time that is to come is not,
>   How can it then be mine?

If everything in Hobbes is material and mechanical, then everything in the poem is immaterial and organic.

In part this is a simple question of what happens to all statements within the quasi-musical discipline of poetry, which part liberates ideas and part destroys them. 'When a thing is too stupid to be said, we sing it'; and conversely to sing a thing may be to make it sound stupid – or if not stupid, then released into a kind of radiant folly. It may be relevant that elsewhere Hobbes admits that he cannot explain music – 'I confess that I know not for what reason one succession in tone and measure is more pleasant than another' – and this issue seems to be supported by Dryden's comment that the philosopher 'studied poetry as he did mathematics, when it was too late'. There appear to be conditions separating philosophy in modern periods from music and poetry, so that if they come together, in – say – the Metaphysicals, the result does not resemble Lucretius or Dante, but has a startled paradoxical self-undermining wit, as of a man who now knows that he is doing the impossible. In such verse, ideas get airborne, or at least stand on their heads. And Rochester's 'Love and Life' does have this Metaphysical wit; its title is borrowed from Cowley, and the whole poem's movement has a quality of strong fantasy, an extravagance in self-commital to paradox, perhaps learned from Donne, whom Rochester sometimes seems to know by heart.

But the change in Hobbesian doctrine in 'Love and Life' goes beyond the effect of what we may call either a 'musical' or a 'metaphysical' discipline. Nominally it is spoken by a libertine, a

---

[1]Thomas Hobbes, *Leviathan*, ed. Michael Oakeshott (1946), p. 16.

rake on principle, a man whose wholly selfish moral presupposi-
tions followed hard upon Hobbesian cosmology and accepted the
practical consequences of disbelief in past and future. But Roches-
ter's libertine first translates philosophical maxims, words used as
counters to win intellectual assent, into factors of human cons-
ciousness; and then, with a kind of sublime or idiot logic, extends
that consciousness into a radical self-undercutting, an intelligence
almost self-destructive. The conclusions of that intelligence might
have surprised even Hobbes. For Rochester's libertine, having no
past or future, has, in all honest logic, no present either: unless we
give the name of a 'present' to the poem itself, which the poet,
however 'courtly' or 'gentlemanly', speaks as out of an essential
solitariness, in a surprise of realization rendered by the abrupt, lucid
monosyllables, that seem to resonate in a void. 'All my past life is
mine no more . . . How can it then be mine?'

One of the 'mob of gentlemen' here speaks with that peculiar
lucidity which is the speech of the inward self, alone; and it is with a
curiously chaste impersonality that the libertine watches the 'flying
hours' carry his life away into a driftage as of dead leaves, of
'Dreams', 'Images', memory. When this same rakish lover turns at
the end of the second stanza, in a beautifully located surprise, to
hand over the poem to its audience and reader, the suddenly-
invoked Phillis, his courtesy and gravity are hardly at all ironic; his
'Miracle', in fact, is one of those most undermining of word-plays,
where a quiet literalism forestalls metaphor, irony grows serious
and pretence turns real:

> If I, by Miracle, can be
> This live-long Minute true to thee
> 'Tis all that Heav'n allows.

The brilliance of this small poem, and what surely explains its
great popularity and its anthology status both in the poet's time and
in our own, is the way it converts a relatively sterile proposition
from Hobbes into a potent human moment. The poem is a 'saying'
that moves itself into action, becoming the fulfilment of the
promise it half makes; its conclusion thus 'seals' the poem like a
personal crest on a document now long crumbled away. Given that
this hypothetical and contingent 'Phillis' is partly a mocking relic of
past tradition, and partly some future dream, this ending makes of
the lines a decisive handing over of the self to some unknown

quantity, the 'present' being only a knowledge of what is unknown. And this sudden, ironic and yet generous self-offering is so circumspectly dealt with as to be able to suggest the perpetual existence of the self as in a void, created from moment to moment as a poem is from line to line. For the poet of 'Love and Life' has, by definition, nothing at all to call his own – neither past nor future, nor any present that he knows, beyond that 'Miracle' of the poem's live-long Minute. Neither a philosopher nor a libertine but something more like an equilibrist, the poet balances in the void, sustaining himself on nothing whatever.

I have been hoping to suggest that Rochester's poems may only safely be said to be representative of the Restoration period if that period is defined very cautiously. The 1660s and 1670s through which Rochester lived and which, in literary terms at least, he helped to create, were something of a cultural no man's land, a pause in time equally out of touch with the past and future, the medieval and the modern. It was an age in which writers began to inch themselves along again, with what Emily Dickinson would describe as 'that precarious gait / Some call Experience'. Rochester's best poems, in short, were probably all written in that decade after the Plague had seemed to empty London, and the Fire to level it. They were written, moreover, for a court presided over by a penniless king back home from banishment and living carefully hand to mouth. The period which we name after its political Restoration has a reality not confined to its King and his court; but it is that court sphere which colours with an intensity beyond its apparent importance some of the best literature of the time. Similarly, though there were a number of different aspects of the world of that court, the one which features most vividly in writers of the period was that which the Marquis of Halifax (elder brother of Rochester's closest friend, and an even cleverer man, perhaps, than Rochester himself) was to call, in his well-known essay on the King, 'His Dissimulation'. In the drafts for his *History* Burnet had given this 'art of concealing' in the Restoration court a historical basis, deriving it from Charles's education at the hands of a Queen Mother determined that her sons should not display the (in the event) fatal unworldliness of their father. Whatever its source, this court dissimulation, evoked in Halifax's brilliant scattered phrases, suggests a kind of evasive darkness that

we should perhaps see behind the sparkle of Rochester's court
verse:

> Men compared Notes, and got Evidence . . . His Face . . .
> would sometimes tell Tales to a good Observer . . . At last it
> cometh to Smile for Smile, meaning nothing of either Side;
> without any kind of Effect; mere Drawing-room Compliments
> . . . there was less Signification in those Things than at first was
> thought . . . He would slide from an asking Face, and could
> guess very well . . . It was a kind of implied bargain.[1]

It was for this world of 'Smile for Smile, meaning nothing of
either Side', that Rochester's love poems were written; his Satires
are 'Notes', 'Evidences', telling 'Tales to a good Observer'. To
describe his verse as a construct from a world of surfaces implies
that it is always close to irony; but the concept of irony can only be
used cautiously of Rochester. For since its Socratic origins true
irony has always served some polemic purpose – its 'lies' have
always functioned to make clearer some truth. Rochester's poems
often have a highly ironic sound, but something like a total lack of
any provable intention (or even tone), except possibly the intention
of hollowing out the surface they so finely construct. Apart from
this latent sense of void, there is no form of what James called
'telling about', 'going behind': only the 'explanation' by 'all the
other things *in* the picture'. Rather than by a smoothness so
excessive as to make us defensive (as in Swiftian irony), Rochester's
poems show intent by minute flaws in that smooth surface, by local
shocks and coruscations of wit. Even where Rochester's tone seems
cool, sweet and safe, his wit leaps to the surface in striking, even
dangerous, disjunctions of language which locally fracture the
style, like the minute cracks that beautify crackleware ceramics. An
apparently 'polite' poem that addresses its subject as a 'Fair nasty
nymph' (as does 'By all love's soft, yet mighty powers') is not
going to leave quite where it was a socially-orientated 'fair' sex that
relies on its unfair fairness of face to get away with murder; nor
does a poem that goes on to advise in the name of hygiene a more
'cleanly sinning' leave either hygiene, or sinning, quite where it
was before. Swift's famous letter to a young woman approaching

[1]Gilbert Burnet, MS draft of *The History of His own Time*, printed as an Appendix
to Ranke's *History of England principally in the Seventeenth Century* (1875), VI, 78; and
Halifax, *A Character of King Charles the Second* (1750), pp. 15–46.

matrimony which primarily advises her to wash often and thoroughly is possibly sensible but not funny in any human way, because some degree of animus towards the female makes itself plain in the intemperate style of a man who is for good or bad never a pure ironist; similarly all the smoothness of even the Modest Proposer only enforces what any reader instinctively knows, that eating people is wrong. Rochester's equally profane and good-taste-violating poem on the 'Fair nasty nymph' is more purely ironic than Swift's letter because it voices no animus at all against women (I think it highly unlikely that the poet had any) – it voices nothing: it merely sets out the flaw in the china in the cool crack about the 'Fair nasty nymph'. Bodies being as they are, it is the social insistence on 'fairness' that is the thoroughly 'nasty' thing.

In very much the same way, but with a more expansively indecorous decorum, the better-known outrageously-ending lines that tell us how 'Fair *Cloris* in a Pig-stye lay' make it their business to flesh out the discrepancies between that 'Fair' and that 'Pig-stye'. But they do no more – they do not satirize; they leave both reader and Chloris 'Innocent and pleased', with their illusions in place even if not quite intact. Chloris ends happy with her fantasy of lust and her virginity both unviolated; the reader ends happy in the belief that pastoral tells him something true about life or love; everything in the pig-sty is lovely. The power of this poem, compared with that about the 'Fair nasty nymph', is the greater degree of poetic acceptance of the mode proposed, the triumphant, non-committal accomplishment of this vacuous, self-deceiving, dishonestly erotic pastoral. How good an actor Rochester really was is unclear – certainly he sometimes loathed whatever he meant by the image of 'this gawdy guilded Stage'; but he was perfect at assuming the pose of a certain verbal style. Thus the charm of the very popular 'Ancient Person of my Heart' is its embodiment of the innocence of tone and terrible social polish that make the deb an evidently unchanging type over several centuries of English social life. The pronunciation of the time brings together in an assonance words as discrepant as the frigidly social 'Ancient Person' ('Parson') and the boldly intimate 'Heart': the comical insistence of this paradoxical refrain – 'Ancient *Person* of my *Heart*' – embodies a social type on the page, as elegant and peremptory as a pedigree cat.

That refrain from the 'Song of a Young Lady' makes relevant here an even more minute detail. In citing 'Ancient Person of my Heart' (with its capital P, capital H), as in most other quotations from Rochester's poems up to this point, I have deliberately used Vivian de Sola Pinto's Muses' Library text (Routledge and Kegan Paul, 1952, second edition 1964), which is now to some degree superseded by David M. Vieth's scholarly modernized edition (Yale University Press, 1968). Vieth modernizes because, as he rightly argues, there is no bibliographical authority for any of the Restoration editions of the poet. But this is helpful proof of the simple fact that, where literature is concerned, bibliography is frequently (like patriotism) not enough. The primary need in presenting a poet is not to obscure his tone; and certain of Rochester's poems are so social in tone as to profit from the retention of that Restoration and Augustan habit of visual literacy, the capitalization of important nouns. Thus, Vieth's able but toneless text renders meditative and inward a poem like 'Upon his Leaving his Mistress', a part of whose flagrant virtue it is to give the whole of social life the look of an open secret, a network of called passwords in a war, a surface of nods and becks which there is no 'going behind, no *telling about*':

> 'Tis not that I'm weary grown
> Of being yours, and yours alone:
> But with what Face can I incline,
> To damn you to be only mine?
> You, who some kinder Pow'r did fashion,⎫
> By merit, and by inclination,   ⎬
> The Joy at least of a whole Nation.   ⎭

The first word the Muses' Library edition follows its 1680 text in capitalizing is the third-line 'Face'; the next in this stanza is 'Pow'r'. All the delicate contradictions of a lover's psychology, which the poem also manages to hint at, the ironies of a Petrarchan self-abasement in the sensitive lover's soul, are shouldered back behind and yet somehow expressed by the heightened capitalized forms of social observances, the agreement that socially it is 'Face' not feeling that matters, it is 'Pow'r' not love that governs ('continually to outgo the next before is felicity'); and in such a context to give or take fidelity is hardly a saving grace – it is to '*damn* you to be only mine'.

Rochester can writer tenderer, more inward poems than this, such as justify Vieth's modernized reading of the poet. One of these more tender poems offers a stylistic detail as interesting as Rochester's use of capital letters: a rhythmic effect that speaks to the ear, as the capitals speak first or primarily to the eye. In each of the two, apparently highly conventional, stanzas of 'My dear Mistress has a Heart', the last foot of each of its four-footed lines is, in lines 2, 4, 6 and 8, a trochee ('gave me . . . enslave me . . . wander . . . asunder'); but lines 1, 3, 5 and 7 truncate their last foot by a syllable, so that 'My dear Mistress has a *Heart*' (not an ankle or an elbow). The result of this delicately asymmetrical scansion is that every line ends with what sounds like an unexplained falter, the odd lines because they have one syllable too few, the even because they have one too many. With a striking technical mastery, this effect of varying but inevitable falter, like a flaw in nature or an irony in the mind or what medicine calls a shadow behind the heart, is repeated conclusively in the structure of the whole; for the sense of the poem's first eight-lined stanza and then its succeeding six lines swells to a climax of feeling, of certainty, that is suddenly undercut by a kind of 'rhyme' the reader had not expected, the repetition at the end of the second verse of the last two lines of the first, a *reprise* like a stammer that turns the whole poem into an echo of its sustaining and yet faltering pairs of lines. And yet again, that falter finally does not seem to matter, because where the first time its rhyme-word 'asunder' occurred, it only half-rhymed with 'wander', here in the repetition it comes to rhyme with 'wonder', so the poem is after all strangely complete.

If 'My dear Mistress has a Heart' is touching and troubling in a way we do not necessarily expect a conventional Restoration lyric to be (so that Victorian critics used to compare it with Burns), the cause is a quality not often found in Restoration poems: its power of latency, its character of reserve. The blank general words with their capitals – 'Heart', 'Constancy', 'Joys', 'Mankind' – are a fine hard surface under which (we delusively feel) the real life of the poem goes on; but we feel that real life at the point of breakage, where the poem falters for an instant and then carries on – where we see the surface as *only* surface, with perhaps vacancy beneath. But for this there are no 'explanations', there is 'no going behind'.

In all these poems, minute technical details – what one might call flaws of the surface – speak of conditions that one cannot consider in a merely 'technical' way. All Rochester's most potent and idiosyncratic lyrics develop this sense of 'flaw' into a condition of discrepancy that almost breaks apart the convention he appears to be working within – almost, but not quite: the result is never true burlesque, only a kind of agitation below the social surface. That agitation, or submerged quality of personal apprehension, can render the actual treatment of a conventional subject quite unlike what a reader might expect it to be. It might be said, for instance, that Rochester approaches the question of the physical in love as a libertine, with a frank and cynical 'realism'. That he has realism is true, but to say so may imply a quality of apprehension quite different from what we actually find. To say that in 'The Fall' Rochester portrays Adam and Eve as a pair of cool libertines caught between the acts is to predicate a poem that has little in common with what he actually wrote:

> Naked, beneath cool Shades, they lay,
> Enjoyment waited on Desire:
> Each Member did their Wills obey,
> Nor could a Wish set Pleasure higher.

The plangency of this comes partly from that negative, 'Nor could', a little like Milton's 'Not that fair field of Enna'. But what is even more striking is the absence of the sensuous, of which the 'puritan' Milton's Adam and Eve in Paradise have far more. When Poussin paints Adam and Eve in Paradise he gives them, over their naked bodies, a hair-style comically close to the great wigs of Louis's court, as though to his mind certain aspects of dress can't be taken off even in Paradise, but are generic to the human estate. Rochester, another court artist, seems to be driven by a comparable yet reversed impulse. It is as if, in order to undress his fallen couple, to get them back towards whatever innocence once meant, *he* has to take off their very bodies, which in this poem are dissolving towards the Platonic condition of shadowy Idea, under trees so abstract as to have grown mere generic 'Shades', dark reflections of themselves, in an experience so reversed as to be only the negative opposite of that dulled satiety which is the one happiness we know. In Rochester's Paradise, 'Enjoyment waited', in a past and future defended from the satisfactions of the horrible present.

If this seems a strained reading of that strange abstract stanza, it should be said that it is only consonant with the poet's representation of physical existence throughout his work: all Rochester's lovers are portrayed, at their most intense, like his Adam and Eve. If these first parents are abstracts, then the poet's typical lovers are simply ghosts, haunting a period of time never 'Now' but only a reflex of past and future. The manner of these poems will make a reader expect an art as of an expert social photographer catching smiling and solid persons in the bright light of the moment: but when looked at hard, these results are all negative. The speaker of 'Absent from thee', whose 'Fantastic Mind' desires only *not* to be a 'straying Fool', makes it his hope, not that he will be true, but that he will betray love *enough* – that he will tie a tight enough knot of punished infidelity to hold himself steady in: as steady as the poem is held by the syntactic knot of the line which sums up the only available alternative of fidelity –

> To wish all Day, all Night to Mourn.

'An Age, in her Embraces past' starts its vagrancies by letting the reader down from the expected summer's night which its erotic context suggests, into its actual 'Winter's Day' of love: a chilly actuality as mistily indecorous to our conventions of love as are the divergencies of the poem's chief character, a Shade of Soul that wanders ghostily through the poem. Its path is indicated by a ramifying grammar –

> When absent from her Eyes;
> That feed my Love, which is my Soul,
> It languishes and dyes . . .

– that becomes a fragmented style from which even the poet dissociates himself contemptuously ('Love-sick Fancy'), thus disintegrating the medium still further. The poem at last rests for its stability on one conclusion only, that 'expiring' truth attained in 'Absent from thee'; here it takes the form of the stoical 'Pain can ne'er deceive', the belief that jealousy at least provides

> Proof 'twixt her and me,
> We love, and do not dream.

The time scheme proposed in this poem comes to rest, not on present moment, but on that shadowy past and future evoked in its last stanza's re-echoing rhymes, 'when past' and 'at last'. It would seem a mistake to write down this lack of the libertine art of present enjoyment to a mere bad mood of love, a passing depression. For this same insubstantial medium may be found in poems that cannot be written off as court lyrics of love. One of Rochester's strongest short poems, 'The Maim'd Debauchee', takes as surface (without quite burlesquing it) the graver heroic style of the period, and its vision extends as wide as state affairs: but it is a fact that its perspective on war and politics is identical with that of the lyrics on love. Immediately beneath the grave, powerful surface, all is a resonant dissolution:

> Shou'd some brave Youth (worth being drunk) prove nice,
>   And from his fair inviter meanly shrink,
> Twould please the Ghost of my departed Vice,
>   If, at my Counsel, He repent and drink.

That the warrior of love here becomes a Ghost of Vice fits the peculiar decorum of the poem, for its situation offers the temporal vertigo of a man who lightens the miseries of present love by toughening himself with the reminder of the prospects of future impotency – the future pleasure, that is, of remembering a then past potency. The fragile, hardly Socratic, self-knowing wisdom which its last two syllables tender ('be wise') is something like the knowledge that human beings love, or lust for power, in order to enjoy looking forward to the pleasure of looking back at the pain of having suffered. It moves in fact from

> My Pains at last some respite shall afford . . .

to:

> Past Joys have more than paid what I endure.

The brute strength of these factual-sounding lines has to be balanced against the shadowy non-existence they record. The poem celebrates fulfilments never more than ostensible. And its title, 'The Maim'd' – or, as Vieth reads, 'Disabled' – 'Debauchee', compacts into a phrase the theme of impotency or emptiness below the surface of an extreme worldly experience.

This theme, brilliantly embodied in the matter of the poem, is oddly reflected too in one specific detail. I am still quoting here from the Muses' Library text of the poems; but in that edition, this poem's climactic stanza will not be found in the text, only doubtfully added to the notes at the back of the book. And even there, it is to be read only in the more decent version which the 1680 text printed, and which Vieth rejects for one hardly printable until a decade or so ago. Thus, earlier versions, extending over nearly three centuries, all give the poem as it were a hole in the page, a void between the lines. The editorial problem, in fact, which begins with a matter as simple as Rochester's use of the notorious four-letter word, properly considered takes us right to the centre of the whole question of his aesthetic purpose, as expressed in the characteristic abstract violence of his style. For an art that so brilliantly and customarily brings together fact and fantasy, the surface and the void, also brings together with particular point the elegant and the obscene. For in obscenity, in the words unprintable – except in pirated editions – even in Rochester's time, the extreme of verbal and emotional nothingness is reached. Whatever the changing proprieties in an age, an obscenity is a non-word, a hole in the page – a betrayal of human sense and meaning to mere grunting phatic gesture.

It is clear, I think, that Rochester, who is sometimes misnamed a pornographic poet, wrote as a man capable of thinking of his obscenities in precisely this way – with the eye and ear of the sensitive man who once came to court not merely blushing but stammering, finding certain things unsayable. Consider the missing stanza from 'The Maim'd Debauchee':

> Nor shall our *Love-fits Cloris* be forgot,
>   When each the well-look'd *Link-Boy* strove t'enjoy
> And the best Kiss, was the deciding *Lot*,
>   Whether the *Boy* us'd you, or I the *Boy*.

It could hardly be said that this gets worse when Vieth reads,

> Whether the boy fucked you, or I the boy . . .

In fact a strong case could be made for feeling that the verse undoubtedly gets better in the more brutal transposition. For that specific, end of the road, last-ditch verbal shock both embodies and in some curious way resolves the other much larger shock which the poem is about: which it is both about, and bespeaks in everything we mean when we gesture vaguely towards its 'mock heroic' or burlesque manner.

A more recent poem, one of Philip Larkin's, mentions the 'long perspectives / Open at each instant of our lives', meaning the deracinating shocks time brings to those whose element is said to be the temporal; and Rochester's 'obscene' stanza provides this among other shocks. It brings to a culmination, just before the end of the poem, everything pastiche in it up to that point: in an imitation of 'antiquity' whose soft delicate indelicate procedure has hardly been improved on in three hundred years of translation, imitation, pastiche and burlesque, up to and even including Pound's reversals and repetitions of a whole century of phoney classicism. Rochester's stanza aches with an almost Virgilian sense of distance, the yearning both of and for the classical, since all epic from Homer on looks back to an earlier innocence only surviving in an epic lumber of weapons, feasts, ships, the nicknames of gods and the code of poets. That loaded long-perspectived classic sense of life in time Rochester reaches back for and wraps around, not a battle or great feast but a memory of private pleasure; and that memory and that pleasure capsize the great mood, bring it down to a ground bass of simple wordless obscenity. This last line is, in its way, perhaps tender, perhaps funny; it also shows reality dissolving, chaos and promiscuity taking over, and sheer nothingness opening all around.

The self-defeating lordly art of that 'unprintable' final line is generic to Rochester's work, which offers many parallels – though not, of course, in such older texts as the Muses' Library, in which a couplet or a whole poem will become that 'hole in the page': as where the poet, skating on the thin ice of obscenity, has fallen in. In all of them Rochester devotes his elaborate talent to capturing both phonetic and semantic nullity: as when he settles the scope of his monarch's affections with a noise as of a mud bath, in 'Love he loves, for he loves fucking much'; or, leaving his club or coffee house one evening, looks back, as it might be down to the bottom of a well, to see and hear the *Symposium* reduced to the sound of frogs –

> Much wine had passed, with grave discourse
> Of who fucks who and who does worse . . .

This reductiveness and this nullity are in fact the heart of the matter, for Rochester can when decorum demands maintain the same brutal art of monosyllables without the aid of obscenity, as when Artemisia gives us the whole Art of Love in wondering whether

The old ones last, and who and who's together.

Similarly, the *Satire against Mankind* says the last word when it paraphrases the whole Hobbesian dance of human society as

Man undoes *Man*, to do himself no good

– an extraordinary complexity of sonic monotony, a concrete music of fallen nature.

To observe the peculiar artistry of Rochester's single-lined brutalities is to understand more clearly what he is doing in whole poems like the extraordinary complex of finesse and unrepeatability, *A Ramble in St James's Park*, whose *Symposium*-like opening pair of lines I have just quoted (from Vieth's edition). The poem is a vision of the social scene as a violent phantasm, with the darkness of night-time London showing through it. Its poised yet perhaps three-quarters-mad speaker has been betrayed by the 'infinitely vile, when fair' Corinna, taking turns with three young blades (a Whitehall gadabout, a Gray's Inn wit, and a Lady's Eldest Son) who may well embody the world, the flesh, and the devil in person; and what maddens the poet to near screaming-point is that this semi-goddess has sold him *for nothing*, as exercise of mere preference of change for change's sake, fashion in love; a preference which therefore brings the speaker in all logic to recognize his equal guilt in similarly loving a mere nothing, a mere love object, a figment of imagination. In self-punishment as much as revenge he curses her with the fate logic demands: she shall 'go mad for the north wind . . . and perish in a wild despair'.

The *Ramble*'s savage, dangerous, yet obscurely innocent fantasy – innocent from the sensed rectitude which its upside-down fury violates, the contained and quashed romantic idealism without which we could not (I think) laugh at that wilfully frightful ending – epitomizes much of what Rochester does in his elegant and obscene writings. If one says 'much' rather than 'all', this is because the violently sustained grossness of the *Ramble*, its comic extravagance or fantasy of wildly pained love, unbalances that poise which the poet more usually maintains. A more representative art may be found in a slighter poem, in the delicate brilliance of the translated 'Upon Drinking in a Bowl'. This poem is from Ronsard's version of the Anacreontic 'Cup' lines. But Rochester's final effect is radically unlike the almost Jonsonian directness Ronsard keeps to here. Its difference will illustrate well enough – better in fact, than the *Ramble* – that art by which Rochester will place obscenity up against a brilliant social surface.

For the poet makes two mutually opposed departures from Ronsard. Taking a hint from Cowley's version of this much translated poem, Rochester gives it a vein of controlled fantasy that Ronsard knows nothing of: he replaces the French poet's sober directions by allowing the poem to mime before us the shaping of the cup, to call forth to the imagination the 'contrivance' and 'Skill' of its 'trimming', the chaste feel of it to the mind as it is 'Damasked . . . round with gold'. Fantasy begins to build on the simpler sensuousness of 'Damask': the 'swelling Brim' holds an almost Mallarméan vision of imagined toasts swimming on the 'delicious Lake, / Like Ships at Sea'; and on this image, the poem flashes through each stanza scenes of War, of the Planets, of a Vine, each perceived only to be rejected. The poem grows and solidifies as the imagined cup, an exquisitely 'holding' structure, is turned before us in an imagined hand. With the sixth stanza, quietly, this whole beautiful structure is tossed away, like a wineglass thrown over the shoulder. Building on a mere hint offered by Ronsard, who introduces a vulgarism ('*Trogne*', 'mug' or 'phiz', for Bacchus's face), Rochester closes:

> *Cupid* and *Bacchus* my Saints are;
> May Drink and Love still reign:
> With Wine I wash away my Cares,
> And then to Love again.

In this last line, where the more seemly Muses' Library text reads 'Love', Vieth follows the 1680 text and prints a cruder monosyllable, mockingly alliterating with 'Cares'. This obscenity must be, I think, what Rochester wrote. He has given this exquisite but shocking small poem a wholly original structure, necessitating two opposed poles: the one creating in fantasy an extremity of imagining; the other with one casually dropped word shattering everything that has gone before. The final dynamic effect of the poem is not unlike the extraordinary structure which Milton's bad angels erect in hell: a brilliant energy of human creation, teetering over a void.

Rochester's biographers have noted that in his last years – his early thirties – his reading turned to history, philosophy and politics; and they have surmised on that basis that had he lived he might have given more time to the public affairs he had profoundly despised earlier. In something of the same spirit Robert Parsons implies that on his death-bed Rochester looked forward to the writing of sacred poetry. Both prospects seem unlikely. Both seem, moreover, to be associated with the kind of anxiety that impels even his best critics (like, for instance, David Farley-Hills in his admirable study) to overstress the 'positive' aspects of his work, either in the direction of making much of the philosophical importance of his ideas, or of underlining the exciting fictiveness of the more substantial poems – of finding in them even the three-dimensionality of the novelist. Both ventures risk distorting the real aesthetic quality of Rochester's poetry. A moment's consideration of some of the couplet poems will show how little truly 'fictive' they are, how little they rest within the play of psychological and social relationships.

Rochester's more overtly satirical writing makes it seem odd that there is still any question as to why he chose Timon as a persona. Shakespeare's character took the covers off the dishes at his banquet to show, beneath, nothing but spangles and warm water; and he looked forward to his removal from the great social scene with the words

> My long sickness
> Of health and living now begins to mend
> And nothing brings me all things.

Of *A Letter from Artemisia in the Town to Cloe in the Country* one might say that all things bring us nothing.[1] Some recent critics regard this as Rochester's best poem, and the quality most admired is its fictive density of substance, its moral relativism. This admiration is responding to something true in the poem which explains its sheer entertainingness; but it is a dangerous admiration that overlooks an essential element of structure. 'Dear *Artemisia*! Poetry's a Snare': and this poem is as reductive, as self-underminingly self-consuming as anything Rochester ever wrote, the seductive promise of whole Decamerons of future stories with

---

[1] I quote the Muses' Library title and text for this poem, while changing the spelling of the name to Vieth's *Artemisia*, for reasons suggested in my discussion of the name's possible source.

which it ends as unaccomplished and unaccomplishable as those
'Promises' and 'Vows' which end 'Upon Nothing': for Rochester
was not a man who wrote the same poem twice. And it is an
unalterable condition of the poetic form that, unlike drama or the
novel, poetry has no free-standing voice, each persona must be
taken responsibility for by the poet – who was, in this case, as
peculiarly well known to the audience for whom he wrote for his
masculine gender as for his aristocratic standing. Rochester never,
that is to say, writes like a woman, only like a man writing like a
woman, and carefully selecting only such female attributes as may
solidify the equation latent in the opening that women are to men
as the individual man of wit is to the rest of society. For, as
Rochester says elsewhere,

> *Witts* are treated just like common *Whores*,
> First they're enjoy'd, and then kickt out of *Doores* . . .
> *Women* and *Men* of *Wit*, are dang'rous Tools,
> And ever fatal to admiring *Fools*.
> Pleasure allures, and when the *Fopps* escape,
> 'Tis not that they're belov'd, but fortunate,
> And therefore what they fear, at last they hate.[1]

From the beginning we hear Artemisia, for all the brilliance of
the impersonation, as Rochester's voice at one remove, and gain
perpetual pleasure at the paradoxical comparisons that continually
arise from his two-faced mask of man of wit and woman; indeed
the pleasure derives from the exact measuring of the distance of that
remove – 'Thus, *like* an arrant Woman, as I am'. This is a game that
grows more difficult, but all the more worth playing, as the
resemblances stretch and grow thin but still sustain through the
inset personae of fine lady and true whore. The poem is composed
of women betraying each other – and the other sex, too, insofar as
it comes in their way – and is thus made up of a descending series of
self-scrutinies, of measurements of the treachery that detachment
from the human self entails, when a writer (for instance) stops

[1]In the last line of this passage from the *Satire against Mankind*, Pinto follows the
1680 text in reading 'And therefore what they fear, at least they hate'. John
Hayward, in his Nonesuch Press edition (1926), reads 'And therefore what they fear,
at heart they hate'. I have silently altered the Muses' Library text here to 'last', a
reading which I propose as possibly underlying the erroneous *least*; in literary terms,
the conclusive ring of 'at last they hate' is both more Rochesterian and more
generally Augustan.

living in order to sigh, in an impossible self-denying act of self-scrutiny, a remark like

> Were I (who to my cost already am
> One of those strange prodigious Creatures *Man*.)
> A Spirit free, to choose . . .

This construct made out of creative treacheries, this descending spiral of darker and darker illusion analysed, may explain Rochester's choice of a name for his heroine. The word 'Artemisia' means the species of bitter herb that contains the plant wormwood, and the poet may have thought this 'flower of Artemis' a good name for his sharp-tongued virginal heroine; but Rochester's impersonation of a female speaker suggests that he remembered the punchline of a story from Herodotus's account of the Persian Wars.[1] Artemisia, Queen of Halicarnassus, saved herself at the battle of Salamis by a brilliant act of treachery: hotly pursued by a Greek vessel and finding her way barred by one of her own allies, she promptly rammed and sank the allied ship. The Greek pursuer assumed that she must therefore after all be Athenian, and turned away; the observers of her own party assumed that the rammed vessel must after all be Athenian, and sang her praises. Xerxes said afterwards: 'My men have behaved like women, my women like men!'

In the circumstances this remark has complexities that resonate in the memory (though Herodotus did not think it his business to notice them); the likelihood is that they lingered in Rochester's, given the subtle and paradoxical games based on wars of the sexes that he goes in for in *Artemisia*, from the point of view of the unsexed, unsocial writer –

> Like Men that marry, or like Maids that woo,
> Because 'tis the very worst thing they can do.

For the poem traces a charming, casual course downwards from disloyalty to criminal treachery. The substance is so delightfully

[1] The relevant parts of Herodotus's *History*, Book VIII, chapters 87–8, here quoted in George Rawlinson's translation of 1858, had not been translated into English before Rochester's death, though there were both Latin and French versions. The story may have reached Rochester indirectly, but it is worth noting that most contemporary accounts support Parsons's description of the poet as 'thoroughly acquainted with all Classick authors, both Greek and Latin', and that Rochester seems to have had no less a taste for reading history than Lucius Cary, who a generation earlier was reading the Greek historians.

'sociable', so randomly entertainingly gossipy, so thick with amusing observations of the known, that we barely notice its structure, which is hardly in fact extrusive: it may even be slightly flawed. But it has without doubt three descending stages. We open with the innocent but wilfully sentimental Artemisia's discovery of solaces for herself – from a social world that both governs and disgusts her – in the conscious follies and illusions of art, turning from a hated passionless love to a loved loneliness of letter writing. From there the poem moves by a refined malice on Artemisia's part to the inset treacheries of the 'fine lady', who is false not only to the other sex – her poor fool of a husband – but even to her own species, preferring the 'dirty, chatt'ring . . . Minature of Man', a monkey to be fondled instead of a human creature to be loved. And she herself glances down with a considering pity to the voiceless, unindividuated, merely type-treachery of Corinna, who – a kind of dark shadow behind the delicate Artemisia – also knows how to use her experience and others' for her own purposes, but who rests, 'diseas'd, decay'd', at the mortgaged bottom of society, 'looking gay', 'talking fine', her every feeling a lie and her whole life an illusion – her child a 'Bastard Heir' to existence itself, the shadow of a shadow of a shadow. The poem climbs down through one level of fashion and fantasy to another, and then another as through a 'snare' –

(*Bedlam* has many Mansions; have a care)

– which catches us and lands us on the brilliant last line:

But you are tir'd, and so am I.
                              Farewel.

In a letter to his friend Savile, Rochester wrote: 'The World, ever since I can remember, has been still so unsupportably the same'. It is on that 'tired' insight into some pure banality in social existence that the poem rests, as on a rock. And later he wrote to the same correspondent, casually: 'few Men here dissemble their being Rascals; and no Woman disowns being a Whore'.[1] *Artemisia* is a kind of undissembled dissembling, an owned disowning, because it is a social construct itself, and gives genuine pleasure thereby: it is a letter to a friend just like these often delightfully witty friendly

[1] *The Rochester-Savile Letters*, ed. J. H. Wilson (1941), pp. 40, 73.

letters Rochester wrote to Savile, or the usually charmingly kind
and nonsensical notes he sent home to his wife. But at the same
time it expresses the weary lucidity of Rochester's insight into the
social self: it is a progressively more ruthless, more searching light
turned towards the darkness that cannot be either 'dissembled' or
'disowned'. And it is on that darkness, the lack of anything beyond
the self-cancelling illusions of the poem, that it rests: there is
nothing else, and nothing is what it is. At the centre of *Artemisia* is
the fine lady who defines the aesthetic which both poem and social
world are content to share, with a line that clearly haunted Swift's
imagination: 'The perfect joy of being well deceiv'd'. So long as the
poem lasts the poet is content to stay within that 'perfect joy', to
follow out to the end his own curiously elegant, undoubtedly
entertaining construct of lies and illusions: one that is successful
enough to make many of its readers ask (as does Rochester's best
editor), 'Which of the poem's many characters represents the
truth?' – when the only answer is, 'Fewer and fewer and less and
less'.

This is something like the answer, at any rate, which Rochester
gives in his most powerful poem, the *Satire against Mankind*, whose
finality is its essential character, at whatever stage of the poet's
career it happened to be written. It is here that a reader may see
more clearly the achievement and the cost of Rochester's peculiar
art of extremity, the intensity he gained by arriving at the point
where something comes to an end:

> Then Old Age, and experience, hand in hand,
> Lead him to death, and make him understand,
> After a search so painful, and so long,
> That all his Life he has been in the wrong.

I mentioned earlier Rochester's use of capitals, and the faltering
rhythm that breaks his strongest lines. The peculiar character and
memorability of this climactic fourth line is the way that capital L
'Life' quietly dissolves into wavering distractedly weak negatives –
Man is not, but 'has been', he is nowhere but 'in the wrong'. This
'satire' is no satire, but simply a poem, which we cannot
understand unless we believe its medium, its verbal surface; and
this poem, which seems to have so much public clarity, in fact
works through a style like a misty secret labyrinth in which the
person who reads well gets lost,

> climbs with pain,
> *Mountains* of Whimseys, heap'd in his own *Brain*:
> Stumbling from thought to thought, falls head-long down
> Into doubts boundless Sea, where like to drown,
> Books bear him up awhile . . .

It is, again, unsurprising that the best part of the poem, its harsh, undeniably conclusive opening prelude, moves from paradox ('who to my cost already am') to net us throughout in a rhetoric whose most memorable effects are all explicit intricacies of verbal surface, like that later famous obsessive passage in which the poet winds his subject, Man, in a knot of monosyllables:

> wretched *Man*, is still in Arms for fear;
> For fear he armes, and is of Armes afraid,
> By fear, to fear, successively betray'd
> Base fear . . .

Perhaps only Rochester among English poets could have got such power from the exploration of that purely negative form of imagination, fear.

It may be asked how a writer whom I have presented as so concerned with 'Nothing' could have made of his work a 'something' still appreciated after three hundred years – indeed, enjoyed and admired now as at no other time since that period of intense success during which the poet himself wrote. I want to finish by suggesting an answer to this question: and it will be one other than the supposal that nihilism as such is peculiarly the concern of the present. Rochester was not a philosophical nihilist, and there is no reason to suppose that, if he were, the modern reader would admire him for it. But the reasons are, I think, in some sense philosophical, so long as we are content to allow that the philosophical can include the highly paradoxical. For Rochester can, like any other poet, be more relevantly 'philosophical' when he is writing entirely playfully, with an appearance of casual randomness, than when he 'thinks' in prose. Rochester's arguments with Burnet, for instance, are well worth looking at: but at their most interesting they only include points that will be put far more forcibly and personally in the verse, even where we might least look for it.

Thus, a reader interested in Rochester's philosophical position could do worse than read the Epilogue he wrote for a friend's comedy, *Love in the Dark* (even the title is Rochesterian, suggestive of that 'mistaken magic' he calls love in 'The Imperfect Enjoyment'), where he mocks the success of a rival company given to effects of flying spectacle:

> Players turn Puppets now at your Desire,
> In their Mouth's Nonsence, in their Tails a Wire,
> They fly through Clouds of Clouts, and show'rs of Fire.
> A kind of losing *Loadum* is their Game,
> Where the worst Writer has the greatest Fame.

These two brilliant images are better than they ought to be – than any casual satire can be expected to be. This is surely because Rochester was himself a kind of equilibrist, an expert in moving high over that vacuity he defines in 'Love and Life': no past, no future, no present to call his own, beyond a 'miraculous' minute high over the crowd. All his verse is, similarly, a 'losing *Loadum*', a card-game like a slow bicycle race where the loser wins, because he does the difficult thing. The French Symbolist dramatist Jarry wrote a blasphemous essay, which is genuinely funny and innocent, called 'The Crucifixion considered as an Uphill Bicycle Race', which gets us within the area where Rochester needs to be considered; remembering Eliot's remarks on the relative spirituality of certain kinds of blasphemy.

Rochester's angry antipathy to the worldly world of success, that world in which for long he was so anxious to succeed and in which he so long succeeded in succeeding, even to the point at which the perhaps comparably worldly Bishop Burnet remarked with some satisfaction after the poet's death, 'All the town is full of his great penitence' – this world-opposing side of his character was clearly far more evident to the other and probably more intelligent attendant on his death-bed, Robert Parsons, his Puritan mother's private chaplain. It was Parsons who brought to Rochester perhaps his only moment of true spiritual vision, by reading to him Isaiah's prophecy of the Suffering Servant, the Messiah who is a man of no importance at all; and it is Parsons, similarly, who in the sermon he preached at Rochester's funeral at once grasped the game of 'losing Loadum' the poet had played morally all his life:

> He seem'd to affect something Singular and paradoxical in his
> Impieties, as well as in his Writings, above the reach and thought

of other men. . . . Nay so confirm'd was he in Sin, that he liv'd, and oftentimes almost died, a Martyr for it.[1]

It was surely this upside-down spirituality, or reversed idealism, that made Johnson among other eighteenth-century writers think that *Upon Nothing* was Rochester's best poem, for it is the single one of all his works which in its startling depth and largeness comes close to that classic standard, even to that image of Nature which Johnson demanded of his poets; for *Upon Nothing* is of course both cosmology and history, a mischievous rendering down of all those Renaissance histories that start with the Creation and end with the present day. Johnson, who had remarked casually to Boswell that 'Politics are now nothing more than means of rising in the world', would have appreciated Rochester's demonstration that *sub specie aeternitatis* they are also a means of falling in it:

> The great Man's Gratitude to his best Friend,
> Kings Promises, Whores Vows, tow'rds thee they bend,
> Flow swiftly into thee, and in thee ever end.

The liturgical cadence here, as in the music of an ancient Latin hymn gone slightly wrong in the translation, gives *Upon Nothing* something of that real largeness often lacking in Rochester's insubstantial verse – a verse that finally seems to hate substance – and makes of this poem an object with the extension of a Rubens ceiling reversed, or a Purcell chorale reset for solo flute. Or, to make comparisons within the poet's own work, *Upon Nothing* is empowered, by its source in the paradoxical encomium, to bring into the forefront those elsewhere entirely latent Metaphysical elements in Rochester's imagination, such as he himself tended to dismiss with irritation as the 'extravagances' of 'my fantastic mind'; elements which make, for instance, *A Ramble in St James's Park*, when it is compared with the reductive and mean-minded work of Butler which it so admiringly seems to copy, an actual if finalizing perpetuation (for all its grossness) of earlier Renaissance modes of idealism, rather than a Butlerian destruction of them.

It is in this high and spacious abstraction that *Upon Nothing* contrasts so interestingly with another 'nothing' poem, the very late translation from Seneca's *Troades*. The best lines of this

---

[1]Robert Parsons, *A Sermon Preached at the Earl of Rochester's Funeral* (1680), p. 9.

translation are those in which the poet picks up and adds to the essential materialism of his source:

> Dead, we become the Lumber of the World;
> And to that Mass of Matter shall be swept,
> Where things destroy'd, with things unborn are kept . . .

Bodies here become disturbingly indestructible, like old dressmak-ers' dummies stacked among the dusty attics of Chaos: the Lumber image has a humorous irritated homeliness in considering physical existence that is the other side of the coin to Rochester's idealism. Clearly, it was the very closeness and actuality of the Restoration poet's sense of the physical and material world – the inevitabilities of his 'realism', the close limits of the only vision he knew, like the small confines of the court he was ironically drawn to – that threw him back on an idealism markedly negative, abstract: such as Rochester himself found in another Roman poet, Lucretius, after whom he splendidly invoked gods who needed nothing, asked nothing, were angered by nothing. And similarly he maintained against Burnet's Christian God – a god deeply marked by that recurring pragmatism that can make English theology, as Col-eridge once remarked, as insistently vulgar as it is realistic – that

> God had none of those Affections of Love or Hatred, which breed perturbation in us, and by consequence he could not see that there was to be either reward or punishment. He thought our Conceptions of God were so low, that we had better not think much of him: And to love God seemed to him a presumptuous thing, and the heat of fanciful men.[1]

It is easier to see, or rather to feel, the flaws in the theology of the time if we turn the kind of over-pragmatism that the romanticism in Rochester was struggling with into its more secular philosophi-cal form: the Hobbesian philosophy that entered deeply into the imagination of the age, even into areas where nothing was consciously felt but angry hostility to Hobbes's premises. Hobbes's philosophy has more power than Burnet's theology simply because it relies more deeply on and speaks more frankly from its age's historical presuppositions than any true theology can honestly do.

---

[1]Gilbert Burnet, *Some Passages of the Life and Death of John, Earl of Rochester* (1680), pp. 52–3, quoted in Farley-Hills, *Critical Heritage*, p. 60.

It is possibly easier to write a *Leviathan* out of mid-seventeenth-century history – out of the disillusioned consciousness of the age – than to create a work of dogmatic theology out of it. Hence the potency of a passage that says:

> The whole mass of all things that are, is corporeal, that is to say, body . . . also every part of body, is likewise body, and hath the like dimensions; and consequently every part of the universe, is body, and that which is not body, is no part of the universe: and because the universe is all, that which is no part of it, is *nothing*; and consequently *nowhere* . . .[1]

Where the religious imagination of a period becomes hopelessly comfortable, a conformist cul-de-sac, more life *may* be found latent in the world of blasphemy or heresy. Thus, even the intensely 'social' Henry James – whom I cite, as having used him elsewhere in this essay – at the end of the nineteenth century turned, like many good writers after him, to the murky world of the ghost story, to express moral and spiritual facts not easy to keep hold of otherwise within the philistine insensibility of contemporary middle-class England. The real subject of *The Turn of the Screw*, as he made clear in a letter, was the appalling exposure of children to lethal adult affections; it was to help him out in saying this, to a society of hard sentimentalists, that he called up the pot-boiling spooks, for whom he apologizes to his correspondent, jokily: 'I evoked the worst I could . . . "Excusez du peu!" '[2] Rochester, two centuries earlier, had 'evoked the worst *he* could': he evoked half-lovingly that 'Nothing' which Hobbes laid down like a Green Belt at the edge of his unimaginably material universe, whose 'body', in the light of what Rochester does with *his* 'Nothing', takes on something of that ghostly immateriality which the poet gave mockingly to *his* 'bodies' – the lovers who haunt his poems.

Such negativism deserves, I think, the highest respect: it should not be brushed aside, in anxious search for more substantial virtues – more positive philosophical values. Rochester's Nothing deserves, what is more, even more respect in that it entails for the poet Something of a losing game, a 'losing Loadum'. To refuse, in all honesty, to trust the only world one has; to find oneself incapable,

---

[1] Hobbes, *Leviathan, ed. cit.*, p. 440.
[2] Lubbock, *Letters of Henry James*, I, 308.

on the other hand, of any other music in one's poetry beyond the crash of breaking glass – this is a fate as grim as that appalling epitaph with which Johnson sums up the fate of Harley: 'Not knowing what to do, he did nothing; and, with the fate of a double dealer, at last he lost his power, but kept his enemies'. Rochester clearly possessed that extreme moral courage that is willing to leave behind a body of work fundamentally 'unlikeable' – that presents the self in it as unlikeable, for the work's sake: a moral courage which is the prime virtue, one would have thought, of all true artists. For, from inside Rochester's work, which is likely to have come from a personality both sensitive and generous as well as honest, no 'nice man' emerges. There is only an image strikingly like that image, now in the National Portrait Gallery, which we mainly know Rochester by: a portrait surely planned and dictated to the painter by the poet himself, and so an actual picture to match those several verse 'Instructions to a Painter' which were a favourite literary exercise in this period. Half turned away from his audience, whom he regards with a sideways and wary inward amusement, the Earl of Rochester welcomes us with an open gesture of his shining silk left arm, which gesture at the same time directs our eyes to his raised right hand holding a laurel wreath high over the head of a pet monkey; a monkey who, like an image in a mirror, gives to the poet with his left hand a torn fragment from the book he grips open with his right. In aesthetic terms, the animal is the focus of the human being, while reversing his every gesture: its little black mask is raised devoutly towards the white unforth-coming stare that the tall young aristocrat directs down on us; the monkey's small chest is slightly unnerving in its nakedness against the costly concealing taffetas that fall from a lace collar over the man's torso. Like his own 'fine lady', the poet is playing with a 'Minature of Man'.

In itself the portrait is a design of pure rebuttal, all dead ends and barriers. It is an impassive self-concealing refusal of disguise, a courtier's serious joke about looking 'frightfully': it takes us back, that is to say, to the elder Wilmot's remark, and summarizes what I have tried to say about an art of social surface. For all such charm as the Rochester portrait has is not a charm of 'personality', but is a matter of the subtle shadowings of the taffeta cascading down below the intelligent but rebuffing eyes of the poet, the silk's beauty sharpened by contrast with the disturbing nakedness of the

small ape's chest beneath its blank dark averted mug. Underneath
the taffeta there is to all intents and purposes nothing whatever: but
the picture is not, for all that, empty – it is full of something, even if
that something is couched in mockeries and denials.

5

Tibbles: A New Life of Pope

Even Swift, who liked to think he was half author of the *Dunciad*, had trouble with its allusions and wrote grumblingly to warn Pope that twenty miles from London 'Nobody understands hints, initial letters, or town facts and passages'. The delighted poet seized his chance and added to his poem for its 1729 'Variorum' edition those profuse helpful footnotes which make the text more confusing than before. Pope glosses, for instance, the first occurrence of the name of the poem's first hero, called in it '*Tibbald*' though we would now write the name of the Shakespearian scholar in question 'Theobald'; and the poet's notes mentions that Tibbald's name was in fact always pronounced so, though written as Theobald. Working on the poem rather more than two hundred years after Pope, the distinguished editor of the Twickenham *Dunciad*, James Sutherland, declined to take the poet at his word, and added a note on the annotation explaining that the name 'really was pronounced' Theobald. Presumably following this lead, an equally distinguished Popian, Maynard Mack, has now in his long-awaited and richly-informative new Life of Pope found a corner in which to extend this editorial scepticism into his own full-blown critical observation: 'Even the name of the hero dunce, Lewis Theobald, though printed out in full, was "translated" (like Bottom wearing the ass's head in *A Midsummer Night's Dream*) into a foolish tumble of syllables rhyming with "ribald" '. Elsewhere in the Life, Professor Mack makes the point that the sheer fictiveness of Timon's villa in the *Epistle to Burlington* 'will be evident to those who have travelled much among English country houses'. It doesn't seem irrelevant therefore to point out that those who travel much by bus in Holborn are likely to hear the conductors, not all of whom can have read the *Dunciad*, calling 'Theobald's Road', 'Tibbles Road'. Interestingly, the *Oxford Dictionary of Christian Names* supports both Pope and the bus conductors, pointing out that *Teobaldus* or *Theobaldus* is the Latin form of the name for which *Tebald* or *Tibald* is the vernacular; it refers to Shakespeare's Tybalt, cites the surnames *Tibbald* and *Tibbles*, and quotes Pope's *Dunciad* note without supposing any irony. As to *Tybalt*, I have myself always assumed that since Mercutio with cheerful derision calls his enemy 'Prince of Cats', 'King of Cats', making allusion to rat-catching and the possession of nine lives; and since furthermore Elizabethans kept what they referred to as 'Tib-cats', then the chances are strong that our still-surviving habit of calling the occasional cat Tibbles dates back at least as early as the sixteenth century. From all of which it seems safe to conclude that the talented Augustan editor of Shakespeare, Lewis Theobald or Tibbald or Tibbles, inherited a name that just happened to be as innocently embarrassing as, say, Thomas Kitten. [1]

The name Theobald/Tibbald was there; Pope didn't put it there. What is difficult about Pope is not his fantasy but his facts. The

[1] Although in medieval narratives of Reynard the Fox the 'Prince of Cats' is called Tybald and must be presumed to be a Tom, the Elizabethan Tib-cat appears to be a female. The early history of Tib-names for cats appears, on the evidence of the *OED*, to be interesting and complicated. The dictionary suggests that in the sixteenth century the Tab/Tibby names primarily denoted the female animal, following on the use of these names (probably contractions of Tabitha) for a woman of low birth, particularly in paired opposition to 'Tom' for the male. By the seventeenth century, and especially after the introduction into England at the mid-century of the 'tabby-cat' from Persia – i.e., the now familiar grey or brown cat, striped or brindled like the cotton imported from Baghdad – the Tibby/Tabby field of names had become so confused as to permit the suggestion, in both feline and human contexts, of mere cattiness rather than any gender differentiation. What remains clear is that it was no particular advantage to an Augustan scholar to bear a name which sounded like a cat's.

That the name Theobald did in fact sound like this is a contention which I support here by the probability that in the past the ancient royal residence of Theobalds was always known as 'Tibbles' (or thereabouts). After this essay was first published in the *London Review of Books*, two (independent) correspondents very kindly sent me evidence confirming this, and I am grateful to both for allowing me to quote them here. Sir Ian Gilmour, whose family now owns the Theobalds Park estate in Hertfordshire, reports that, like many others of those who live on or near the estate, his family have inherited the pronunciation of its name as 'Tibbles'. This circumstance is given a provenance in Pope's own lifetime (if not before) by a note quoted by Mrs Christina Colvin from the Edgeworth family papers. The note, written before 1768, and composed by and in the hand of Richard Edgeworth, grandfather of Maria, records that 'William Edgeworth [*c* 1726] bought a country house called Tibbald's Park near Theobalds in Hertfordshire, held by lease from the Duke of Portland . . .' (Bodleian MSS Edgeworth [uncat.]: typed copy of the Black Book of Edgeworthstown, fol. 73.)

poet might have told Mack that no 'translation' had taken place, that not he but Nature had made Theobald/Tibbles write like a tom-cat. The sense of the amazing nature of Life's observable quantities, of the things that are actually there, fills the *Dunciad* – this gritty and atomistic masterpiece dense with people, streets, dead dogs, data, 'Millions and millions . . . / Thick as the stars', 'As thick as bees', 'As thick as eggs': a whole world thick with itself, with books, words and above all names:

> Twas chatt'ring, grinning, mouthing, jabb'ring all,
> And Noise and Norton, Brangling, and Breval,
> Dennis and Dissonance, and Captious Art,
> And Snip-snap short, and Interruption smart.
> Hold (cry'd the Queen) a Catcall each shall win . . .

A Catcall is that shrill hostile whistle from the gallery, but also (perhaps) the noise that Tibbles makes. 'Captious' is an odd and difficult word too; the dictionary defines it as 'Fallacious, sophistical . . . trying to catch people in their words', which is what Pope and Swift did *par excellence*. If Pope's verse and Swift's prose are the great literary achievements of the earlier Augustan period, it is because both learned how to live within yet to master their culture's dominant premise that truth was observable fact. That mastery involved for Swift the formation of a style that could be called uncannily plain, and for Pope the regular claims he makes to an 'Honest Muse': neither manner is free of ambiguities. In Pope's case there is a parallel between the elusive simplicities of his work (how do you pronounce 'Theobald'?) and the complex relation with the world of public fact maintained by the poet in his private existence. The one thing that most people know about Pope's life is that he called in his private correspondence by trickery in order to publish it with improvement. No period has writers who play more difficult games with fact and factuality than the Augustan. This helps to make Pope the most interesting and problematic of subjects for biography.

Biography is itself perhaps the most Augustan branch of literary studies, being an offshoot of History; it isn't surprising that Boswell's *Life of Johnson* competes with Gibbon's *Decline and Fall* for the title of the greatest literary work of the eighteenth century. Professor Mack acknowledges this affiliation with History as he makes tribute to helpers in the Preface to his Life of Pope:

dear Daughters of Memory, Muse of History, Muse of
Biography (if any), speak loud as many of their names as you can
. . . sing rapturously these . . .

But in doing so he compacts some of his problems. A literary
biography, being part of History, must serve the facts: the great
pleasure of this fascinating form is the sense of seeing objectively
and externally a world hitherto known from the inside of the
subject's own experience. Yet as well as the facts there are always
the Muses, any biography's ambition to be a thing in itself, even an
art-work in itself. Mack's Life of Pope achieves this ambition – it's
a thoroughly readable and enjoyable book. Its 800 pages (with
Notes and Index, 975 in all) don't seem excessive; the narrative is
conducted with large assurance and urbanity, and manages to
communicate a great deal of information without weighing
anything but lightly on the reader's attention. As biographer, Mack
probably gets both confidence and continuity from the purpose
stated in his Preface: 'There are few poets who cannot use an
advocate'. For, although the poet has had enthusiasts, the general
biographical tradition – in our own time relatively fragmentary –
had tended to borrow the toughness of Johnson's short and classic
Life, written some forty years after Pope died, without necessarily
possessing the Augustan critic's very great intelligence, judgement
and wit.

Mack's intention has been to write a Life of Pope that will be
popular in a number of different senses. He has wished not only to
be read with pleasure, but to tell a pleasurable story – a story of
Pope's great success as a writer, not merely in England but more
widely throughout Europe; to show the poet as essentially, despite
his faults, a richly likeable man, perhaps more widely befriended
than any other English poet; and to indicate that his life and
character made him, not merely a literary man in a narrow sense,
but something of a culture-hero for both his own time and our
own. In this portrait there may be noted a stress which illuminates
the observation that 'Poetry for [Pope], as for his great predeces-
sors, is emphatically more a social than a personal institution' – a
debatable point when made concerning Pope, but perhaps relevant
to the book's own approach. Mack states his purpose as the giving
of 'a comprehensive account of the man in his times'. There seems
to be something static in the phrase which is matched by the

general movement, or lack of movement, the sense of relished vista in the book as a whole. A reader learns in the first few pages not the least fascinating of the innumerable pieces of information which the Life has to offer – that Pope's maternal aunt was wife to the man who was perhaps the finest English painter of the seventeenth century, the miniaturist Samuel Cooper; and the Life itself, illustrated by many portraits – both reproductions and verbal descriptions of the poet's host of friends – is not unlike a collection of Augustan miniatures. Its spacious, slow-moving and sociable construct calls back an older sense of the eighteenth century as an 'Age of Elegance', a period when the increasing wealth of civilization was fostered by the 'Peace of the Augustans'. Mack's easy grip on his materials – in a sense he has neither story to tell nor thesis to argue – leaves the identity of his subject both as man and poet free to be uncertain, to develop, expand and dissolve into what might rather be called 'Pope's world' than 'Pope'. Louis MacNeice once referred in a poem to what he called the 'tea-coloured afternoons' of Poussin's paintings. That there is something of the tea-coloured afternoon in Mack's biography is not inappropriate to its subject. And it certainly adds to the pleasure of what will clearly be an extremely popular biography, likely to remain for many years the definitive Life of Pope.

It is because the book will be read so widely, will prove so influential and will last so long, that there is room to voice a few regrets. Everything, even the enjoyable, has its price, and the price of the pleasures of 'advocacy' can seem at moments a high one; an advocate after all is only a man paid to tell lies on one's behalf in a court of law. The claims in short of the Muse are not always compatible with those of History. A certain kind of Popian fact gets lost in this golden and likeable Life of Pope; and the facts that get lost are valuable and interesting facts, in no way merely diminishing to the poet. One single case may be cited, partly because the Muse comes into it.

Part of the charm of this biography is its profuse illustration. Since cost-cutting (the book is remarkably low-priced) seems to have proscribed an index to the illustrations, finding one of these pleasing images can occasionally be tiresome, and when found it may prove to be poorly reproduced. This is the case with one of the poet's most interesting portraits, now in the National Portrait Gallery and reproduced on page 342 – so darkly as to make it unsurprising that Mack twice calls it 'teasing' in his discussion of it. The poet's friend Charles Jervas painted it, probably in 1717, when Pope – aged twenty-nine – was deep in his translation of Homer, a lengthy task that not only sealed his fame as the country's leading poet (he was admired by good judges when still under twenty) but secured him the fortune which made him free of patrons for the rest of his life: the first poet, he liked to think, who had ever thus earned his independence. Understandably, a bust of Homer stands on a bracket in the upper left-hand corner of the picture. Below it, the slight, bewigged figure of the poet fills the centre of the composition, perched with dignity in a sumptuous high-backed leather chair, his white face resting on his right hand, whose wrist is cuffed by a wonderfully fine cambric shirt. Behind the back of his chair, on the right and balancing the Homer but a little lower down the picture, a girl with her back to us stands on tiptoe in stockinged feet on a footstool, reaching up or lifting down a large book (invisible in this reproduction).

Mack describes this young woman as pushing 'up and away some sort of drapery or heavy curtain, almost as if she were engaged in an unveiling'. There is a certain oracular heightening here, reflected in Mack's whole sense of the picture, as indeed perhaps in his image of Pope throughout the Life. The 'Muse' reappears. The biographer identifies the young girl as either 'the poet's Muse', or as Teresa Blount, the elder of two sisters of good Catholic family with whom Mack insists Pope was in love – and certainly the younger, Martha, became his close friend for life. But it is unlikely that either the Muse or Teresa would have agreed to be painted in the posture and dress of a serving-girl. For this is surely what the girl lifting a book behind the chair is; just as the curtain she draws can be no more than a common shield against the sun once used in great houses to protect their more valuable books and pictures (its presence here probably indicates that the book, presumably written by Pope himself, *is* valuable). The girl herself, one would guess, is only ambiguously valuable, 'a treasure'. For her pleasant, crude and dark-skinned face (for centuries before 1900 the English upper classes believed working-class people to be actually darker in hue, owing to a genetic inheritance of lives of sunburned outdoor labour): her simple clothes, shortened skirts and stockinged feet – shoes politely removed before ascending the posh footstool – all indicate servant class. It seems clear that the

poet has posed himself between Homer and a serving-girl, a pairing
faintly echoed when Johnson speaks of *The Rape of the Lock* as
admired 'by readers of every class, from the critic to the waiting-
maid'. The phrase comes from his Life of Pope, which, elsewhere
using a published account by just such a serving-woman, released
into biographical tradition what may in any case have been a kind
of legend quite consciously furthered by the poet himself – the idea
of a great man's dependence on faithful female menials has a quality
Pope would have liked. Johnson speaks of the 'perpetual need of
female attendance' on the part of a writer never strong or well
(born of ageing parents, developing early what we now believe to
be a spinal tuberculosis contracted from a foster-nurse, and further
weakened by a bad accident in infancy, a trampling by a vagrant
cow, Pope was a delicate – though decidedly beautiful – child, and
an incapacitated adult, in middle life crippled and often in pain).
Johnson tells how, all his life, not only at home but in the houses of
his increasingly grand friends, Pope would call for the day-long
and even night-long ministrations of coffee-bringers and other
helps, the more willing for being charmingly thanked and very
well paid.

In other portraits, Pope chose ironically to pose himself with one
of his vast, muscular, adoring and adored dogs (about whom Mack
has some excellent stories to tell) gazing up towards the poet's
small, deformed person. In this image Pope has surely 'framed'
himself between what he saw as the defining laws of a limited life.
Before him stands a cold marble bust; behind, a female servant.
The poet's cheek leans on his hand in the ancient pose which
Panofsky's study has taught us to recognize as that of the artist as
Melancholy Man.

Should Mack be mistaken here, the slip is of no importance
amidst the splendid wealth of information he offers us. Yet the
character of the error is interesting. There is a kind of significant
factuality about the serving-girl, both as an aesthetic image and as
what she represents, particularly to an Augustan consciousness.
The avoidance of this factuality, and in its place the stress on a
Muse or mistress – like the similar neglect of the reality of
'Tibbald's' name – suggest to what degree this Life by a scholar
leans towards 'the Muse' and away from the facts of History. There
is a sense (as Peter Ackroyd cogently observed in his Life of Eliot)
in which every literary biography is something of a tightrope-walk

between these two poles: a sense in which, that is, all biographies are really re-interpretations on the part of each individual biographer of what he or she takes the word 'Life' to mean. If Mack's sympathetic romanticism provokes thought here, it is partly because, by the chance of that brilliant fluid intelligence that seems to surround Pope always like a flood of varying light, the very topic of Pope's picture appears to present its own counter-statement to that made by Mack's 800-page biography. If Jervas's portrait has any meaning, it must be that the poet, alas, *has* no 'Life'.

Though Mack claims that the elusiveness or reserve of his subject's personality is peculiar to himself, this 'most perplexing aspect' could by contrast be said to be congenital to most poets: who exist with intensity to other generations only by their work. Their 'Life' has a tendency to contract to an intellectual or literary centre more properly the concern of the critic: or it expands to a far periphery that has less to do with a 'Life' than merely with 'life'. Or this can be put another way. Poets like Milton, or Byron, are exceptions; most poets, being 'inward', don't do that much actual living – or, as Pope said, 'contemplative life is not only my scene, but it is my habit too'. In the Introductory chapter to his intelligent, stimulating study, *Pope's Essay on Man*, A. D. Nuttall puts it crisply if slightly more objectively when he summarizes the poet's life after youth as 'a steady march of major works and a most unedifying and intricate mess of quarrel and intrigue'. Mack's 'advocacy' of the poet makes him choose to interpret this history in terms of a psychology less literary than largely social. 'The poet in his world' consists of a man for whom we could and should feel an understanding sympathy. But the biographer interprets such terms as 'psychology' and 'social' in a fashion in itself fairly tendentious and personal. He explains much of Pope in the light of two main dominating conditions, personal (the debility of his health) and social (the exclusions forced on him by the fact that his parents belonged to the Roman Catholic Church – the poet for instance could not attend University, nor at certain periods live in central London). The feeling we are tacitly asked to render Pope divides between the admiration deserved by a successful public man, and the pity we owe to a human being whose personal unattractiveness so little encouraged that triumph.

This reading makes sense; but it omits some things that fill the verse (as well as the Jervas portrait) with reserve, with irony. Again, one specific, slight but interesting case may illustrate this mixed inflation and reduction Mack seems to be unconsciously carrying out on what might be meant by a creative writer's 'psychology' or 'society'. Early in the first book of the *Dunciad*, which Pope first brought out in 1728, when he was forty, a reader meets a pair of lines which have all the peculiar Popian blend of fantastic imagination, humour, and implacable 'factuality', (what Swift would have called 'town facts'). They tell us that even the dull City of London businessmen (whom Pope calmly takes as symbols of those who pursue the trifling squalors of the pleasures of this world) have their own 'dreams'; for, after the riotous feasting of the Lord Mayor's Banquet,

> Now May'rs and Shrieves all hush'd and satiate lay,
> Yet eat, in dreams, the custard of the day.

These surely hysterically funny lines Mack 'personalizes', tracing the reference back to Pope's happy and cherished babyhood and boyhood: 'One cannot help wondering whether Pope's characteristic later association of poetic rewards with custard and puddings [he quotes from the *Dunciad*] had its origins in an extra or more tempting slice of egg-pie (for such custard then was) rendered to a small boy for "good rhymes" ' – i.e., by the poet's father. Yet it's not too difficult to learn, from early plays and joke books if from nowhere else, that a vast custard-pie – into which a clown jumped – was once the grand climax of Lord Mayor's Banquets. Here it becomes a wonderfully funny and poignant image of the gross and mean and unimaginative pleasures that life can bend people to, a 'dream'-custard. Like the use of the name 'Theobald' and of the figure of the servant-girl, the custard-pie is an example of Pope's grappling with the real stuff of existence, and transforming it – by a kind of 'mental fight', by a life's reserved skill and labour – into an inimitable poetry.

These slips, or this reduction in the significant range of Pope's 'social' world, seem to arise from something missing in the biographer's sense (a lack perhaps owed to his concept of a popular audience) of the primacy of the poet's life *as a writer*. To that intense centre, everything can prove relevant; it is only if we try to focus externally 'the man in his time' that a certain incoherence takes over, and everything collapses into a 'climate of opinion'. It is not that Professor Mack is unaware of the problems of writers, both in Pope's time and in our own. Thus, he speaks of

> the by no means always successful struggle of the serious writer to keep from drowning in a Sargasso sea of soft porn or other eyewash prepared to formula for the tired typist home at tea-time.

The possibility that this phenomenal sentence is merely parodic, a mockery of the base civilization which gives the modern writer his troubles, ebbs under the realization that the remark is hardly worse than the half-page in which we are told that Walpole 'was not . . . a mere opportunist: he had a genuine paranoia about Jacobitism that could raise oaks out of acorns in his mind overnight'; that 'the Court, having been kept abreast of developments, had made a killing before selling out'; and that George I, 'though hardly brilliant, was bright enough to know that his hold on the affections of the English nation was just now something less than ironclad'.

It remains an oddity of the Eng.Lit. academic life that the authority who has given us, in his remarkably handsome and informative edition of some of the poet's manuscripts, *The Last and Greatest Art*, evidence of Pope's own endlessly self-correcting and self-refining perfectionism, can himself as Pope's biographer write as he does here. There is in the Sargasso sea of eyewash a real failure to understand that individual, inward apprehension of language which constitutes the reading and the writing of literature; to understand that a reader's response to such sentences must be a dazed chaos of killings and sellings, of soft porn, of oaks and acorns for the tired typist at tea-time. A certain side of English studies even now, after many critical revolutions, assumes that 'style' is to be deprecated as being a faint grace incommensurate with true scholarship or historical intelligence. But the fact is that style *is* historical intelligence. The 'Muse' has in cold fact its own facts, its own History, its own laws of nature which may not be violated: for a breast is not oak or iron, nor is eyewash what any typist, however tired, has for tea.

Literature has its own factuality that forbids loose talk of the Muses; in other words, words matter. The 'tired typist home at tea-time' is the corpse that has floated out of that true factual poem, Eliot's *The Waste Land*. The idiosyncrasies of Professor Mack's writing extend themselves into his treatment of the fragments of other writers' writing that surface through his text in incessant quotations – quotations not so much buried as washed-up. Thus, a passage in Pope's *Satire II* is called

> one of the most charming pictures in English poetry (visionary, to be sure: a man's reach should exceed his grasp, or what's a heaven for?) of a way of life in which limit has become freedom, the dancer indistinguishable from the dance . . .

Certainly there is enthusiasm and energy written into this, and it is no crime to mix a metaphor or cross a quotation. But do Browning or Yeats actually help us to see Pope better? – that is to say, is it the poet, or something else, which the enthusiasm and energy are actually 'advocating'? Again, the *Epistle to Arbuthnot* makes way for Milton and (presumably) Beethoven:

> It is from this succession of opening chords – harsh, studiedly impatient – that the mind makes its way to its famous close, in calm of mind, all passion spent.

This is Pope merely being used to illustrate some quite general or social concept of 'culture'. Elsewhere, Mack fuses Swift's 'Only a woman's hair' with Donne's 'bracelet of bright hair about the bone', thus merging two writers who seem to me radically unlike; uses a line from Shakespeare's sonnets, 'in disgrace with fortune and men's eyes', to gloss the equally unShakespearian critic John Dennis in his brutal, difficult, intelligent and tragic old age; and trails a hash of Dylan Thomas's resonant phrases ('those short days when Time lets us play and be golden in the mercy of his means') across the end of the section dealing with Pope's work in the 1720s, thus bringing together two poets almost ideally incompatible.

In all these cases the biographer seems to lose his grip on the real literary identity of every writer involved. He is caught in a quandary that makes him fail to write sense, in a fashion interestingly close to what occurs when he tries, as he does pervasively through this Life, to use Pope not as a poet but as a kind of culture-hero. Struggling as 'advocate' to make us think well or better of his subject, on some terms other than those that result from our reading of his poetry, Mack effects a bewildering collapse of the principles of his argument into a mere 'climate of opinion' surrounding 'most of us' – though it is a paradoxical feature of this book to show a pervasive and very decided antipathy to the modern culture of 'most of us', to write as

'an astringent observer of our own cultural scene'. Thus, speaking
of Pope's definition of the perfect critic in the *Essay on Criticism*,
Mack adds: 'Pope shared with most of us a total inability to attain
this ideal'. But can it be true that the author of that extraordinarily
accomplished and gifted poem, the *Essay on Criticism*, had as *total* an
inability to criticize poetry perfectly as non-poets have? Similarly,
the Grotto which Pope carved out of the basement of his
Twickenham house, and which Mack has written of elsewhere
with more point than here, is described as 'a diverting toy, no
doubt, for the child in Pope, who as in most of us, never grew up'.
Certainly the Grotto is grotesque, and it remains ridiculous that,
together with Pope's garden, it probably helped to make formative
changes in English taste influential in Europe at large; but does this
allow us to confuse that clear child's vision never lost by creative
persons with the lack of psychological maturity some adults suffer
from?

My point here is not that the intention of 'advocacy' can prove
curiously reductive of the subject it seeks to defend. Rather, that it
is dangerous for any literary biography to lose its proper focus on a
writer. That focus, taking as its priority the writer's work, includes
as wide as possible a relevance from the historical period which is
the work's context. Only then shall we genuinely see 'the man in
his time'. Mack's opening sentence, indeed his book's opening
paragraph, is a half-echo from Dickens: 'It was the best of times
and it was the worst of times.' This is a shrug, and shrugging,
though an available social gesture, doesn't do for explanation.
Mack's Life gives us so much, and makes vivid so much in the
poet's existence, that to ask for more is unjust. Yet the word 'Life'
does entail interpretation – Mack interprets as much as any
biographer. And the element of what I have called 'fact and
factuality' that is pervasively blurred or neglected here as a factor of
interpretation is of quite primary importance in the Augustan
period. This biography, with all its excellence, ignores the very
quality that made Swift and Pope the major artists that they are.

The earlier eighteenth century was a period that presented quite
exceptional difficulties for the making of poetry. It was not
precisely what Arnold called it, an age 'of prose'; but his objection
made sense, and continues to make sense in the mind of every new
reader who is struck by a kind of oddness, a going against the
grain, in Augustan verse. Certainly the culture was one that, in

theory, adored and admired poetry. No reader of Roger Lonsdale's
New Oxford Book of Eighteenth Century Verse – a collection too large
and too rich to be more than mentioned here – can remain ignorant
as to how far through Augustan society at large the passion for
poetry spread. The major difference between this volume and its
predecessor (apart from the coherence achieved in the present
collection in terms of temperament and taste – Lonsdale's anthol-
ogy shows an attractive feeling for disadvantaged groups like
women and animals) – lies in the fact that the editor has extended
the *Oxford Book* by about one poem in four, the new work having
come from manuscripts or collections not re-published since their
first appearance. This 'resurrected' verse – the word is the editor's –
offers a fascinating insight into a great social scene of women,
labourers, army officers, and clergymen all zestfully putting pens
to paper: and in the process giving us invaluable information on the
activities and interests of the period. But this is what we get:
information. The verse Lonsdale finds for us is certainly interesting
– to read once; it increases our knowledge of the society of the time;
it aims to inform, and it does inform, and thus fulfils and exhausts
its use in so doing. But that is not quite what we mean by poetry:
which, in all periods, is re-readable by virtue of its rare capacity not
just to inform but to embody an inner dimension as of individual
inward experience, so that every new reading is a new meeting, a
rediscovery.

Both to express *and* to surpass the peculiarly limiting demands of
the culture of the time – this was an art given to very few writers.
In a well-known comment from his Life of Pope, Johnson observed
with dissatisfaction that the two greatest writers of the period
preceding his, Swift and Pope, 'had an unnatural delight in ideas
physically impure'. This is true, but even truer if we leave aside the
immediate literal application and the moral censure that goes with
it. Both Swift and Pope *were* 'unnatural' and 'impure' as writers,
because it was vital to corrupt and complicate and undermine the
inhibiting restraints of their own highly external, politicized culture
in order to 'tell truth', as good writers can tell it. (It is this that
earlier criticism used to recognize in its conventional, sometimes in
a way unhelpful, stress on the frequent satiric and parodic modes of
the time. The best Augustan writing need not be 'satiric', but it
does possess the inward obliquity which the ironical modes
suggest). No good art of the age can survive *simply* by virtue of

those qualities which Lonsdale's kindly Introduction defends in his rediscoveries, 'freshness' and 'immediacy'. All the really good work by Swift and Pope is definitely 'odd' – partly because it works through and makes ironic use of those Augustan criteria which commend the equivalents of freshness and immediacy.

There is a sense in which Mack's advocacy of Pope's warmth and sweetness of nature fails to meet all these facts: for the verse fed on the alternative truth of his character, which was undoubtedly charming and affectionate, but also devious, elusive, and cool. It is a simple fact that there is no outstanding love poetry in the true Augustan period, and that the culture did not lend itself easily to any greatly feeling mode. The problems of the Augustan love-medium are revealed nowhere more interestingly than in the poem Pope probably wrote in the year Jervas was painting his portrait, 1717, the *Elegy on an Unfortunate Lady*: which, tender and beautiful as much of it is, had such difficulty dramatizing personal feeling through the (in practice) highly unstable characters of the heroine, the villainous uncle, the lover and the poet (and *are* these last two the same?) as to earn Johnson's heavy rebuke: 'A poet may be allowed to be obscure, but inconsistency can never be right'. Like Pope's other but even more chaotic and sexily frigid poem of passion, *Eloisa to Abelard*, the *Elegy* gains something from being compared to a casual verse letter, written in 1714, that is none the less more moving in its flawless poise: *To Miss Blount, on her leaving the Town, after the Coronation*, a poem that takes its power from its refusal to write or mean love. Love as the 'fond virgin' feels it becomes a haunting, teasing, touching parallel, only, for whatever it is that Miss Blount feels in the imagined tedium of the country, and for whatever it is that the poet feels, remembering her, in the suddenly greater tedium of the town:

> Vext to be still in town, I knit my brow,
> Look sow'r, and hum a tune – as you may now.

The tenderness of this enchanting 'town and country' poem is all obliquity, all wit, all imagination.

This emotional tone in Pope is often attributed to personal characteristics explainable one way as simple coldness, or another way as homosexuality. Johnson's Life speaks of the number and lastingness of Pope's friendships, a theme Mack takes up too, and makes indeed the centre of his book: a welcome attempt to rectify

the image of a man evidently vivid in his affections, and never –
though attacked in his time for almost everything else – accused of
loving his own sex. Since he was clearly a poet not only interested
in human beings but one of the most brilliant psychologists who
has written in verse, Pope's difficulties in expressing feeling are best
discussed as in his period something other than idiosyncratic. It
may not be irrelevant to point out that the greatest prose work of
Pope's time, *Gulliver's Travels* (published two years before the 1728
Dunciad) has a quite comparable quality of emotional strangeness. It
is a book which lives by its heroic heartlessness, its austere
acceptance of a universe reduced entirely to physical fact, to a
concept of data as 'those things outside the self'. Swift suffered
from vertigo all his life; and it is perhaps surprising that no
biographer has, so far as I know, noted that this vertigo gets
extrapolated into his trick, in the *Travels*, of shocking the reader by
the conversion of moral madness into a dizziness of sheer 'sense', a
disproportion only stated as a matter of scale, status or measure-
ment. When a malefactor is executed in Brobdingnag, 'the Veins
and Arteries spouted up such a prodigious Quantity of Blood, and
so high in the Air, that the great *Jet d'Eau* at *Versailles* was not equal
for the Time it lasted': Swift approved neither of barbaric public
executions nor of the pretty fountains at Versailles, a palace whose
years of building killed large numbers of its starving labourers.
Considering the reductiveness that makes this tough game possi-
ble, Johnson (again) was in a way right when he grumbled about
the *Travels* that 'When once you have thought of big men and little
men, it is very easy to do all the rest'. But it is from this very
coldness, this hard limitation of means, that the work builds up that
power of unspoken, disallowed, as it were illegitimate feeling,
which underlies the end of the story like a planted explosive. When
the horse at last says to Gulliver, as he departs from Houyhnhnm-
land, 'Take care of thyself, gentle Yahoo', the remark is almost
enough to make a reader burst out crying – it so touches a nerve as
to seem one of the greatly feeling things in Augustan literature; but
it does so because of the coldness and emptiness all around. This is
one of the facts implied by the truth of Johnson's 'unnatural'.

I earlier mentioned Johnson's tribute to Pope's art of friendship –
an art that becomes one of Mack's central themes, the creative
emotional centre of his book. Yet Johnson perhaps is right too
when, somewhat before his praise of Pope as friend, he drops a

word concerning the social sphere in which many of the poet's friendships were pursued: 'His admiration of the great seems to have increased in the advance of life', and 'To his latter works . . . he took care to annex names dignified with titles'. Pope's friendships are not accounted for entirely without some mention of that romanticism which played a part in them, and of that strong 'worldliness' (it is hard to find a better briefer term) which played a part in the romanticism. The great Bolingbroke was one of the people whom Pope loved most, and his 'greatness' surely had its place in Pope's not-altogether-worldly, but not-altogether-un-worldly love. Mack quotes a fascinating discussion between Spence and the poet that reveals an intense reverence, not remotely homosexual in feeling, but startlingly 'spiritual' ('I really think there is something in that great man which looks as if he was placed here by mistake',): clearly, a deep romanticism even to the point of spirituality may attach itself to the most worldly of persons and concerns in an unromantic age.

I stress the worldliness, because it is surely significant, à propos of the *Essay on Man*, that its poet – who, as A. D. Nuttall remarks, 'always writes well when he thinks of small animals or insects' – was urged towards an *opus magnum* by this Great Man among great friends, Bolingbroke:

> Employ not your precious Moments, and great Talents, on little men, and little things: but choose a Subject every way worthy of you; and handle it, as you can, in a manner which nobody else can equal, or imitate.

Professor Mack shows signs of believing, in his discussion of the poem in this biography, that the *Essay on Man* was indeed that *opus magnum*; the same case is made perhaps even more strongly and warmly in his Twickenham edition Introduction to the poem, which now takes its place at the centre of Mack's gathering of reprinted essays on Pope and allied subjects, *Collected in Himself*. Yet, spacious and weighty as is Mack's praise of the *Essay on Man*, he never really comes to terms with Johnson's well-known judgement on the work – that, despite all the splendid rhetoric, there is falseness somewhere, lack of sincerity: 'Never were penury of knowledge and vulgarity of sentiment so happily disguised'. Johnson's dry critique at least supports and explains a profound feeling hard to lose: that Bolingbroke could hardly have given a writer worse advice than this, even though it probably echoes the advice given by the 'great' to the arts in all periods. Pope spent the second half of his career desperately trying to follow it. *The Rape of the Lock*, which is about 'little things', was the last (when Pope was aged twenty-six) satisfactorily finished work that the poet managed in his career. For this is surely the shape of Pope's career, an ironical design which the writer himself must have observed, but which Mack doesn't quite trace: that the poet spent the first half writing to achieve a 'greatness' which he spent the second half trying to prevent from destroying his writing.

If 'feeling', 'imaginative insight' has been dispelled from early Augustan literature, what flows in to take its place is surely that manipulation of worldly energies in society which can be called politics in the widest sense (and the study of Augustan literature invariably involves the political). Both Swift and Pope struggled intensely for success; Swift adored, with whatever ironical intonations, the brief period during which 'the Court serves me for a coffee house', and Pope (again, with whatever ironical reservations) wrote in the Preface to his 1717 volume of poems that 'the privilege of being admitted into the best company' was a chief reason for pursuing success as a writer. Such success, such friendship with the great, seems then to have accrued to itself something like our own social myth of romantic love, in defining happiness in a context as generally 'social' as was the Augustan. It is worth noting that, when Pope once threw a friendly dinner for some of his intimates, the four writers among the five distinguished men present there were all bachelors – Pope, Swift, Congreve and Gay, the exception being Bolingbroke; yet none was discernibly homosexual. Congreve's life held two deep and abiding attachments to women; both were mutual, though in neither case was a marriage feasible in worldly terms. Yet Congreve was the least ambitious, the most withdrawn from the world, of all these five.

Any reader of Pope's verse knows at sight that this is a brilliantly, studiedly worldly man (even his all-but-invariable use of the established couplet mode hints this to the reader). One of the strengths of his verse is the direct relationship it maintains with a given social world, a relationship which helps to explain its great early and continuing success. *The Rape of the Lock* could not have been written other than by a man exquisitely habituated to the world around him; verse has hardly ever expressed a finer social comedy. But it remains an interesting fact that those about whom the poem was written were not entirely pleased with it. This 'worldliest' of men maintained the tenderest of regards for his elderly parents, not to mention his friends, not all of whom were great, and his dogs – he was in fact intensely pained by the suffering of animals – and the little estate he cultivated with such pride was in the end not in London itself but out in the river 'suburbs' (the term is only just not anachronistic at this period) at Twickenham. Certainly the poet lived there a rather comfortable, well-off life, with Homer on the one side and the servant-girls on the other, and continual jaunts to the houses of his grander friends. But he also wrote the most effectively dangerous, offensive, poem ever published, about which his biographer frames the question:

> Publishing the *Dunciad* was in many ways the greatest folly of Pope's life . . . What can possibly have impelled him to do what he did?

Mack's answers, including 'Sheer arrogance . . . that "saving-remnant" syndrome . . . the usual compulsion of men who are physically very small', perhaps show the limitations of a narrowly 'psychological' or 'social' explanation. I began this discussion by mentioning Theobald's (or Tibbald's) name. It is an oddity of the *Dunciad*, alluded to in passing by Johnson but not made much of by critics after him, that the second major version of Pope's poem, published with revisions and extensions into a fourth book in 1742 (Pope was to die in 1744), drops the name of Theobald in favour of that of Colley Cibber, a genial actor in no way a scholar – yet the poem hardly alters the Theobaldian circumstances. Therefore, as Johnson points out, 'By transferring the same ridicule from one to another he destroyed its efficacy'.

From this it is fair to assume that Pope also cared less than might be imagined for any local, attacking or satirical force inherent in his poem. The alternative Mack sets up to a merely vindictive purpose is that large, even religious intent to put a whole culture on its feet, which has become the major theme of Pope critics in justifying the poet's actions. Thus:

> Are these repeated intuitions of a Ruining City and an oncoming Great Darkness by any chance true apprehensions . . . or are they simply, as in the Cave of Poverty and Poetry, the half formed maggots of overheated poetic brains?

This is a thinking close to the Augustan division of possibility into either 'fact' or 'fantasy'. One might say, rather, that Pope was struggling to overcome the division, that the poem is powered at the centre by conflicts and interdependences much more deeply personal than the idea of 'social' poetry allows. Johnson gives us the terms for this when, two or three lines before his trenchant remark about the poet's 'admiration of the great', he tells us that, none the less (and his phrase seems to me magnificent) 'Pope never set his genius to sale.'

Pope admired the great: and he never set his genius to sale. This is not an easy attitude in the Augustan period, or in any other. But it is within the span of this complex, conflicting, even anarchically principled 'worldliness' that Pope's poetry acts itself out; and it is by the difficulty of the integrity of this balance that we recognize his high powers, and define what made him inimitable to the decades of couplet-writing poetasters who followed him. Early in his Life, Mack regards compassionately the young poet's

> unexplained bouts of irritability, sweeping irresistible impulses to throw a few bricks at the stained-glass attitudes of the excluding Establishment . . . though I do not in any way wish to mitigate his responsibility for his actions.

I have to say that I find this nothing but imperceptively diminishing beside the tough 'hostile' generosity of Johnson's 'Pope never set his genius to sale.' Moreover it does less than Johnson to explain the nature and power of the poet's most impressive writing. Consider a line like that in the first paragraph of the *Dunciad*'s first book: 'Still Dunce the second reigns like Dunce the first'. Certainly we can explain this in terms of Pope's Tory antipathy to the Hanoverian King Georges, and yet the charge of the line goes well beyond politics. Indeed, to undermine politics is precisely what it does. Its words work together, so that 'Dunce', involving with 'reigns', 'second' inbreeding with 'first', indict the working of all power in a fashion not very far from Shakespeare's Timon, who rejects the power localized in all wealth, thus:

> The learned pate
> Ducks to the golden fool. All's obliquy . . .

In the eighth chapter of the third book of *Gulliver's Travels* Swift 'evacuates' human history; life as mere existence in Time is lived by the terrible Struldbrug. He is writing here in a tradition which includes the Rochester of 'Upon Nothing', Erasmus and More – the masters of both Swift and Pope – and ultimately Socrates. Pope's *Dunciad*, which is similarly something other than prophetic, works by the same radical principle of subversion. It exposes worldly rituals of status, folly 'High on a gorgeous seat'; all ambitious arts in the end reduced to a pissing competition, all impurities yawning to death at an 'uncreating word'. The poem's close has its own dark exhilaration, and a cleared air as 'The sick'ning stars fade off th'ethereal plain'.

This extremity or violence is not Pope's characteristic mode, though he can master many. He is perhaps most fully present in the more relaxed of the late poems: in for instance the dazzling, nervous, humorous, exacerbated *Epistle to Arbuthnot*. This highly 'social' poem (it has the two lethal portraits of Atticus and Sporus) is at the same time intimate, even autobiographical; its theme is simply writing, and it begins with a decisive withdrawal from society ('Shut, shut the door, good *John*!'), for the 'world' is really only a world of mad, bad poetasters. A little further into the *Epistle*, Pope tells us with grave pathos that

> The Muse but serv'd to ease some Friend, not Wife,
> To help me thro' this long Disease, my Life.

Mack's biography gives valuable insights into that limited 'Life'. But it can't do what the *Epistle* does. For the poem reveals directly that creative vitality in Pope which kept his crippled existence going for fifty-six years: longer, not only than stronger members of his own circle, like Gay, but even – it is odd to reflect – than Shakespeare himself, dead at fifty-two.

6

Keats: Somebody Reading

Perhaps as a result of the lingering Symbolist inheritance, the aesthetic notion of most potency at present is the idea that the work of art is in some sense about itself. Even in the fine arts, apparently most in love with the visible world, the great painter will be said to paint himself in every portrait. The exquisite old lady reading in a pool of light holds the stillness of Rembrandt himself as he paints, and Velasquez looks back at us through the eyes of a court dwarf. This self-involvement may all the more readily be found in literature since most poets tend to be experts on themselves. Outgoing and unegoistic as he was, Keats shows himself in his letters to be endlessly articulate on himself and his writing, and the poems, too, can be read as something like works of criticism. Many critics see 'On First Looking into Chapman's Homer' as the earliest evidence of Keats's genius, and the sonnet treats with Renaissance magnificence that peculiarly modern subject, the poet as reader of poetry. Or again, the remarkable fragment which, only two and a half years after the sonnet, marked the beginning of Keats's last and 'living year', 'The Eve of St Mark', could easily be re-titled 'Portrait of the Artist as a Young Woman Reading': so suggestively inward and original is its image of a young person wholly absorbed in a poem, one chilly spring evening in a small country town, where she sits by the window in an old house trying to catch the dying light

> With forehead 'gainst the window pane . . .
> All was silent, all was gloom,
> Abroad and in the homely room;
> Down she sat, poor cheated soul,
> And struck a lamp from the dismal coal,
> Leaned forward with bright drooping hair,

> And slant book full against the glare.
> Her shadow in uneasy guise
> Hover'd about, a giant size . . .

It's hard to be surprised that 'The Eve of St Mark' was never finished, or to be much interested in guesses as to how the story would have gone on, when the poem seems to fulfil itself in this portrayal of a young reader. There may well be an interesting gloss on the poem, which helps to confirm this sense of it, in a letter written by the poet only a few weeks later. The Keats brothers' younger sister, Fanny, lived separate from them in the house of their guardian, but was faithfully kept in touch with by John: who here writes cheerfully promising to get his sister anything she would like, barring 'livestock' – always better and more kindly left in its natural environment:

> – though I must confess even now a partiality for a handsome Globe of gold-fish – then I would have it hold 10 pails of water and be fed continually fresh through a cool pipe with another pipe to let through the floor – well ventilated they would preserve all their beautiful silver and Crimson – Then I would put it before a handsome painted window and shade it all round with myrtles and Japonicas. I should like the window to open onto the Lake of Geneva – and there I'd sit and read all day like the picture of somebody reading.

Casual as this is, it turns into a virtuoso exercise in the use of the conditional tense; and the final flick of irony is like a lightning flash. The happiness of goldfish and the happiness of young readers (whether Fanny or John, who perhaps meet in the heroine of the earlier poem) are alike a dream, a 'picture' cut off, like the existence of so many unfortunate domestic creatures, from the sources of life.

In true Symbolism the concept of a world limited to self-reflection led to Mallarmé's well-known utterance: '*Mon art est un impasse.*' That Keats, too, knew about *impasse*, however, does not make him the first of the Symbolists. The letter suggests how far from simple self-involvement any form of self-portrayal may be in the work of a major artist; self-portrayal may, in fact, be the most direct route to the dismissal of self-absorption. In an earlier letter Keats had said in passing: 'There is something else wanting to one who passes his life among Books and thoughts on Books.' That judgement, and the irony in 'the picture of somebody reading', touches and colours the beautiful image of the girl in 'The Eve of St Mark'. However tenderly delineated, the romantic young reader is also found 'dark / Upon the legend of St Mark'; her eager strained gaze leaves her 'dazed with saintly imageries' and a 'poor cheated soul'; and as she stoops abstractedly to her book she is mocked by the great shadows of herself that gesture behind her. Peacock invented the name, for philosopher-poets like Coleridge, 'Flosky' or *philoskios*, 'lover of shadows'. It is from the artist in person that we may find the greatest uninterest in art in general, and the most intent capacity to treat his own self in his work with an unilluded detachment. The really striking thing about a great painter's portraits (to return to the fine arts) is not the degree to which they look like the artist, but the degree to which they don't. All vision is limited by the imprisoning self. But the great portrait can make it seem that for an instant the impossible has happened, and the painter has got outside, into the 'real'. The old lady and her book and the light that joins them are *there*, and if she is (as she is) in some elusive sense like Rembrandt, then the strongest likeness is to that part of the painter which by its attentiveness becomes free: free, that is to say, of itself. In something like the same way, the intense existence of Velasquez's court dwarfs depends on the differing perspectives contrived by the artist – sometimes, like himself, they seem smaller than a mastiff, sometimes larger than their King and Queen; and these perspectives release them from the indignity of their normal social selves.

A Keats poem too may have liberating perspectives. The 'Ode to a Nightingale' is much liked by most people who read any poetry at all, yet it is not obvious why it is a great poem; nor is it obvious how it manages not to suffer from the intense romantic egoism its substance seems to involve. The answer, I think, is a matter of its creation of perspectives on the self like those that open up a great portrait or self-portrait. The Ode may begin with the clamorous self, the self that 'aches' and is 'emptied' and has 'sunk', but it ends somewhere surprisingly far and farther out. The clue to this movement (which is confirmed as well as threatened by the flight of the bird at the end) is the odd striking word dropped into the Ode's second line, the word 'hemlock'. It was, I believe, because the poet so needed this particular word for an opiate that he allowed himself to half-quote an earlier half-line of verse, 'like as if cold Hemlock I had drunke' (from Marlowe's version of an Ovidian comic lament for sexual impotence), only doubtfully to his purpose, but rememberable as having used this particular noun. Keats wanted it for reasons that can be discovered simply by quoting the word experimentally in public. From most reasonably literate people it will produce one of two automatic responses: either 'Keats' or 'Socrates'. Keats himself mentions Socrates in the long journal-letter written to his brother and sister-in-law in America during the spring of 1819 (when both 'The Eve of St Mark' and the letter to Fanny were also written), the letter that concludes with the first of the Odes, 'To Psyche'; and the poet refers in it to Socrates as being one of the only two cases (the other being Jesus) he happens to know of, of what he calls 'hearts completely disinterested'.

The word 'hemlock' moved into the Ode because it carried with it the whole context of the undeserved death of Socrates. And, as the letter makes plain, the death of Socrates served in its turn as a motif for a burden of feeling which was already a vivid fact in the poet's consciousness, and which was to weigh on him almost unendurably during his last embittered and angry year of life: the sense of existential injustice. It seems clear that to Keats, as his life darkened, the theme of the unjust rewards of selflessness became both a simple personal misery and a more impersonal moral outrage. In this Ode, that double sense is both an intensity and a largeness – both a 'selfness' and a 'selflessness'. As soon as the note is struck, in the opening lines, of a suffering miserably and frankly personal –

> My heart aches, and a drowsy numbness pains
> My sense, as though of hemlock I had drunk

– the poem begins to extend and purify itself by association with the not-self, the 'other', the far off and classic case of injustice endured. That movement from the self is intrinsic to Keats's nature. Its lack of natural egoism is glimpsed in the trivial fact that the manuscript of the poem shows him apparently to have begun at first with the odd bald phrase, 'Heart aches'; and similarly (if conversely) it is striking that the poem was given in the drafts the Johnsonian 'grandeur of generality' by being named 'Ode to the Nightingale', before the poet corrected this in the published version to the more characteristically modest, casual yet specific 'Ode to a

Nightingale'. Both these minor evidences from the manuscripts help to support the sense of a cheerfully self-denying character to the poem, and of a natural adherence to the sense of the real. The Ode moves at 'hemlock' from the egoism of pain to the concept of some good outside the self. It starts seeking to justify (in an almost Miltonic sense), in terms of a reality represented by the poisonous if natural plant hemlock, that equally natural truth grasped by the human imagination: its inalienable possession of some innocent, primary and bird-happy state, the thing that

> In some melodious plot
> Of beechen green and shadows numberless
> Singest of summer in full-throated ease.

The strength of the 'Ode to a Nightingale' is its power to reconcile – obliquely and naturally, as its shadows suggest sun – two primary human facts, all that is focused in 'hemlock', on the one hand, and in the bird's song, on the other. Its logic works by rejection and a kind of attrition: but a sumptuous and benign rejection and an attrition ('I cannot see what flowers are at my feet') that brings the searching imagination to its true end in sympathy. Poetic happiness finds out where it belongs, which is, oddly but naturally, with unhappiness, in company with those who are sad or deprived, who resemble the poet only in the fact that they too gave attention to the bird's song:

> The voice I hear this passing night was heard
> In ancient days by emperor and clown:
> Perhaps the self-same song that found a path
> Through the sad heart of Ruth, when, sick for home,
> She stood in tears amid the alien corn.

It is at this point that the poet achieves a going-out comparable to that of the great portraitist: the Ode moves beyond the bounds of the romantic-personal and translates self into other selves. In the distance bridged between 'hemlock' and 'emperor and clown' (and Socrates was, among other things, a kind of emperor and clown) misery becomes conscious of its human context, and writes itself a history. In the Old Testament Ruth it finds a satisfyingly human and specific symbol (she was merely obdurately kind to her mother-in-law): but her name means 'pity', and her tears, like rain, bring on a harvest, however alien. It is therefore not very surprising that Keats closes his stanza with an image easy to think of as peculiar to him, one of windows opening.

The opening in this case brings with it the 'perilous' and the 'forlorn'. The earlier invocations of the imagination in the form of a reader by an open window included a window merely painted or a reader finally mocked (because no more than a 'picture' or a 'poor cheated soul'). Here the window truly opens, and there results a loss of self that is perilous and forlorn. I suggested a note of dry reservation in Keats's letter to his sister. In a letter written in September 1819, after he had composed his last Ode, 'To Autumn' (which in effect brought his creative life to an end – in the winter that followed fatal illness declared itself), there is a comparable but more direct reservation. Keats wrote: 'Some think I have lost that poetic ardour and fire 'tis said I once had – the fact is perhaps I have.' This element of serious doubt about himself needs noting, despite the fact – or perhaps even because of it – that it seems to find little reflection in many of the more orthodox Keats studies that have appeared over the last half-century or so. The image or 'portrait' of the poet to be found there is essentially of a career more or less exemplary in its development and progression. The writer matures triumphantly but steadily from Sensation into Thought, discovering how to make a true philosopher out of a mere poet, and in some sense a 'modern' philosopher too, almost Symbolist in the austerity and extremity of his last poems: one whom fatal illness cut off as he was producing his most perfect and brilliant work, 'Lamia', 'To Autumn' and 'The Fall of Hyperion'.

But Keats's writing life and his personal history (his 'biography') are extraordinarily interdependent, and they make together a very much more complicated image than this. The packed brevity and the increasing difficulties of the poet's three-year writing span give some sense of his struggle to achieve and maintain that sense of the reader by the open window, that balance of inward with outward, of imagined and 'real', which forms the character of his best writing: exact feeling fills images from life, 'And gathering swallows twitter in the skies'. Everything about the living quality of Keats's lines suggests how fully dependent their poise is, for all their intense literariness, on the poet's own nature and the life he actually lived. And everything in Keats's history similarly suggests that, though reserved and imaginative, he was also an outgoing spirit, sociable and hungry for experience: a London-born and bred

man, interested in the world at large as well as possessed of a
conscience that reckoned human claims important. When in his last
year Keats lets fall in a letter the sentence 'Upon the whole I dislike
Mankind,' it brings a distressing sense of the sickness of mind that
had come to him. It measures, that is to say, the results of the fact
that the larger world which Keats thought he so hungered for had,
until the minor success of the 1820 volume when he was too ill to
write, brought little but opposition to his radically original genius.
During the year (1819) in which Keats was writing his Odes, only
months after the attacks on him by the Reviews, the world in
general seemed first to threaten his continuance of the literary life;
then of any professional life (he could not find suitable work); then
of his emotional life (marriage depended on earning-power); then
of life, simply, as his health failed.

It is the pressure of these circumstances, the natural need for a
world that also destroys, which gives to Keats's work during this
supreme but also distraught year its power, scope and complexity:
above all, its quality of heroic but hopeless struggle. The more he
reforms and refines his work the more his, and its, spirit fails.
Fidelity to experience, refusal to let go the hold on a reality at that
moment wholly menacing, brought the poet to accept the
frightening possibility that he had genuinely lost himself, that he
had exhausted ('perhaps I have') his creativity. It seems to me to be
this possibility that induced the fatal illness, and not illness that
simply stopped Keats writing. And there is something in the last
poems that seems to betray this defeat, and particularly in the
strange deadness of the (however beautiful) 'Lamia' and 'The Fall of
Hyperion'. Even 'To Autumn' may give pause to a reader. Most
mainline criticism tends to accept Robert Bridges' estimate of this
Ode as perhaps the poet's most perfect work. Among more recent
critics, Bernard Blackstone and Harold Bloom have stressed its
absolute superiority to the other Odes. Certainly 'To Autumn' is
flawless, one of the poems in literature that one would least want to
raise doubts about. And yet perfection is always a questionable
quantity, especially in the case of a Romantic writer. (Blake, urged
to admit the finished quality of a painting that he disliked, asked
innocently: 'How these things could be finished when they are not
even begun'). Conversely, there is something terminal in the
perfection of 'To Autumn'. At moments it seems 'good' in the way
that a child will be called 'good', when what is really meant is that

its spirit is broken. In the Ode's perfection is something of defeat. Its first stanza wholly lacks a main verb, being quietly dominated by those suggestive but failing and trailing parts of speech, the present participle and the infinitive; both the second and third stanzas begin with a question in effect rhetorical, whose ironical intonations ('Who hath not seen thee . . .?' and 'Ay, where are they?') sound a note both withdrawn and concessive; and the poem's habit throughout of over-running lines sustains a mood of odd poised weariness, something next door to surrender ('to load and bless / With fruit'; 'may find / Thee'; 'keep / Steady thy laden head'; 'borne aloft / Or sinking'). 'To Autumn' is magnificent poetry, but it is a poetry of losing ('perhaps I have') maintained with unshakable control and reticence.

Helen Vendler's more than sixty-page chapter on 'To Autumn' is the culmination of her exercise in the close-reading of Keats's Odes; and she follows modern critics in seeing the poem as itself the culmination of Keats's own writing life. Wonderfully full and dense with observation as this last chapter is, she does not notice that lack of main verb in the opening stanza of 'To Autumn', just as earlier she does not pause on the word 'hemlock' in the 'Ode to a Nightingale'. The critic's sense of these two poems dictates, in short, what she finds in them; and that sense is itself dictated by her choice of thesis. This is, with a certain congruence, the argument that the Odes are essentially self-reflective on the part of the poet, 'a form of intrinsic self-criticism'. This position, too, has its logic, since the Keats of most recent academic criticism is himself a kind of critic, self-reforming by those powers of will and rational judgement always more critical than creative, and making this struggle articulate in his superb letters. Helen Vendler defines her place in this tradition: 'The complexity of Keats's reflective and constructive acts is now generally admitted . . . we all know now, thanks to a long tradition of criticism, the outlines of Keats's concerns. But I think we have not yet fully seen Keats's views on art.' Her study is concerned with the ways in which the Odes may be said to be 'views on art'. Moreover, since 'views', unlike experience in general, are capable of improvement, of education, the shape of Keats's career during these months is described as a curve of self-improvement and of self-education. Helen Vendler's argument is that all the Odes before 'To Autumn' are a necessary programme of trial and error, a series of closed avenues by which the learning poet came at last to see his way clear to 'To Autumn'.

But this progressivist account of Keats's writing life is crossed and complicated by something quite different. Helen Vendler also sees each of the Odes as, in a sense, both self-sufficient and the focus of everything else in the poet's writing career. The movement from the first to the last of the major Odes is a movement through time which is only accretive, never destructive; the poet, unlike Louis Philippe, learns everything and forgets nothing; 'To Autumn' becomes the focus and fulfilment of everything that is Keats, and (because this is at moments a source-study) of everything that is a good many other writers as well. This last Ode, and Keats's consciousness, and also the book that Helen Vendler is writing, all together approximate to an image that at one point she turns to examine, Moneta's 'hollow brain' in 'The Fall of Hyperion' (on which she adds a chapter to those on each of the Odes): an image in which a single human memory becomes the location of all history itself. In this way Helen Vendler has managed to cross an academic thesis with a Symbolist work of art. She defines what she means by 'close-reading' as 'the illusion that one is composing' the work in question: a definition she borrows from Paul Valéry, who is, with Wallace Stevens, the tutelary deity of the book. *The Odes of John Keats* is itself certainly and thoroughly 'composed': it is thick with often beautiful clarities of perception organized into sometimes compelling coherences of theory; it all co-ordinates, it all – in a sense – works.

But only in a sense. With all its gifts of sensitivity, the book as a whole manages to add to the problems of Symbolism all the problems of an academic thesis – for a thesis this study is, in its intransigence as well as its efficiency. A thesis will all too often rival Symbolism in the stasis it imposes on the nature of its subjects. The more Helen Vendler strives for the 'ultimate embodiment' of art in her study (a phrase she uses in her first sentence), the more she reduces Keats to the 'picture of somebody reading': for her book, it might be said, gives to the poet only the self-absorption of a reader reading, and not the in fact very different self-knowledge of a writer writing, that power which infuses the image of the reader whenever we meet it in Keats with its light but serious derision. One could say that the critic's very reverence for the poet, her anxiety to rectify the indignities of history and rewrite his life as an image of consciousness triumphant, is an insistence that endows him with a security and a lifelessness he was never near possessing. Hers is a study that refuses to accept the risk and the openness of the poet's own 'perhaps I have'.

In her introduction the critic defends this procedure as a hostility to the 'haphazard' in criticism:

> It was in fact Keats's choice of subjects for the odes that originally perplexed me: why did he write on a quality (indolence), then to a goddess (Psyche), then to a nightingale, then on an urn, then on an emotion (melancholy), then to a season (autumn)? The usual critical accounts made these choices all seem relatively haphazard, depending on a nightingale in a plum tree or a visit to Haydon's studio or a walk to St Cross; but I believe an artist's choices are never haphazard, though the occasioning motive may seem so.

The word 'haphazard' here could almost be glossed 'historical'. And the passage makes a useful focus for the difficulties Helen Vendler gets into, throughout her book, in her treatment of the historical.

The Odes of John Keats chooses to make the claims of history seem out-of-date, to set itself within an area of discussion for which the sense of what used to be known as history is meaningless. This decision produces a complex of problems of very different kinds, ranging from the odd judgement to the plain error. An example of the first is the treatment of other critics. In the first few pages of her book Helen Vendler introduces a substantial list of what she calls the 'classic studies in Keats' up to the present day: this manages to leave out what is in my view the best, and certainly the most fructifying, single essay on Keats during this century, John Bayley's *Keats and Reality* – a study acknowledged as seminal by two critics (Christopher Ricks and John Jones) whose admirable books declare themselves indebted to it, and whom Helen Vendler does include in her list. Presumably her hostility to *Keats and Reality* (she disagrees with its author twice and sharply) springs from John Bayley's attempt to call into being the 'real', the externally perceived and historical poet, and to do so in the course of a deliberately unmethodical and unsystematic personal critique.

But this is only a minor problem in what is in fact a much larger intellectual context. Helen Vendler's antipathy to the 'haphazard' is in itself both sympathetic and 'impossible' (Keats once remarked, in what is perhaps his most important utterance during this last year of writing: 'I would mention that there are impossibilities in the world'). Being against the haphazard is justified to the degree that, in that criticism is a system or a science, it must be opposed to the random; the intellect's job is to find answers, and it has to begin by discovering for itself those areas in which answers are to be found. But insofar as criticism has little point unless devoted to an art contingent on life itself (because on language), then the random or haphazard is not a fault in method but a law of the very subject. The critic's stress here on the poet's 'choice of subject' can't help but raise an echo of Johnson's derisive 'choice of life' in *Rasselas*: it translates, that is to say, a definitively deprived young writer into one of that tale's protected royal innocents (it seems symptomatic that the critic later insists on the 'ascetic' nature of the language of 'To Autumn' without pausing to distinguish between 'ascetic' and 'half-starved', which is what, in both an actual and a metaphorical sense, the poet was who wrote it). It is also an interesting fact that, though better-fed, the poet Paul Valéry never chose a subject in his life, he just let them, so he said, turn up. Helen Vendler's definition of the poet is of a 'chooser', and it leaves far too little room for the factor in human life of the unchosen, the choiceless and the unalterably 'haphazard' which is one of the faces of the natural. If the 'Ode to a Nightingale' is much better and more interesting than the critic makes it sound (in the Ode Keats 'continues his inquiries into the nature of art'), this is because it has more power than its critic, first to recognize the paradoxical necessity in life of the haphazard, and then to transform that haphazard into necessity. It is the fidelity of this process that keeps the poem, to use Keats's only half-mocking image in his letter, 'fresh' and 'well-ventilated', that preserves for ever all its beautiful 'silver and Crimson'. Helen Vendler's Keats is by comparison airless, and perhaps also just a little beautified.

The kind of difficulty that the abjuring of history gets the critic into can be illustrated from one quotation, the opening sentence to her chapter on the 'Ode on a Grecian Urn':

> We must presume, since Keats went on after writing the 'Ode to a Nightingale' to write the 'Ode on a Grecian Urn' (as near a twin to the earlier ode as one poem can be to another) that his

experiments in analysing, distinguishing and objectifying his thoughts and feelings about creation, expression, audience, sensation, thought, beauty, truth and the fine arts were still in some way unsatisfactory to him . . .

This is really not unlike the proposition that most people have a second child because they can't stand the first: an objection to which not merely the logic of the passage makes it vulnerable, but its language. Helen Vendler seizes on 'twin' because it momentarily gives emphasis to her argument that one of these odes is very 'like' another: but an obstinate, ineradicable physicality and historicity in the word and what it means make the whole idea unworkable. What can perhaps be done in *Four Quartets* (or even, when one comes to think of it, in a twin-laden *Comedy of Errors*) to prove that a thing both is and is not timeless can scarcely be done in an academic thesis. But this difficulty is intrinsic to Helen Vendler's whole intellectual position in this study. Every time we reread a literary work, we do so 'as if' we had forgotten its true ending; and we are able to do so because human beings are, unfortunately, creatures that forget, just as literary works change and are lost with time. We can never be absolutely certain that *Othello* might not end happily this time. Helen Vendler is involved in a process rather different. She operates with the benefits of the 'illusion of composing', while simultaneously assuming the detached, superior and retrospective advantages of critical judgement, from which position 'To Autumn' may be used as a vantage-point to measure the failure of the other Odes to be itself. To try to cross the methods of the scholar and the critic, the critic and the creative writer, in this way, is to enlarge the scope of the study and perhaps to refine the nature of the thesis: yet the book fails, quite extensively, to convince, and it leaves behind an intermittent, almost pervasive sense of wrongness.

That sense of wrongness occasionally becomes both solid and local. The book contains slips or mistaken conjectures which are, considering the fineness and penetration of much of the writing, surprisingly frequent and surprisingly simple. What makes it worth mentioning any of them is the degree to which their occurrence is involved with the rebuttal of the historical, of the 'haphazard'. Sometimes these are small matters: in discussing the rejected first stanza of the 'Ode on Melancholy', Helen Vendler is caught out by the differences of Regency English, or perhaps merely of English English, taking 'Though you should . . .' to mean 'You must . . .' instead of 'Even if you did'. In 'To Autumn', Keats's English climate seems to offer as much difficulty as his subjunctives in the earlier Ode. In analysing the first verse of 'To Autumn', the critic pauses over the 'incidental oddity' and the 'puzzling anomaly' of the fact that, as she sees it, Keats has there reversed the normal pattern of the seasons, so as to follow the autumn harvest by a further spring-like blossoming of flowers ('to set budding more, / And still more later flowers') – his reason being (she argues) that to retain the natural sequence of the year would be to allow its fruits to die back into the earth, promising a further spring. And 'We are emphatically not permitted to see any further season . . . One cannot deduce more than the poem allows.' This may or may not be so. But the argument loses its strength if the critic happens not to perceive that Keats is here 'first following Nature', and tracing the natural course of an English autumn: for in England September is the golden month of late flowers. In literary terms, this is the country of Betjeman's *A Few Late Chrysanthemums*, or Barbara Pym's *A Few Green Leaves*.

The haphazard, that is to say, is a part of the literary. Something in Helen Vendler's image of the poem collapses with the removal of her conjecture about the poet's conscious change: Keats becomes again what in a sense he always was, the poet of a changing climate and of transitional phases, subject like many of his countrymen to affliction by melancholy and hope. Two of the most magnificent lines he ever wrote, from his second early sonnet on Homer, derive from just such a sense of changing weather, a sun-and-shadowed climate:

> Ay, on the shores of darkness there is light,
> And precipices show untrodden green.

In the same way, the image of 'To Autumn' shifts with another detail of disagreement. Helen Vendler lists a number of female goddesses as sources for the figure of Autumn. If Autumn is female, and if she requires a source, I suspect that source is more likely to be a figure hardly a goddess at all, but one involved with Keats's own 'haphazard' history of reading and writing – which is to say the Psyche of Apuleius's *Golden Ass* (whom it is surprising to find omitted here): a profoundly human and fallible young girl who spends much of her story stumbling tired, pregnant and patient across the countryside in search of her god-husband, and who is helped to find him by the kind creatures and powers of nature. This stress on the merely natural and enduring perhaps helps to explain Keats's alteration of one word in the last line of his poem:

> The red-breast whistles from a garden-croft;
> And gathering swallows twitter in the skies

so that the birds were not 'gathered' but 'gathering'. The present participle becomes the most exquisitely disturbing word in the whole serene poem, because of all that it communicates of incipience in time, of the survival of selves beyond the present self, even of open windows looking over perilous seas of hope. One might go still further and speak of a 'gathering' quality in the Ode as a whole, reflected in the new rhythm Keats found for its stanzas. Helen Vendler's is a study perhaps not much interested in poetic rhythm and metre, in themselves the forms through which poetry most lives in time. She does not at any rate mention, for instance, the (to me) extraordinary effect of the change made by 'To Autumn' to the ode-stanza as Keats had established it up to this point: the addition of an extra line after his ninth in each verse and rhyming with it as in a couplet. As a result, in each of the three stanzas, the poem seems to be slowing to a standstill, to be stopping (on the words 'cease', 'look' and 'croft'); then quietly to find the strength to outgo that ending, to overspill into the retrospectively rhyming 11th line, that brings the stanza home: 'For summer has o'erbrimmed . . .', 'hours by hours', 'And gathering . . .'

Precisely because it does so 'move in time', embraces history in its process, the structure of a Romantic poem is in no way easy to define. It is on the question of structure that Helen Vendler places her greatest emphasis, perhaps seeing her proposals as the most innovative part of her thesis:

> If there is any single part of this book that I feel confident about, it is the discussion of the structure of the odes and of the appropriateness to the matter of each ode and to its view of art. These discussions lead to the end point of the book: Keats's powerful discovery, in the ode 'To Autumn', of a form of structural polyphony, in which several structural forms – each one autonomous, each one pregnant with meaning, each one

continued for the full length of the ode – overlap in a palimpsest of effects.

In a way, the two most interesting words here are 'polyphony' and 'palimpsest': for their flattening effect as images demonstrates how difficult the critic's task was in producing what might be called her symbolic unification – and of course how difficult in its turn Keats's own task was. This quality of flattening, of static simplification into the one-dimensional, also attaches to the solution Helen Vendler produces. She proposes that the Odes may be distinguished one from another by an identification of their structure in terms of what she calls 'figure'. Thus Keats is evoked as meditating 'To Autumn': 'Will he choose reduplication, as in "Psyche", or reiteration, as in "Nightingale"?' These terms might be called 'consciousness figures', since they really represent our consciousness of different forms of reduplication in 'To Psyche', our consciousness of different forms of reiteration in 'Ode to a Nightingale', and so on; and the problem is, as with all readings, that consciousnesses may differ. Conversely, where the terms do work, they have the effect of narrowing the work of art within the sphere of a common agreement. In general, the systematic clarity or quasi-scientific impersonality of these terms may entail tendentiousness: they suggest excess where there may be bounty, or perfection where there may be thinness. Thus the critic condemns a quality of discreteness in both the 'Ode to a Nightingale' and in the 'Ode on a Grecian Urn', and argues from it a superiority in the more evident because more 'figural' integrity of 'To Autumn'. Having called the 'Ode to a Nightingale' 'reiterative' after some of its tropes, Helen Vendler goes on to find it therefore lacking in necessity: 'This ode could go on for ever . . . Structure is sacrificed here . . . the poem risks becoming obvious'; 'the ode shows signs of improvisation, notably in its passage from a sunlit day to a midnight scene (with no apparent allowance for the passage of time).' Of the 'interrogatory' 'Ode on a Grecian Urn', similarly: 'We are shocked . . . by the language of the close of the ode . . . The language of the close of Urn cannot be entirely assimilated to the language used earlier in the ode, and this is a flaw.'

In fact, all these remarks seem to me untrue, all the criticisms based on false premises. The language of the 'earlier' part of the 'Ode on a Grecian Urn' seems to me wholly lacking in the quality of the 'entirely idyllic' which the critic attributes to it – a phrase like the extraordinary description of a bride's state as 'still *unravished*', heralding as it does the plain suggestion of mass rape in the first stanza, needs far more sensitive analysis than it is usually given by critics. But the point at issue is the more general one. Helen Vendler's terms give her the opportunity to make some striking and fascinating distinctions between the poems. But by and large they are guilty of the great vice of the Academy – that of applying systematic method in contempt of the true nature of the subject. Where integrity is identified with 'assimilation', life must be condemned as 'improvisation'. These abstracts, moreover, by their de-naturing property, assist images like 'palimpsest' in edging the Odes towards a purely visual medium, and away from that auditory factor in them which is at least as important. The Odes demand to be listened to quite as much as to be read; the poet who wrote them was to say regretfully only a few months later that had he had any ambitions surviving, these would have taken him in the direction of composing 'a few fine plays'.

We get nearer, I think, to this auditory, even dramatic quality in the Odes by remembering a suggestion made in turn by both Garrod and Ridley: that Keats made the stanza, used in all the Odes after the 'Ode to Psyche', by breaking down the sonnet as he inherited it, primarily from Shakespeare. This idea seems to me to be strongly supported by a sense, open to any reader, that Keats got himself into decided difficulties with the first of the Odes, the 'Ode to Psyche', and that he realized from these difficulties that he was in need of some lyric form more public, more resonant, and perhaps more dramatic to balance the inward and personal side of his new kind of poem. This matter becomes blurred in Helen Vendler, partly because she follows Blackstone in placing the 'Ode on Indolence' first. We don't in fact know the precise dating of any of the Odes except the last, 'To Autumn', although some internal and external evidence supports the generally accepted sequence to be found in both Keats's major recent editors, Allott and Stillinger: which places 'Indolence' after 'Psyche', 'Nightingale', 'Urn' and 'Melancholy'. The 'Ode on Indolence' itself speaks of its season as 'May', and we know from the letter to the poet's brother and sister-in-law that the 'Ode to Psyche' was already written in April. Helen Vendler sets this fact aside on the ground that 'though it was written down as late as May, the experience which gave rise to it is related in March,' and 'the core of the ode remains his lassitude in March.' The March experience is in certain of its details different from the poem; and Helen Vendler's argument, moreover, makes a distinction that is surely disturbing between 'written' and 'written down', between the words of a poem and its 'core' or 'experience'. The real problem is, however, that she seems in some curious way to be disagreeing with the poem itself, which makes a *Hamlet*-like delay and procrastination a part of its very substance. Again, the weakness of the Ode, coming between the power of the 'Ode on Melancholy' and the fineness of 'To Autumn', perhaps suggests rather a mind tiring more than just beginning; and a part of that weakness is the thinness of a subject limited to the self. The 'Ode on Indolence' is an example of what really did happen to Keats when he was confined to a stifling self-consciousness.

It is the 'Ode to Psyche', clearly, which is a starting-point; and its intensely personal substance taught Keats his need for a more external model, for a form that would help him more to a public voice than the sensitive Pindarics of Collins were doing. The clue to this is the end, which promises

> And there shall be for thee all soft delight
> That shadowy thought can win,
> A bright torch, and a casement ope at night,
> To let the warm Love in!

Startlingly, if understandably, Helen Vendler identifies the poet with Cupid and the 'Love' with Psyche: but it is Psyche who, here as in her legend as Apuleius tells it, waits in the dark room for her invisible god-lover, Cupid or Love, to enter. The end of the Ode is wonderfully inward and sensitive, but as a result the poet has helplessly invoked a state of reverie in which the self before the window of reality is all too like a woman awaiting sexual fulfilment: an innocent embarrassment of the kind that Keats often made himself vulnerable to. Hence the recourse to the more safely magisterial tone and stance of the sonnets, which we hear in the later Odes. In Shelley's 'Epipsychidion' an island is described as 'beautiful as a wreck of Paradise': one might adapt this fine phrase and say that Keats's large, grave and extraordinarily influential ode-stanza, which can be heard through a century and more of English poetry from Arnold through Yeats to Larkin, is in itself 'beautiful as a wreck of the sonnet'. Listened to, Keats's stanza re-echoes with the cadences of Shakespeare's sonnet, that survives through the first six lines, troublingly starts to founder, yet discovers in its disintegration a new brief balance and power. In a late poem directed to Fanny Brawne, Keats used the strange and striking phrase 'live a wreckèd life' (altered by editors to 'wretched', perhaps unnecessarily); it may be that the 'wreck' of the sonnet seemed to the poet the right form for the wreckèd life.

So much for the source of the single stanza; to explain the form taken as a whole by the Keatsian ode some extension is demanded. My own view is that the sound of the sonnet-sequence held Keats's imagination. For the music of the Odes is not just a matter of each stanza, repeated: it is rather that each of these Odes gives out, when listened to as a public rhetoric, the special auditory effect of a sequence of sonnets. Arresting as Helen Vendler's account of the form of each is, it postulates unity as the final ideal; and it does not confront the fact that even the most integrated, 'To Autumn', holds discreteness within itself as a vital necessary pulse or rhythm In this as in every Ode after the 'Ode to Psyche', there is a silence, a breaking or a turning-aside between every stanza, as between every sonnet in Shakespeare's sequence. This is completed and intensified by the different and self-contained substance, and even style, of each stanza, a difference and self-containment as great as it can be without destroying the harmony of the whole. Some essential part of the character and of the beauty of these Odes – especially of the 'Ode on Melancholy', the 'Ode to a Nightingale' and the 'Ode on a Grecian Urn' – derives from this harmony of differences. This is true of 'To Autumn' too, whose quiet and contained quality only intensifies the sense of new beginning with each of its three stanzas. 'Who hath not seen thee oft?' and 'Where are the songs of spring?' –both questions, abrupt and innovative, tacitly surprise; and the two inter-stanzaic pauses are like crevasses, vital landmarks in the poem's spiritual geography.

It is interesting that this structure of linked pauses, this holding-together of great autonomous units of creativity (which commemorate, perhaps, the principle of the haphazard in a life lived), occurs formally in the Odes alone; in 'The Eve of St Agnes', for instance, the story proceeds evenly and cohesively from stanza to stanza. If the Odes have a 'story' to hold us, it must be in their re-creation of the movement of the living mind, remaking itself at every pace forward, so that every new stanza is also a self-losing.

We hear something of that loss at the end of the 'Ode on Melancholy', perhaps the poet's most superb and unnerving ending:

> His soul shall taste the sadness of her might,
> And be among her cloudy trophies hung.

Helen Vendler tries to join this last stanza to that preceding it by taking its sudden and inward opening ('She dwells with Beauty') as referring to 'thy mistress': but it must surely refer to Melancholy herself. The misunderstanding underlines the risks of the Odes, and thereby adds something to the vertigo of the poem's ending: which records the sense of enormous difficulty overcome, yet perhaps ('perhaps I have') overcome in vain. For it fuses sudden dissolution of the self (in 'cloudy') with exhilarated ascendance (in 'trophies'), the two marrying in the uncertainty of 'hung' (as a criminal? Or merely as a picture – 'of somebody reading'?). The lines, which echo one of Shakespeare's sonnets, echo something else in Shakespeare less easy to be lucid about. The real life of Shakespeare's sonnets lies within the silences between each, where the mind may be felt as recouping itself and reforming its fictional inventions – it waits, as it were, in the wings of reality. By imitating this movement, Keats acquires as well a profound potentiality: we feel that every stanza is a journey into art from the shadows of the historical, and back into the silence of the life lived. Lived or died: there is a full Keatsian irony in that 'cloudy trophies hung.'

7

Browning Versions

James Thurber's best-known cartoon has an impassive little man introducing his spouse to a dazed friend with 'that's My First Wife Up There, and This Is the *Present* Mrs Harris'. The first Mrs Harris seems to be crouched on all fours on the top of a very high (glazed) bookcase, just behind the second Mrs Harris. This image has found an appreciative audience even among those not particularly interested in American humour of the 1930s. In part this large appeal probably derives from a real social sophistication concealed in the innocence of the drawing. The linguistically prim social formula of the caption underwrites the wild surprise both of the occasion in itself and of its medium, Thurber's own very peculiar and vestigial draughtsmanship; together they cover the way in which our formulaic social manners have to contend with the extreme *ad hoc*-ness of experience – a first wife on a bookcase, crouched to spring, or embalmed, or perhaps just teasing.

But one would go further and say that this social joke in fact works in linguistic terms: that the whole cartoon is a sober pun on 'Up There' and on 'Present', and indeed on the entire verbal gesture of introduction. We expect an introduction not to introduce *so much* – not to take us in so far; from 'Up There' we look for a portrait, and we scarcely want any art-work to be as much 'present' with us as is the first Mrs Harris, up on that bookcase. In fact this linguistic quality seems to me to extend as far as the literary (Mrs Harris was the potently invisible friend of Dickens's Mrs Gamp, and Thurber was a writer before he was a cartoonist); more, that the 'extra' dimension in this cartoon came about because its essential idea had first been established by another and earlier writer. Somewhere at the back of his mind Thurber was surely remembering, with profit and perhaps with gratitude, a poem by an inventive, a hugely fructifying writer widely read sixty or eighty years ago when

Thurber was young, although out of fashion for at least the last half-century. Browning's 'My Last Duchess' begins, with a fine surprising immediacy:

> That's my last Duchess painted on the wall,
> Looking as if she were alive. I call
> That piece a wonder, now . . .

– the sixteenth-century Duke of Ferrara speaking with a flamboyant strength that Thurber's capitals echo at a distance; and the Duke, too, ends by introducing a second wife in circumstances felt as not altogether usual:

> his fair daughter's self, as I avowed
> At starting, is my object. Nay, we'll go
> Together down, sir. Notice Neptune, though,
> Taming a sea-horse, thought a rarity,
> Which Claus of Innsbruck cast in bronze for me!

Browning's 'My Last Duchess' is an oddly tricky poem: very striking in its own right, it yet hardly proclaims the fact that it *is* a good poem, and even less suggests the reasons why it should be so. And yet it has a potency that makes one understand how it could generate out of itself so successful an image as the cartoon has been, in a different medium, and for an age and a continent so different from its own. In this, the poem is characteristic of Browning's work as a whole, and of the problems it seems to present to criticism. Such essays as have lately been written about 'My Last Duchess' – for something like a critical revival is happening in Browning studies, one marked and accompanied by the accession of new editions – do little more than try to base an ethical conclusion on what they take to be the psychology of what they take to be the Duke's 'character'; and though such probings are often acute and sensible, they hardly advance understanding of the poem beyond the critical consensus of Browning's lifetime, that the poet was of course not a poet at all but a prose-writer, indeed a novelist. This antique tradition (the term is precise, since the poet died nearly a century ago in 1889) has probably continued silently ever since in the conventional handing-over of the poet, all through the period of his unfashion, to the innocent and the unwilling, to the school-child and the under-graduate, presumably on the supposition that Browning is securely far from all such troublesome complications as anything in the nature of the aesthetic would entail. The Thurber cartoon at least does better than that – which is why, I think, his 'quotation' from the poet is worth remembering: it mediates aesthetically what it has clearly seen aesthetically. Speaking less clumsily, one might say that in the cartoon itself a magnifying glass will not make really clear whether the Mrs Harris on the bookcase is animate or inanimate, is glaring or just glass-eyed. These things are not important; the drawing has to be let speak for itself. To 'read' it at all is to recognize how much is entailed by *style*, both the farcical personal style of the drawing and that severe social intonation that the caption implies: the two in special combination constitute Thurber's own style. Browning's poem is richer in details of sense-experience than most cartoons will be, but all the same it offers no more than meets the eye.

What the eye sees is a (relatively) short poem that all the same bears one or two delusive attributes of drama. It is headed by a quasi-speech-heading, 'Ferrara', and it is consistently couched in that essence of Browning's stylistic character, the sound of a voice talking in an intensely recognizable human situation. To this degree the poet is, despite all his older reputation for obscurity, a very simple poet – the kind of human being who enters a room talking. In Browning a temperamental downrightness and impetuosity meet and fuse with the common Victorian preference that literature should be public and popular: with the result that his first lines tend to put us into the presence of all that is there to be communicated. In this case the opening line is appropriately a form of social introduction. To say all this, however, is not to predict a drama: the very strength and self-consistency of that voice which begins talking brings with it the inheritance of Romantic poetry, which is a subjective mode – and nothing that follows in the poem is in itself free-standing and extraverted enough to break down that in fact private and poetic communication. For a speech-heading is not a stage-direction, nor is a voice a character. Earlier periods can sometimes startle us by their possession of what we think of as 'modern' attributes, just as the present is often archaic and retrospective; Browning is (we can say if we want, though the comparison may not be fruitful) making a new metaphor out of fragments of old forms and genres, as Eliot and others were to do eighty years later.

The only literal way to take a metaphor is not to make the

mistake of believing it to be literal. The Duke's situation is confined to that brilliant imagined voice: he will never really come down the portrait-adorned staircase into the actuality we stand on. Browning was later to say of *Sordello* that 'The historical decoration was purposely of no more importance than a background requires': background and foreground are metaphors too – what the reader of 'My Last Duchess' sees and hears is a voice, which is less sixteenth-century Italian (Browning's pervasive easy humour emerges here in the relative insignificance of the trappings) than nineteenth-century Victorian, indeed the voice of the poet's or the reader's contemporary moment. Poetry itself is to Browning 'How it strikes a Contemporary'. The voice's inflections are, if we like, upper-class or at least authoritarian English of reader or writer's own period, with a powerful assurance written in every phrase, but most in that still encountered idiom by which proprietorship is signalled by the addition of 'my' to properties sometimes unexpected: my plumber, my milkman, my archivist, my last Duchess. Person at once converts into owned object ('his fair daughter's self, as I avowed/At starting, is my object'). This proprietorship, whether of wife or of painting, is so marked that we may for a moment think that the Duke himself is an artist: as the wife is no more than a painting, 'looking as if she were alive', so is the Duke for an instant something very like a highly successful and established Victorian artist, Ferrara, RA, receiving in his studio, the 'introduction' of his wife commuting to the Private View. But his Italian Renaissance prototype would of course in practice scarcely have been a professional painter in this way. Therefore someone must be introduced to do the actual work, hence the existence of Frà Pandolph:

> . . . I call
> That piece a wonder, now: Frà Pandolph's hands
> Worked busily a day, and there she stands.
> Will't please you sit and look at her? I said
> Frà Pandolph by design . . .

It is in the interest of both the poet and the Duke himself to keep the Friar's part in things as small as possible, so that his work on the portrait is diminished to that contemptuous 'busily *a day*'. Reading the poem naturalistically, editors and critics have found 'problems' in it, of which this is one: how did the Friar manage it in a day?

Another is what discoverable 'design' the Duke can have had in so naming him, for the poem itself does not appear to disclose it. But, just as the 'day' is really the measure of the Duke's dismissal of the true artist, so is the 'design' really the difference between the creative idea of the quiet, almost invisible Friar painting in the background, and the Duke's insistent will to turn attention solely on himself ('none puts by/The curtain I have drawn for you, but I'). Thus, in the manner of any work of literary art, words like 'day' and 'design' do trace back into truth, but not into an imported psychology: to suppose that is to ignore the working of an aesthetic medium, just as the Duke treats with contempt his aesthetic workmen. We cannot, in short, know much about the dramatic plot, the precise fate of the last Duchess or the putative future of the next one (and Browning is very unlikely to have known it either). What we can say is that from the moment that the Duke fuses together woman and portrait into that fatal image of ownership, 'My Last Duchess', – 'There she stands/As if alive' – the poem finds a language vividly metaphorical to the point of drama, in which to speak of both love and art in terms of the power they both yield. From first to last, the Master (both Maestro and tyrant) is the Duke himself: 'That's my . . . for me'. But while we read, we cannot usefully distinguish between Browning's voice and the Duke's – between the authority of the writer and the tyranny of the despot. Because this is true, all critical accounts that attempt to settle finally the moral status of the Duke are in themselves pointless: he is made of an ambiguity. Even while we follow the quasi-history of the Duke's destruction of his wife, we acknowledge that his servants are Frà Pandolph, preserver of the natural life of art, and Claus, the bringer of a bronze-like immortality. And more, that such servants have it in themselves to perpetuate, even against the will of the Duke – indeed through that same incisive intense voice of authority that is his – and even through deathly forms, all the natural life that is in the fluid evanescent actualities of the Duchess's existence, 'the faint/Half-flush that dies along her throat',

> The dropping of the daylight in the West,
> The bough of cherries some officious fool
> Broke in the orchard for her . . .

Any genuinely literary work achieves conviction because of some harmony between ends and means, between meaning and medium. From this point of view there is no real discrepancy in referring to Browning's poem, with all its vivid realism, as something like a striking 'Legend of Art'. In effect, the Duke is simply a bad artist – the bad Artist, one might say: in the game for what it satisfies of his instinct for power. To this degree, the judicial presence of silent figures like Frà Pandolph and Claus of Innsbruck prompts the conclusion that Ferrara is less 'maker' than mere sterile dilettante, officious critic and connoisseur ('here you miss/Or there exceed the mark'). As such, the character clearly influenced a second writer, earlier than Thurber and – it has to be said – much more distinguished: for the Duke of Ferrara surely fathered Gilbert Osmond, Henry James's lethal dilettante in *The Portrait of a Lady*: a man who at first represents 'the artistic life' to the naive heroine, but whose antiquarian talent proves in fact confined, in a penetrating image, to tracing the common coinage of the world around him, just as Ferrara ends triumphantly with 'cast in bronze for me!' These interconnections are perhaps mere random accidents of literary history. Yet they also suggest something of the curious power of this relatively short poem by Browning: its power, and its nature. Realistic as the Duke's story seems, the suggestiveness of Browning's image can be measured by comparing it with an actual novel-character – with that, for instance, which seems to have provided the other side of Osmond's ancestry, the character of Grandcourt in *Daniel Deronda*. Grandcourt is a brilliant social creation, with interesting psychological depths, but without that resonance that makes the Duke almost a simplified 'mask' – a royal mask speaking of the ambiguities of the Palace of Art. 'My Last Duchess' is, one might say, a striking art-work written in opposition to Art.

'Art' is to a large extent the invention of the nineteenth century; and it may be said to explain why the Victorian period produced no really great poets, only two figures as considerable, in their different ways, as Browning and Tennyson are. The enormous expansion of the ordinary culture of the age could be assimilated with some directness into the developing form of the novel: but it left poetry with peculiar problems. Tennyson met them by creating a post-Romantic verbal 'magic' so intense as to equal what it usually could not include, the sense of the real; thus, Mill described his gift in 1835, some ten years before 'My Last Duchess' was published, as a 'power of *creating* scenery, in keeping with some

state of human feeling; so fitted to it as to be the embodied
symbol of it; and to summon up the state of feeling itself, with a
force not to be surpassed by anything but reality.' This imposition
of inward feeling on the external explains the extraordinary
'beautifulness' of Tennyson's writing, his spell-binding aestheti-
cizing of all subjects, even the death of his own son at sea
recorded in a painfully beautiful dream-like image. Tennyson's
verse is only the most masterly and most distinguished of all
Victorian poetic forms 'for working on the world' – the phrase
being Bishop Blougram's definition of religious faith, 'the most
potent of all forms/For working on the world.' Or one might
apply to late nineteenth-century Romantic poetry an innocently
dangerous sentence let fall by another of Browning's characters,
Mr Sludge: 'Really I want to light up my own mind.' The
equivocal qualms with which we listen to Blougram and Sludge
suggest something of Browning's odd and striking position as a
writer. Post-Romantic art created for itself a 'Palace of Art' as
refuge from the philistinism of an emerging industrialism. But
certain natural impulses and principles in Browning made that
'Palace' quite as antipathetic as its alternative – perhaps rather
more so. Everything he writes shows how strong was his
inheritance, of radical and independent Puritanism from his
Scottish–German Calvinistical mother, and of radical and inde-
pendent liberalism from his power-hating father, who had for-
feited his own paternal inheritance rather than continue to work
for slave-owners. To the enormously talented, well-read if self-
educated Browning, poetry and the love of the arts in general
seem to have come as both the possession of power and the hatred
of power: as an art that opposed Art.

   This is, I think, the reason why his 'Art'-loving but destructive
Duke of Ferrara brings to Browning's verse the sudden sense of the
poet's having for the first time found himself as a writer, as an
artist. The cause is not merely the form with which he had
experimented, that of the dramatic monologue, but the theme to
which that form's dubieties were so well suited: the ambiguous
nature of art and the artist. Browning was an undisciplined poet,
who seems never (amiable as the characteristic is) to have taken
himself seriously enough to know what it was he could best do. He
went on for years grinding out his talentless plays, and brought out
the *Dramatic Romances and Lyrics*, in 1845 when he was already

thirty-three, only at the urging of his publisher; and it was ten more years – 1845 – before his best collection, *Men and Women*, followed. But all the most striking poems in these volumes involve 'dramatic characters' like the Duke; and all are 'Portraits of the Artist' like 'My Last Duchess'. They are not precisely indictments, not even satires, but dark studies, at once complicated and comic or tragicomic, of the Artist's negative shadow: of 'Artistry' in a writer as a vice, a lie or delusion. Closest to 'My Last Duchess' in *Dramatic Romances* is 'The Bishop Orders His Tomb at Saint Praxed's Church', where the corruption of the creative holiness into a near-murderous connoisseurship flares out in images whose violent precision has made them famous:

> Some lump, ah God, of *lapis lazuli*,
> Blue as a Jew's head cut off at the nape,
> Blue as a vein o'er the Madonna's breast . . .

In *Men and Women*, the Duke's nearest match, or rather converse-image, is Andrea del Sarto 'Called "The Faultless Painter"'): a gentle, sympathetic and helplessly weak man, whose 'Artistry' is in fact the aching reflex of an acute if delicate worldliness, focused on the white image of his commonplace treacherous wife. 'Fra Lippo Lippi' ('poor brother Lippo') has this same self-betrayal mark with its dishonesties a stronger more genial man, both relishing and distracted by the echoes of street-songs that mockingly interrupt his half-factitious self-revelations ('I'm a beast, I know'). In 'Bishop Blougram's Apology' as in 'Mr Sludge, "The Medium" ' (from the next volume, *Dramatis Personae*, published nearly ten years later in 1864) as also in what is in some ways the most brilliant of all these monologues, 'Caliban Upon Setebos', Browning retains the theme while adventurously leaving behind the literal persona of the artist. Sludge and Blougram together are only metaphorically 'artists' in their amazing hold on us, professionals whose devotion to their 'calling' empties the air around them of all vestige of living truth: while they talk, existence becomes pure fiction, mere aesthetic soliloquy. And Caliban dreams most vividly of all of them, inventing his God in a reverie:

> Setebos, Setebos, and Setebos!
> 'Thinketh, He dwelleth in the cold o' the moon . . .

To Browning's Caliban, an innocent and monstrously articulate animal, God is an Artist who makes and breaks by his dazzling and terrible will alone, 'Loving not, hating not, just choosing so'.

To describe the poet's strongest creations as dark images of the Artist is perhaps to give them some essentially modern colouring of paradox – to make them sound like that critical version of Eliot's *Quartets* which stresses their self-critique, their self-parody. Certainly there are sides of Browning's work that make it possible to understand how he so bewildered his contemporaries, who by and large refused to read him for the first thirty-five years of his career, and after this long period of failure acclaimed him rather as a source of wisdom than as any kind of poet. That aspect of the poet which so startled or bored his own period one can perhaps describe as 'modern'. And certainly his brilliant and incessant experiments with style, reflecting at once both his indiscipline and his generosity, make him many times over a technical progenitor in the simplest sense: inventing styles and tones and manners, colloquial cadences and throwaway jokes, he seems sometimes to be discovering much of the technique of modern verse. This creative influence can 'work' even when his own poems don't: the heavy-handedly sprightly religious meditations in *Christmas-Eve and Easter-Day*, written probably under persuasion from his wife, managed to teach W. H. Auden the sparkling metric of his *New Year Letter* (sometimes wrongly described as 'Augustan octosyllabics'); and the over-long, over-dense, rather boring 'Fifine at the Fair', one of the late narrative poems, in some extraordinary way strikes notes that make it sound as if Browning has invented the whole of modern American verse style. From this point of view, the recent beginnings of rediscovery of Browning as a poet by (particularly) American critics seems hardly surprising; nor does the remarkably high status conferred on him by (for instance) Harold Bloom:

> Browning, in this editor's judgement, is the most considerable poet in English since the major Romantics, surpassing his great contemporary rival Tennyson, and the principal twentieth-century poets, including even Yeats, Hardy and Wallace Stevens, let alone the various fashionable Modernists whose reputations are now rightly in rapid decline . . .

Such an estimate may do justice to the scale of Browning's

work. Whether it comes to terms with Browning's actual identity as a poet is much more doubtful: for Browning's authenticity, which is really the only thing that matters in a poet, depends, I think, on his being in fact neither 'great' nor in any important way 'modern'. A generous power-politics is here perhaps being allowed to push aside criticism; a 'poet' is being confused with a 'figure of cultural importance', and even that figure may be being translated into modern American. For the Englishness of Browning seems to me for good and for bad a factor of peculiar significance – and even more, his character as a Victorian Englishman. He is a writer who, more than many, demands to be seen in his own 'milieu and moment': the world of middle- and upper-class English philistinism, of easy gentlemanly superiority to the arts and to intellect. Browning seems to have reflected with a peculiar simplicity and directness most of the important cultural strains of the Victorian England which came into being in his young manhood: a world which, as his dramatic monologues reveal, he inhabits most intensely even where he most intensely criticizes it. If the fourteen years of residence in Italy which his wife's ill-health necessitated gave the poet a focusing detachment from his society, this is none the less not quite the same as dissociation.

If this point seems to need stress, it is because most that is good in such criticism as the poet has received in the last hundred years has tended to find a role for him as a writer by isolating him within his period (those who by contrast see him as some kind of typical Victorian do so as a formula for demolishing him). This worry about the ways in which Browning really fitted into his time appears to have been initiated by Henry James, who with G. K. Chesterton, is still unsurpassed as a critic of Browning. James witnessed the somewhat uproarious spectacle of Browning's social success during the last ten or twenty years of his life; and the sensitive and sophisticated American critic was at one with those many of his English Art-loving contemporaries who experienced – and expressed – some shock and disappointment at seeing from close quarters the creator of Pompilia shouting red-faced, genial, noisy and spitting slightly, over his post-prandial cigar. James's discomposure went so far as to make him develop a theory that there were two quite distinct Brownings, the public and the private, the social and the artistic. He may well have used his story 'The Private Life' to perpetuate this legend of the artist's 'secret' or 'buried' self.

James's literary power has bequeathed the legend to Browning criticism ever since. It supplies the thesis of the most recent biography of the poet, Donald Thomas's quietly lucid and understanding *Life Within Life* – the best and most straightforward of the modern lives of Browning. But the thesis seems regrettably mistaken, in that it generates and enforces a wrong notion of 'poetry' as well as of Browning: poetry as absolutely distinguished from the normal world in which the writer lives. In his early years Browning himself was tempted by the 'magical' notion of poetry, and the result was the mediocrity of the earliest long poems and then the powerful impossibility of *Sordello*. He becomes both better and more recognizably himself the more he struggles – as do none of his contemporaries – to bring the living and immediate and 'modern' life of his time direct into his poetry.

Certainly Browning possessed reticences as a man. But when he finds himself as a writer, nothing in his style – except perhaps its excellence is altogether outside the mainstream sensibility of his age. He accepts, both from principle and from temperamental affinity, the dominating element in Victorian culture that is public and (the word has to be used) philistine. The poet's very best writing, his most *authentic* verse, includes that public and philistine self: the self that Henry James and so many others saw as red-faced, genial, noisy and spitting slightly. One of the most famous and surely the most amiable of remarks ever made about a poet was let fall by Lockhart, Scott's biographer, who said: 'I like Browning. He's not the least bit like one of your damned literary men.' One couldn't put the point better when discussing Browning's literary personality. As a poet, Browning is good, because he's not the least bit like one of your damned literary men.

There are, of course, disadvantages and difficulties in the case of an 'Artless' artist. For his first thirty or forty years as a writer Browning was essentially a failure – not, probably, because he was too 'modern' for his audience, but because he showed the age itself with a clarity for which it was unprepared: to the unimaginative there are few things less easily readable than the mirror held up to nature. When the poet did meet success, in his last ten or twenty years, it was as a sage or mage more than as a poet. Similarly, for most of the last fifty or sixty years, literary criticism has largely ignored Browning: there is no place for him in a Modernist or post-Modernist critique. The situation has been interestingly reflected in its scholarly parallel: in a period distinguished by high-powered definitive editions of the English poets, there has been no new and complete *Browning* after the one begun while the poet himself was still alive. But just as a certain new critical interest in the poet seems to be beginning, so also is the textual situation altering. In 1969 appeared the long-awaited first volume of the Ohio University Press *Browning*, under the general editorship of Roma A. King, jun.; the most recent volume, the fifth, brings the reader from 'A Soul's Tragedy' to the first volume of *Men and Women*. This fifth volume incorporates some changes in editorial policy and personnel that reflect the rough reception the Ohio *Browning* has met. Reviewing its first two volumes, one of its severest critics, the late John Pettigrew, found that they didn't make him want to modify the statement that 'there is nothing remotely like a good scholarly edition of the works.' It was, in fact, the problems of the Ohio *Browning* that made the editors of the Oxford *Browning* turn back to much earlier conceived but relegated plans for a similar multi-volume edition, so Ian Jack tells us in the General Introduction to the first volume, which has just appeared, and is devoted to *Pauline* and *Paracelsus*. Meanwhile John Pettigrew's own admirable edition in two volumes, completed and supplemented by Thomas J. Collins, and published by Penguin and Yale, includes all the extensive poems of Browning's later maturity except for *The Ring and the Book*, already edited for the same series, the 'English Poets', by Richard D. Altick; it omits the plays after *Pippa passes*, but adds poems uncollected by Browning himself, and also, in an appendix, the prose 'Essay on Shelley'.

In his brief but dense and elegant Preface, John Pettigrew manages to allude to the difficulties encountered in annotating Browning in a manner that evokes the literary character of Browning himself:

> The ideal Browning annotator needs – besides sympathy – to be thoroughly at home with music, art, and seven or eight languages and literatures, to know the Bible and the plays of Euripides and Aristophanes (and Victorian scholarship on them) by heart, to be intimately familiar – for a start – with Keats and Shelley and Donne and Milton and Homer and Anacreon and Alciphron and Herodotus and Thucydides and Horace and Shakespeare and Wanley and Quarles and the *Illustrated London*

News and Johnson's *Dictionary* and the fifty-odd – very odd –
volumes of the *Biographie Universelle* . . .

This is Browningesque; this is, as it were, Browning. Pettigrew
adumbrates here our sense of how the poet offers pleasures that lie
outside the narrower definition of the 'poetic': facts and fictions,
data, quotations, learning, knowledge always broadening and
broadening out – just as the poet made sure that, whatever poetry
was, verse was an inventive brilliance of metrics and rhetorics and
linguistics endlessly extended and adventured on. But the editor's
light comment implies more. Plenty of the English poets have been
widely learned men; more than a few, moreover, acquired their
education in a manner not unlike Browning's own – which is to say
by reading at large through the enormous and recondite library of
his gentle, sensitive and talented clerk-father. What makes the
unschooled Browning special is hinted with pleasant wit in the
following up of Horace and Shakespeare by Wanley, whom the
DNB locates as an Augustan antiquarian. The Victorian poet too,
so the paragraph seems to say, surely – in Jonson's phrase for
Shakespeare – 'wanted Arte': or lacked or didn't care for whatever
it is that makes the learning of other poets more lucid, more
systematic, more available to annotation. Pettigrew's light allusion
to what is 'very odd' in the sources just happens to echo the word
Henry James was to choose in his affectionate and informal
obituary summary of the poet: 'None of the odd ones have been so
great and none of the great ones so odd'.

In short, no account of (or denial of) Browning's 'greatness', no
arguments for or against his standing as a 'considerable poet', will
satisfy unless they take stock of this 'oddness' of Browning's: his
particular authenticity as a writer. The poet's own contemporaries
recognized it, and attributed it either to his not being a writer at all
or, if they liked him, to his being a writer of something else
disguised as poetry. The very inclusion of Browning in James's
Notes on Novelists suggests how near the critic came to agreeing
with Wilde's witticism about Browning being celebrated 'Ah, not
as a poet! He will be remembered as a writer of fiction' – as one
who used 'poetry as a medium for writing in prose.' The
conclusion that the poet was incapable of the lyric was a truism of
the time; to some extent this meant an inability to arouse, or to
seem to be arousing, simple emotion on simple subjects; and to

some extent it posited an incapacity on Browning's part to shape and limit his writing in a fashion that observed the more obvious formal laws. It was this last charge that G. K. Chesterton was meeting when, in his splendidly generous and strongly intelligent study of the poet, he defended Browning as a great master of form, so long as we define the grotesque as a major poetic form.

But there is casuistry as well as truth in this, and Chesterton's talk of Toby jugs does not really solve the problem. A jug is to be drunk out of, and a poem is to be read. The fact is, that while a Toby jug may *be* drunk out of, Browning's longer poems – and they make up a large part of his poetic output – are normally anything but read, and, having just read through them, I do not find this a fault in the modern reader. They are the work of a man of great talent, an interesting and a highly sympathetic man in addition; they have splendid things in them over and over again; and they are still not readable. The fault lies with that aspect of the ordinary philistine Victorian mind that could not help believing that 'More Means Better', that could not stop demanding longer and longer poems for larger and larger audiences, without for a moment coming to terms with the aesthetic problems posed by very extensive works of art. The famously obscure early *Sordello*, a tortuous though often striking tale of mediaeval Italy, is for these reasons hardly more difficult (i.e., no less so) than the pellucidly-told and modern-circumstanced *Inn Album* or *Red Cotton Night-Cap Country*.

In no long poem of Browning's – and this is true of his short ones as well – is it really very easy to know what precisely is going on: so much for his fictive gifts. It seems that verse narrative, like any other verse of length, requires respect for certain kinds of necessity: a reader has to be told what he needs to know before the current of the verse carries him past the point of no return; and this demands of the poet either egoistic intensity of will (to govern both his materials and his audience at once) or deep familiarity with ancient narrative structural formulae, which will do the same work for him. These necessities Browning disregards or does not possess or positively disapproves of, with a result that, to a degree startling in a writer celebrated for his grasp on human psychology, the long poems ignore or even offend reader-psychology.

This is true, to my mind, even of *The Ring and the Book*. The two books 'Caponsacchi' and 'Pompilia' are remarkably good, compacting into themselves the heart of the simple story of love unfulfilled but self-transcending; deep and moving and exciting too, they probably constitute the poet's most solid success. But the retelling of this same story, in its lineaments both bald and cruel, more than ten times over through the medium of speakers foolish and boring when not actually incapable of truth is – despite the linguistic and rhetorical brilliances and the neat angles of character that occasionally occur – largely unendurable, the kind of bright 'idea' that comes to a civilization simply out of touch with the realities of art in practice. One can almost think Guido's self-description meant to echo defeatedly the structure of the whole: 'I am one huge and sheer mistake'. James wrote the perfect review of the poem when, in *Notes on Novelists*, he circled the work with gloomy, delicate prevarication: 'We can only take it as tremendously interesting.' Interesting is what it is, and what really good writing perhaps is not: a bright idea is often a bad idea as far as poetry is concerned. In its lack of correspondence with the actual, *The Ring and the Book* – for all its genuinely impressive theoretical magnificence – is reminiscent of other and baser Victorian misunderstandings about the nature of the aesthetic, from wax-flowers under glass to models of the Crystal Palace constructed out of matchsticks.

All these problems arise from Browning's peculiar relationship to what his age regarded, admiringly but in practice reductively, as the 'magic' of poetry. Both temperament and principle urged Browning to resolve the enclosing pressures of Victorian philistin-ism and of the 'magic' it made of literature, by embodying them – by dramatizing their clash, in poems of an intensity the writer could never have achieved in actual drama. The result is a potent and idiosyncratic pseudo-realism, which is at once a hatred of Art and a creation of art-works. The verse emerging from the struggle, characteristically lacking most recognizable forms of inward aesthetic necessity, takes on those effects of spawning undisciplined scale, and of randomness within it, that Pettigrew's editorial note gestures at: a poetry, like its sources, of 'fifty-odd – very odd – volumes'. And yet the oddness is without doubt poetry: a poetry which extends, as all good poetry should, our sense of what the art consists in. It is Henry James (yet again) who gave the strongest sense of its elements, when – all doubtfully and critically reviewing *The Inn Album*, Browning's late strange sensationalistic yet also tedious yet also brilliantly original if endless narrative verse account of a *crime passionel* in outer Surrey – he concluded:

> The whole picture indefinably appeals to the imagination. There is something very curious about it and even rather arbitrary . . .

'Even rather arbitrary': the phrase is important, helping as it does not merely to extend but to explain the presence of the 'curious' and the 'odd' in Browning, a presence evident to so many of his more appreciative readers. The arbitrariness is the poet's own salute to that truth, that reality which not only – in his view – lay fruitfully beyond the sterilities of Art, but which condemned it. Thus, to return a last time to 'My Last Duchess', it is striking that precisely those randomnessess that the Augustan Pope gives to his Belinda as symptom of her shallowness, the Duke angrily gives to his Duchess as unwilling testimony of her natural truth ('she liked whate'er/She looked on, and her looks went everywhere'). We can hardly fail to understand that it is the quick changes of life and truth which animate the Duchess, and bring rage and despair to the tyrannous Artist-Duke. It is not surprising, therefore, if Browning's own style characteristically 'goes everywhere', random and richly-spawning and inventively indecisive, perpetually converting itself away from ideation towards what the poet himself called 'word pregnant with thing'. One of the things that commands respect in 'Pompilia' is the central and moving respect the poet himself gives to the girl's own pregnancy, which becomes, in the poem, an essential moving force, the power of life's elusive creativity.

And yet that power always comes to Browning in the medium of a breaker, a fragmenter. When one of his friends voiced doubts about the subject of *The Ring and the Book*, Browning tried half-inarticulately to silence her – and he was more intelligent than she – by vehemently stressing the 'Truth' of the 'Old Yellow Book' on which the story was based. The true context of that truth-book he describes in the poem:

> Mongst odds and ends of ravage, picture-frames
> White through the worn gilt, mirror-sconces chipped,
> Bronze angel-heads once knobs attached to chests,
> (Handled when ancient dames chose forth brocade),
> Modern chalk drawings, studies from the nude,
> Samples of stone, jet, breccia, porphyry . . .

The life that exists beyond Art is, to Browning, curious and arbitrary, a chaos of fragments that wait – like the elements of the poet's own hyphen-jointed speech – to be worked together by love into a mosaic of truth. In this sense the whole seventeen volumes of Browning's work are 'odds and ends of ravage': here a beautiful half-dozen lines, there an anecdote from the *Biographie Universelle*, jokes, metres, wisdom, a human voice – as it might be after dinner – entertainingly, inexhaustibly, formlessly talking and talking. As he said somewhat desolately to his loved and far more successful poet-wife, 'I only make men and women speak – give you truth broken into prismatic hues'.

'Truth broken': the arbitrary is built deep into the basis of all Browning's work. If he had moments of despair when he contemplated the story of *The Ring and the Book* – whose source-materials he tried to give away, before he wrote it, to both Trollope and Tennyson – it was because he quailed before the essential randomness in it, the great rubble of data and crime and history that had to become a kind of miracle, a 21,000-line work of love; which was what he meant by referring to 'my great venture, the murder-poem'. And the making of this, often thought Browning's greatest poem, was – I would suggest – a good deal more arbitrary than scholars like to think. It seems to me probable that an accidental encounter played a large part in its inception. Browning bought the gathering of documents he called the 'Old Yellow Book' in 1860, but he did not start to write until October 1864: clearly he was finding difficulties in beginning. But, sometime in the spring or summer of 1864, he met the young Ellen Terry at Little Holland House, where she had gone to live earlier that year.

She was sixteen (though she and everyone else thought she was fifteen), and had just married G. F. Watts, a morose and slightly neurotic man in his late forties. An observer at the wedding spoke of the 'atrabilious bridegroom . . . and the radiant child bride'. Ellen Terry herself said that at marriage she had 'never had the advantage . . . of a single day's schooling'; her parents arranged the marriage, which proved unhappy and broke up something over a year later. I suspect that Browning, who was both a compassionate man and one recently widowed, discovered within the first few minutes of his encounter with this extremely beautiful young girl, that Life, and not the Yellow Book, had found his Pompilia for him and begun his poem. At all events, in the autumn he began his four years of intense work on it.

I mention what may be the fructifying power of this brief encounter to suggest how vital to Browning was the sense of the arbitrary in life. It seems to me to mark and shape his whole poetic career. The problematic character of that career can be summed up briefly by noticing that 1864, the year that he met Ellen Terry and settled down to beginning *The Ring and the Book*, is the year at which the old Oxford Standard Authors edition of *Browning* stops. But in the Penguin and Yale near-complete edition, the second of the two near 1200-page volumes *begins* with the long poem Browning published in 1872, *Fifine at the Fair*. It will not do to say simply that the poet 'went off': I myself prefer any of the later poems to *Pauline* or *Paracelsus*, except for the weak *Ferishtah's Fancies* or the tedious *Parleyings*. There are at best superb and at worst interesting passages to be found throughout all the others. None the less, neither such volumes as the Oxford Standard Authors *Browning*, nor the general reader is wrong in thinking that, huge as Browning's output is, his best work falls within a relatively narrow channel: being written between say, 1844 and 1864, and really only comprising *Men and Women* and some outworks. Only in this area does there occur something like real artistic intensity. It was brought about, I would say, by causes in themselves arbitrary, or at any rate external to the poet's self, and their convergence has elements of the accidental. The first of what seem to me these operative facts is the pain of professional failure. By 1855, when *Men and Women* was published, *Sordello* had sold only 157 copies out of the 500 printed fifteen years before. One reviewer greeted the appearance of *Men and Women* with the comment, 'It is really high time that this sort of thing should, if possible, be stopped'; another added, more temperately, 'There is no getting through the confused crowd of Browning's Men and Women.' Browning pretended not to care, but malevolent human stupidity is always hard to take, and he clearly minded it a very great deal.

The minding was intensified by an odd fact, one always treated by the poet himself with the maximal simplicity, generosity and cheerful admiration that made a large part of his unusually amiable and open character: his wife was about the most successful and respected poet publishing in England, and had just all but beaten Tennyson to the Poet Laureateship. It is, of course, the poet's marriage to Elizabeth Barrett from 1846 until her death in 1861 that constitutes the second operative fact: one would guess that this warm and vivid relationship acted on Browning's direct and responsive nature so as to produce a condition of continual emotional 'openness', availability to feeling. Central as it was in his life, the relationship with a loved and famous invalid kept his emotional nature acutely alive: so that even while his private happiness compensated and reassured him for his public failure, in one unavoidable sense it exacerbated that sense of failure – that capacity in him to feel the failure.

The result is, that in these central decades that surround *Men and Women*, Love and Art become in his poetry interlinked sources of pain and pathos: a pain and pathos that are all the more effective as a reticence below the cheerful jingling matter-of-factness:

> Laughs with so little cause!
> We devised games out of straws.
> > We would try and trace
> > One another's face
> In the ash, as an artist draws . . .
>
> Then we would up and pace
> For a change, about the place,
> > Each with arm o'er neck:
> > 'Tis our quarter-deck,
> We are seamen in woeful case.
> > Help in the ocean space!
> > Or if no help, we'll embrace.

The situation in 'A Lovers' Quarrel' could be said to be not altogether clear, so that if the poem were more ambitious or less haunting it might like so much else in Browning get called 'obscure'. But the obscurity, the arbitrariness, has become co-substantial with the poem itself, which catches some comic and yet desolating mundanity in love, its existence trapped in the house and yet exquisitely, purposelessly out of time – *wasting* time, playing games, remembering. Here, as in so many moments of *Men and Women*, Browning reminds a reader of a remarkable passage he wrote in a letter to Elizabeth Barrett in the months before they married: 'I fancy myself meeting you on "the stairs" – stairs and passages generally, and galleries (ah, those indeed!) – all, with their picturesque *accidents*, of landing-places, and spiral heights and depths, and sudden turns and visions of half-open doors into what Quarles calls "mollitious chambers" – and above all, *landing-places* – they are my heart's delight – I would come upon you unaware on a landing-place in my next dream!'

All Browning's best moments are 'landing-places' in a dream, stairs and passages and galleries on the way to nowhere. 'Yon looking-glass gleamed at the wave of her feather': there are few ghosts in Browning, but it would not be surprising if it were he who taught Henry James how to invent his daylight spectres in 'The Turn of the Screw', so striking and so – with all its mundanity – imaginative is Browning's poetry of the empty indoors. The poet has happened, under the pressures of love and failure, to convert his own Artlessness to 'sudden turns and visions into half-open doors', a philistine art full of the bewilderment born of the ordinary:

> We shall have the word
> In a minor third
> There is none but the cuckoo knows;
> Heaps of the guelder rose!
> I must bear with it, I suppose.

It is a curious fact that Browning is a master of the art of minor thirds – curious, given his equally real character in the brisk and boisterous vein, a producer of poems like 'Waring' which still (to my mind) amuse and energize and exhilarate. But it is the co-existence of this sturdy commonplaceness of mood that makes the 'minor thirds' so suddenly touching and undermining, so dramatically effective. To some degree, this is a matter of brilliance in catching human half-tones, the smile of the defeated ('The chance was, they might take her eye'), or the honesty of the imperfect: 'Well, I forget the rest'. This last is an example of Browning's peculiar truth of endings: like that of the over-long, over-popular 'By the Fireside', which concludes its philosophical aspirations with the wonderfully self-undercutting

> And the gain of earth must be heav'n's gain, too;
> And the whole is well worth thinking o'er
> When autumn comes: which I mean to do
> One day, as I said before. .

Browning can get this subtly-modulated shock-effect by ending with a question: the dim and rambling 'Master Hugues of Saxe-

Gotha' is abruptly irradiated by its closing 'Do I carry the moon in my pocket?', and equally 'out of the blue' is the way the knotty, discursive and actually rather muddled stanzas of 'Popularity' rise at the end with their burst of splendid rage on

> Who fished the murex up?
> What porridge had John Keats?

The aesthetic effect of this last stanza, which seems to me considerable, lies in the way the poem finds a place for the superbness of purple dyes, but brings that spendour back to the 'porridge' of a Cockney poet. A contemporary of Browning's tells the story of how

> On another occasion I heard him smilingly add, to someone's vague assertion that in Italy only was there any romance left, 'Ah, well, I should like to include poor old Camberwell'.

The Camberwell Browning was born in was at that time by way of being a leafy village. None the less, its present sound of South-London suburban is to the point. All the apparent sources of the romantic in Browning, all the Italian Renaissance goings-on, are only costume drama, personal props for getting his audience to listen to him without the exercise of illegitimate 'magic'. The real centre of his art is pure Camberwell: a medium quite consciously unpretentious, at home in its location on the outskirts of things. Indeed, it is from this sense of the self-dependency, the accepted limitations of his craft that the deeper notes of Browning's poems come. One of his most powerful tragi-comic creations is his Caliban, brooding metaphysically as might some unhappy vocal bulldog on the Dark God of its daily existence:

> here are we,
> And there is He, and nowhere help at all.

> 'Believeth with the life, the pain shall stop.'

The mask of Caliban moves and amuses, surely, at least in part because we see under it a poet coming to terms with the awful situation of living humanly as Artist without, so to speak, any ethical or magical equipment for it. This self-appraisal is clearly the secret too of 'Childe Roland to the Dark Tower Came'. Much discussed though the poem has been, it is curious that no critic or editor seems to have noted the point of the title's being a quotation: a quotation, what is more, spoken by a character (Edgar in *King Lear*) disguised as a madman, and himself giving all the signs of quoting from some ballad or romance. The title acts as one of Browning's 'half-open doors' into long disappearing corridors of quotation upon quotation, the great tradition of poets interlinked one with another only by the high hopelessness of the enterprise they share. The first line of the poem is, symptomatically, 'My first thought was, he lied in every word'; the whole could easily have been signed with Sludge's phrase, 'Cheat's my name'; its style throughout is a dense amalgam of Browningesque *ersatz*, of amazingly suburban Victorian journalese, Artless talk, that will suddenly narrow and focus on some deep-needling poignancy:

> What with my search drawn out through years, my hope
> Dwindled into a ghost not fit to cope
> With that obstreperous joy success would bring,
> I hardly tried now to rebuke the spring
> My heart made, finding failure in its scope.

This easy experienced rasp is the sound of Browning writing at his best. He would not have been Browning had he not entertained the large hopes incorporated in poems like *The Ring and the Book*, but it is not discordant with that ambition that he should also be the man who released for poetry words like 'cope' and 'scope' and 'obstreperous' – Camberwell words, and one would have said impossible in verse..It is this side of Browning that makes a reader warm to him now. A lot of his best lines hardly seem, for good and for bad, to be 'poetry' at all: they are, sometimes disturbingly, more like a voice straight out of the past, accidentally silenced and then eerily revived by some trick radio-wave: 'I must learn Spanish, one of these days'; 'You have seen better days, dear? So have I.' At these moments, Browning speaks our language, or we speak his: for the poem acts as one of his 'half-open doors' in time, and it doesn't much matter which side one is. In 'How it Strikes a Contemporary' (the 100-line poem that is perhaps my own particular favourite out of all his work) this simple communicating door opens up vistas surprisingly large: past and present, Spain and England, art and politics, time and eternity. The man whom the poem describes ('I only knew one poet in my life:/And this, or something like it, was his way') is really the Duke of Ferrara's antitype, just as the poem is a quiet answer to 'My Last Duchess'. There is no Duchess, no Ambassador; indeed, nobody seems to be speaking in it, only thinking aloud; and nothing really happens, except that a person, who might be someone like Cervantes, that type of the totally unpretentious and unlucky original genius, goes for what feels like a nineteenth-century walk around the town where he lives, with an old dog at his heels, up an alley 'that leads nowhither', on to the promenade 'just at the wrong time'. He's an almost invisible presence, his 'scrutinizing hat' throwing a shadow under an old house left to crumble away, his 'stick' trying the mortar of a new one being built:

> He stood and watched the cobbler at his trade,
> The man who slices lemons into drink,
> The coffee-roaster's brazier, and the boys
> That volunteer to help him turn its winch.
> He glanced o'er books on stalls with half an eye,
> And fly-leaf ballads on the vendor's string,
> And broad-leaf bold-print posters by the wall.
> He took such cognizance of men and things,
> If any beat a horse, you felt he saw;
> If any cursed a woman, he took note . . .

Browning names the town Valladolid, but it could as easily be Camberwell – or anywhere where the reader happens to be, for it is of course the reader who is the true 'contemporary'. And, though the poem has no Duke to call 'That piece a wonder now', it strikes us as a remarkable enough testimony to Browning's art as a maker.

8

The New Style of *Sweeney Agonistes*

When, in the late eighteenth century, the neo-classical system of genres began to break down, formal satire ceased to attract major literary talents. But the satiric impulse itself did not of course disappear. Satire became an incidental element: it no longer prescribed its own form. Much of the best Victorian satirical writing is found in prose fiction (an obvious instance would be the American chapters in *Martin Chuzzlewit*). In the present century only Wyndham Lewis could be called a thoroughgoing satirist; and he too uses the novel as the vehicle for his satiric vision. T. S. Eliot's earliest important poems, 'The Love Song of J. Alfred Prufrock' and 'The Portrait of a Lady', seem also to maintain a relationship with prose fiction, most notably that of Henry James.

But the novel was never Eliot's preferred form. The manuscripts of *The Waste Land* show him attempting to revive the high Augustan modes of satire: attempts rightly dropped from or radically altered in the final version of the poem. The satiric life of *The Waste Land* is in fact strongest where it is most contemporary in reference and most dramatic in presentation. For it was a dramatic medium that the satiric impulse in Eliot seemed most naturally to demand. Conversely, when, a few years later, he made his first strictly dramatic attempt, the result was two fragments of verse dialogue which are best understood in terms of their satiric hinterland. *Sweeney Agonistes* is essentially, and to an almost Jonsonian degree, intended as 'satire-drama'. Indeed, Eliot achieved his breakthrough into drama not by virtue of a painfully-acquired stagecraft, but by the discovery and mastery of a new and essentially modern satiric style.

The dramatic art was clearly attractive to Eliot. And yet it was in other ways alien to a writer as obdurately inward, as introspectively private as Eliot's particular gifts and principles made him. It may be this mixture of attraction and alienation that produces the characteristically dramatic flavour of Eliot's verse *outside* the theatre; exquisitely reserved in its flamboyancy, reticently exact in its expressiveness. But such a 'dramatic' quality has little to do with a working dramaturgy. Symptomatically, all the later part of Eliot's career shows a gradual fissuring of the poetic and the dramaturgical. His later poetry has a tendency to become the more insistently inward: hence, perhaps, his sense of achievement in the amount of the fully 'public' he managed to bring into his last three *Quartets*; and the theatrical verse struggles against the problem of rhetorical thinness.

Much of Eliot's energy in the making of his plays seems to have gone into that dramaturgy which clearly provoked and delighted him by its difficulty. Play-craft was slowly and laboriously acquired, and remained a conscious, even a public matter, with advice and assistance taken from bystanders. It hardly seems surprising that criticism of the plays has followed Eliot in this. Much of the best work has explicated the plays in terms of conscious purpose, often confining itself to what might be called Eliot's 'spiritual dramaturgy'. One of the best studies, Carol H. Smith's *T. S. Eliot's Dramatic Theory and Practice* (Princeton, New Jersey, 1963), stresses that Eliot 'has chosen poetic drama to accomplish his purpose because it can reach a wider public than other poetic means and, more important, because of the possibilities of creating in drama a total dramatic world in which to demonstrate the divine plan' (p. 29). Almost all academic criticism of the plays has been drawn in this way to a faithful mirroring of Eliot's overt purpose: as if it were conscientiously, and sometimes very successfully, building up his working notebooks for the period covered by the play in question. Carol Smith's account of *Sweeney Agonistes* concentrates on Eliot's conscious effort to revive an ancient ritual drama of death and rebirth; another equally able and representative account, Sears Jayne's 'Mr Eliot's Agon', reads more theologically, seeing in Sweeney himself as much of Christ as of Orestes.[1]

Such accounts no doubt reflect Eliot's purposes. But the poet himself has with some force undermined the role of intention in the

[1] *Philological Quarterly*, 34 (1955), 395–414.

making of poetry. And it must be added that, if his dramatic work were exactly like what it is often described as being, it would be intellectually fascinating and thoroughly dead in performance. There have always, of course, been good critics and readers who feel that this is precisely the case. In his short discussion of Eliot's work in the theatre, John Bayley found the plays in the end no more than 'a game of moral philosophy in the theatre . . . cut off in technique and theory from the source of everything spontaneous in his art'.[1] But a good deal has happened in the last twenty years to make this seem more questionable. In the period since his death, the writer's extreme authority has ebbed; and as a result the verse is coming to be appreciated more simply on its own merits. Productions of the plays seem to be improving, a matter not to be entirely dissociated from this lapse of reverence, and response to the plays in performance is surely both sharper and warmer. The Round House *Family Reunion* was as successful as it was brilliant, and a recent production of *The Elder Statesman* was throughout both more detached and more profound (though with the same leading actor, Paul Rogers) than on its first production twenty years ago – and perhaps also more appreciatively received by its rather smaller audiences. Both plays have been seen to 'work' to a remarkable degree; and such success could not be predicted from the usual academic account of these plays.

This is especially true of *Sweeney Agonistes*. The first of Eliot's plays, it is also the most fragmentary; it possesses least of that 'play-craft' which later work may show. And yet it is interesting that a few critics have seen it as peculiarly dramatic in its own way. In the essay already quoted, John Bayley finds it an exception to the general rule of Eliot's practice, possessed of what he calls an almost 'Brechtian' vitality. Katharine J. Worth, too, praises *Sweeney*'s purely theatrical expressiveness, its derivation (as she sees it) from 'music-hall and minstrel show': '*Sweeney* is very much a play of breaking out and acting out rather than talking out'.[2] This remark suggests some of the problems of this more recent essentially 'theatrical' approach to Eliot's plays. Sympathetic as Katharine Worth's appreciativeness is, this strong stress on what she calls 'the

[1]'The Collected Plays', *The Review* (Eliot Number), 4 (November 1962), 3–11 (p. 6).
[2]*Revolutions in Modern English Drama* (1972), p. 58; see also 'Eliot and the Living Theatre' in *Eliot in Perspective*, edited by Graham Martin (1970), pp. 151–55.

music-hall experience' in *Sweeney Agonistes* fails (to my mind) almost as much as does the 'spiritual dramaturgy' approach to respond to the actual linguistic quality of the work. Symptomatically, Katharine Worth protests at the inclusion of *Sweeney Agonistes* among the 'Unfinished Poems' (rather than with the plays) in the 1969 Collected Edition of Eliot. Both 'spiritual dramaturgists' and theatrical experts alike seem to me to have left aside what makes *Sweeney Agonistes* peculiarly interesting, its character as dramatic *poetry*: a medium that brings Eliot's play-writing into being. Not only have critics failed to appreciate this new and rather startling medium; it has been made the object of savage attack:

> 'Fragment of an Agon' is defective in execution (save the mark) because the farcical music-hall style, without any indication that Sweeney is deliberately talking down, is an improper vehicle for this serious theme . . . The critic with no interest in Eliot's idea might find the work strained to grotesqueness by its subject matter, and the only audience likely to be gratified is a morose one with a taste for the frivolously macabre. Eliot's failure seems the more abysmal when the theory from which he was working is traced to its apparent model – De Quincey's essay 'On the Knocking on the Gate in *Macbeth*'.[1]

What is getting signally ignored in this account of *Sweeney Agonistes* by Grover Smith – and indeed more than ignored, positively reviled – is that aspect of art that we like to summarize vaguely as its *medium*. Poetry or drama rightly consists (this seems to be the notion) in a 'serious theme', in 'Eliot's idea'. The whole concept of style is here degraded and trivialized into something artistically shallow and superficial. Even Carol Smith, who writes much more appreciatively of *Sweeney Agonistes*, speaks of its 'comic surface', a covering under which the real stuff of interest, the ritual drama of death and rebirth, lies snugly awaiting discovery. Such language is sometimes enforced by the needs of finer analysis; but it is always dangerous. An uninterest in or cavalier approach to Eliot's literary or linguistic medium leads to errors which may seem slight but which generate an always-increasing departure from the actual work of art. One such trivial error, which, however, bears directly on what *Sweeney Agonistes* is (to my mind) effecting as a work of art, occurs in another of the essays on the play which I have already mentioned, Sears Jayne's study of what he sees as the play's context of Christianized classical learning as reflected in its epigraphs. When its second section, the 'Fragment of an Agon', was first published in *The Criterion* it was glossed as being 'From *Wanna Go Home, Baby?*'. Jayne concludes: 'The title *Wanna Go Home, Baby?* implied that the language of the play was to be that of the London pub in the 1920s' (p. 397). A title so provokingly flamboyant is certainly likely to imply something, but that it could hardly have implied this, the Supplement to the OED might have told Sears Jayne, listing as it does three uses only of 'Baby' in the slang sense of 'girl' before 1930, and all of them from *American* texts only. The surprise Jayne's remark must bring to an English (or Londoner's) ear is supported by information from another, quite different source: an unpretentious but lively and useful scrapbook on the period put together by Alan Jenkins which tells us decisively that 'the word "baby" as an endearment ("Yes, Sir, That's My Baby") never caught on in Britain, so that unsophisticated British listeners, confronted with a song-title like "I Wonder Where My Baby Is Tonight?" tended to imagine a wayward infant in diapers knocking back cocktails'.[1] And, for what it is worth, though my own memories do not reach back with much effectiveness before the 1940s, they do recall enough from that period of G.I.s and transatlantic hit-tunes to preserve *Baby* as a kind of ideograph of pure (or impure) Americanism. Eliot's earlier proposed title, *Wanna Go Home, Baby?*, suggested, in short, an Americanism all the more highlighted by its linguistic formality: cadenced, derisive and self-conscious.

The 'Americanness' of *Sweeney Agonistes* is indissociable from its meaning, and I shall return to this subject. For the moment it is enough to remark the kind of error that arises when a reader, however expert in other areas, is not much interested in *listening* to poetry. His or her interest must necessarily move to what – if not heard to be there – is by contrast presumed to be there. Hence the concern of much academic criticism with the plot of *Sweeney Agonistes*. In the course of his interesting account of the play, Jayne summarizes some of its plot as follows: 'God, then, invites Doris to

[1] *The Twenties* (1974), p. 151.

the divine union mentioned in the epigraph; pleading physical illness, Doris puts him off until Monday, the day after the Sabbath, in order to have the week-end free for "created beings"; in so doing she has chosen spiritual death (this is why she draws the coffin card)' (p. 407). One would not want precisely to contest this as an account of what may be happening in Eliot's play-poem; in outline the plot sounds likely enough. But if this summary is true, God must be Pereira; and if God is Pereira, God is a ponce. If Eliot can compare the Church to a hippopotamus, he can also (presumably), compare God to a ponce. But 1927 was, after all, the very year in which the poet was baptized and confirmed into the Anglican Church. Any account of the play which stresses such peculiar and yet such purposive meanings as these does not seem consistent with such an act of public profession as that.

It is possible to form ideas about Eliot's 'purposes' (ritual or Aristophanic, Christian or classical) which apply very well to some aspects of these dramatic poems; but if pressed home the results are ridiculous or, in the proper sense, improper. Something of this realization may lie behind the warning note which the poet had appended to the fragments when in 1954 they were included in a collection of one-act plays: 'The author wishes to point out that *Sweeney Agonistes* is not a one-act play and was never designed as such. It consists of two fragments. But as the author has abandoned any intention of completing them, these two fragmentary scenes have frequently been produced as a one-act play.'[1] For there is, one suspects, *no* body of learned materials related to the titles and epigraphs that can be used to make good sense of the dialogue without deformation and impropriety of this kind; and, similarly, no proposed plot adds much to the two fragments as we have them. This seems to be true even of Eliot's own plot-draft as it survives in the Hayward Collection at Cambridge. This draft includes a proposed 'Murder of Mrs Porter' by Sweeney. That almost every reader given to such surmises seems in the past to have assumed that Sweeney's victim was Doris does not prove that *Sweeney Agonistes* is incoherent nonsense; but it does or should arouse some scepticism as to the exact relation of the drafts to what in fact got written. These Hayward Collection drafts have against an earlier form of the title and epigraphs a note in Eliot's hand,

[1] *Twenty-four One-Act Plays*, edited by John Hampden, revised edition (1954), p. 346.

saying 'Probably precedes the fragments themselves', as though he too were testifying to changes in the materials as they gradually evolved. Such comments underline, that is, the realization that *Sweeney Agonistes* is like every other poem (and to a lesser extent every other play) that Eliot wrote, in its disjunction between what can be formulated (in terms of 'draft', 'plot', formal and rationalizable 'purpose') and the words that found themselves spoken, the lines that got themselves written. The gradual emergence of what Eliot came (after 1932) to call *Sweeney Agonistes* illustrates how vital it is to leave room for discontinuities in its development: how like, that is to say, the work is in this respect to what we now know of the composition of *The Waste Land* and of *Four Quartets*.

This is perhaps the place to recall briefly what we know of the emergence of *Sweeney Agonistes*. We are lucky to have a contemporary reference to its beginnings, though this needs to be treated as cautiously as all the other materials involved. Eliot happened to visit Arnold Bennett and mentioned his plans, and the event was recorded in Bennett's journal (entry for 10 September 1924). The visit is often made to sound purposive, as if Eliot went to Bennett (whom he knew only slightly) specifically to talk about his play; whereas the context makes it plain that the occasion of the visit was merely to solicit an article for *The Criterion*, and what followed was generated partly by the poet's anxious and urbane courtesy, and partly by the novelist's rather vain, though genial, aggressiveness. Bennett bluffly attacked what he called the 'Wastelands'; Eliot hastened to assure him that he had definitely given up that 'form of writing', 'and was now centred on dramatic writing. He wanted to write a drama of modern life (furnished flat sort of people) in a rhythmic prose "perhaps with certain things in it accentuated by drum-beats". And he wanted my advice. We arranged that he should do the scenario and some sample pages of dialogue'.[1] In the next month Eliot sent the scenario and samples, had them criticized, and returned thanks, describing himself as about to reconstruct the play according to Bennett's advice. Nearly three years later, in June 1927, Bennett was writing to ask whatever became of the 'jazz play'. He was apparently unaware that such of it as was ever to exist had been printed in the numbers of *The Criterion* for October 1926 ('Fragment of a Prologue') and January 1927 ('Fragment of an Agon').

---

[1] *The Journals of Arnold Bennett*, edited by Newman Flower, 3 vols (1932–33), III, 52.

It is worth, I think, laying out this train of events in some detail, so as to ponder the interesting gaps and silences that occur within it. Carol Smith is of the opinion that the two *Sweeney* fragments as we have them were those sent to Bennett in October 1924, and this may very well be so. But there are discrepancies which at least ask to be noticed. Bennett may of course be subject to slips, and the journal account somehow suggests a successful and busy man who was not condescending to listen very hard; all the same, the errors (if they are errors) are odd ones for an extremely capable literary man to make. *Sweeney Agonistes* as we know it does not precisely involve 'furnished flat sort of people', which suggests a down-graded Somerset Maugham world, and more importantly it is not in prose, however rhythmical. Interestingly, another fragment does survive (usefully reprinted by Carol Smith in a footnote, as well as in the programme to the Stage Sixty Theatre Club 'Homage to T. S. Eliot'), and this fragment *is* in prose. It is a finale in which Time enters, 'closely resembling Father Christmas', and speaks in a style which Carol Smith calls 'not quite consistent with the rest of *Sweeney Agonistes*' (p. 63). This is a large understatement: the passage is in fact a piece of lightweight, second-rate, and (one would have said) entirely derivative Audenesque prose. Since this fragment was never published with the other two but only included by Eliot in a 1933 letter to Hallie Flanagan on the occasion of her Vassar production of *Sweeney Agonistes* in that year, it is clearly possible that it was written after the other two. I in fact find it difficult to believe that Eliot did not add this 'Father Christmas' finale some time after December 1928, when Auden sent him for publication his *Paid on Both Sides*, in one of whose prose passages a 'Father Xmas' figures. At all events this Audenesque prose fragment, while it does not offer any clear evidence as to the actual dating of the two verse fragments, does, if it postdates *Paid on Both Sides*, suggest a work that emerged through different stages and versions. It should encourage, that is, a proper hesitancy concerning Eliot's 'intentions'; for the concept of a single purpose, deriving from a single occasion, becomes as untenable as the notion of a single preserved 'draft'.

Introspective verse like Eliot's (and even a rhetorical drama like his, in so far as it approximates to literature) is clearly always so much of a difficult struggle towards daylight that it is vital for a reader *respicere finem*: to read the words as they emerge on the printed page. Whatever its origins or authorial intentions, *Sweeney Agonistes* begins in print in 1932, when it took the form in which we read it now. And as it stands we read first the section which Eliot evidently wrote first, the 'Fragment of a Prologue' that shows Doris and Dusty at home to their gentlemen friends. Those who attempt to tell the story of *Sweeney Agonistes* have most trouble with this first fragment, for such action as the play might be said to have only gets going (or gets staying) when Sweeney himself appears in the 'Fragment of an Agon'. Eliot, too, deprecated the claims of the first fragment, with that impulse in him which always came to prefer his own 'later stages' as the more articulate and rational, as against the perhaps more obscure if fruitful opening moves. On the other hand, if there is no plot, a good deal is at least *going on* in the 'Fragment of a Prologue'. From the very beginning the poem manifests a furious tragicomic energy. Energy need not be identified with activity, nor activity with action, nor action with plot, for us to use the word 'dramatic' here: for the intensity is integral with anything we can conceive of (in Eliot's work at least) as an event reflecting relation between the characters. To put it in a phrase, *Sweeney Agonistes* starts with something like an electric shock. Drama moves consequentially, and the opening of *Sweeney Agonistes* makes drama out of the mere astonishing linguistic sequence, from the title through the epigraphs to the dialogue that begins. Eliot's final title, *Sweeney Agonistes: Fragments of an Aristophanic Melodrama*, is powerfully yet frigidly intellectualist; the very word *Agonistes*, with its shadow of Milton's austere unworldly drama, 'never intended for the Stage', and the faint suggestion of 'agonies', darkens the opening like a cold cloud passing over: a darkening intensified by the epigraphs, the first a quotation from Aeschylus ('Orestes: *You don't see them, you don't – but I see them: they are hunting me down, I must move on*') and the second from St John of the Cross ('*Hence the soul cannot be possessed of the divine union, until it has divested itself of the love of created beings*'). Obliquity here complicates negation, as the mind is lost in the structures both of quotation and of argument, in a rhetoric both conditional and abstract. By the time we arrive at the sub-sub-title, 'Fragment of a Prologue', the opening introducing-apparatus has taken the form of an enormously top-heavy structure: which mutates into the Senecan stichomythia of 'DUSTY. DORIS' as the play begins:

DUSTY: How about Pereira?
DORIS: What about Pereira?
                I don't care.
DUSTY: You don't care!
                Who pays the rent?
DORIS: Yes he pays the rent
DUSTY: Well some men don't and some men do
                Some men don't and you know who
DORIS: You can have Pereira.

The extreme formality of this opening can hardly fail to draw to
our attention a simple fact: that there is a difference between
'reading' and 'reading in'. The prolegomena reflect (as they attract
and justify) the work of scholarship and criticism; in some real
sense a Christian ritual drama 'lies behind' Sweeney Agonistes, as
Eliot's chosen epigraphs from Aeschylus and St John of the Cross
'stand above' his printed fragments, and as the word 'Aristophanic'
follows the title he finally settled for. The difficulty occurs when
the two kinds of material are brought together (as Grover Smith
indignantly recorded): when the superstructure comes in contact
with the dialogue. For not to record a hilarious discrepancy is, in
some sense that matters extremely in literature, not to read the
work at all.

   That Sweeney Agonistes might be funny (extremely funny – and
consequently, and equally, touchingly sad) is a truth not often
admitted in orthodox accounts of the poem. This can only be
because those who write them do not attend to the actual words: do
not notice details like, for instance, the impassive lack of
punctuation, which 'answers' the appalling self-contradictory
super-literacy of the opening with a subliteracy in the circumst-
ances almost refreshing. A kind of implicit production-note that
works equally well on the page or audibly, this absence of pointing
makes the girls seem startlingly to be writing *their own dialogue*.
Given the extreme intellectualism of the context, this makes Doris
and Dusty appear alive and kicking in a world of glossaria: mere
commentary, notes and queries. The complex split in sympathies
involved here provokes a violent laughter, that specifically 'hysteri-
cal' or sad laughter that attends the girls throughout, a tribute to
their capacity to collapse empty cultures. This can perhaps be put
more technically: the vitality of Eliot's writing in Sweeney Agonistes

derives from a tension here represented as distance between styles, something anticipated in the satirical styles, burlesque and mock-heroic, of *The Waste Land*. The move into formal drama only accentuates the distance between, and yet the close marriage of, the 'commentary' on the one hand and the agents on the other: the great Christian-classical panoply, and the two girls' squeakily obdurate voices, as basic, as classic in their way as the *Choephoroi* in its way ('I don't care!' and 'Who pays the rent?'). It is a part of the construction of this echo-chamber that the given passage from the ancient tragedy ('You don't see them . . . but I see them') just happens to use a form of helplessly self-repeating monosyllabic utterance not unlike the illiterate tautologies of the chattering girls. To marry them truly, to raise the 'low' to the power of the 'high', is the task Eliot has set himself.

Grover Smith has regretted that Eliot made the mistake of utilizing a 'farcical music-hall style' which was improper for the work's 'serious theme'. This is near to the art of sinking in criticism. For throughout *Sweeney Agonistes*, as in these few opening lines, Eliot is moving burlesque towards a brilliant and new dramatic poetry. He is discovering a voice that permits him to do what is most necessary for any dramatist but perhaps for any poet most difficult: to create an idiom that will lastingly give utterance to lives and beings quite unlike his own. He has done so by giving a grave intellectual context to a medium unused in serious English drama, certainly in verse, for centuries: the medium of the comic demotic. And he is enabled to do so because he has learned to call into account a peculiarity of personal situation: his dislocation between two available traditions. The intellectual context is only as alien to the two girls as the character of Sweeney is to that of Doris; or as the ancient European tradition is to the new American, and each equally far away, each equidistant as it were, from the expatriated unacademic Eliot of the 1920s.

For this is (or so I would suggest) the heart of what Eliot is doing in *Sweeney Agonistes*: he is making a dramatic voice for himself by 'calling in the new world to redress the balance of the old', writing, one might say, a European tragi-comedy in American. I have tried elsewhere to suggest that Eliot had originally hoped that *The Waste Land* might bring together a 'poetry of America' (in the rejected opening section) with a 'poetry of Europe'; just as we should perhaps see him in *Four Quartets*, and especially of course in 'The

Dry Salvages', 'domesticating' French Symbolism, humanizing and Christianizing it by rooting it in English and American landscape and history.[1] *Sweeney Agonistes* has a place in this exceedingly ambitious programme. It brings together a great if largely 'dead' European culture with a vital if debased modern American speech, marrying (one might say) Seneca to Doris. And like many other large national and racial resettlements, the job is done essentially at the level of language. To appreciate the scale of the enterprise, it will be necessary to pause and consider rather more exactly the language of these two fragments.

I have already referred in passing to Sears Jayne's assumption that *Wanna Go Home, Baby?* calls up 'the London pub of the 1920s': an assumption worth noting, because it summarizes the major critical response to the fragments' language, invariably gestured at as 'the common speech of the time'. The exactness of Jayne's slip is fruitful and helpful. For one of Eliot's problems as a dramatist was of course that of localization, of being able to show his characters in terms of a specific habitat: a task made peculiarly difficult by his own cultural displacement, however central that displacement was (in other senses) to a great period of expatriation and exile. All Eliot's poems in fact manage to generate an intense sense of place, without at the same time making it at all easy to say where the place in question actually is.

Sweeney Agonistes is certainly no exception. Jayne's allusion to the 'London pub', though falsely dependent on *The Waste Land* and (I believe) wrong in fact, since the poem does not take place in a pub whether or not in London, at the same time has some point. Many of the speech-intonations of Doris and Dusty certainly seem to be those of smartened-up South London: Balham or Tooting, say, around 1920, and gone up in the world. Sweeney himself equally certainly has relations in or with a distinctively suburban seedy squalor. The murder he is haunted by is of a piece with those great grubby 'mere English' murders, often for love and often by poison, that filled *The News of the World* through the 1920s. This is a milieu of lower-middle-class violence that evidently fascinated Eliot, perhaps by virtue of the way its mixture of the genteel and the seamy offered challenge and resistance to the beglamorizing tastefulness of late

[1]'Eliot's Marianne: *The Waste Land* and its Poetry of Europe', *RES*, 31 (1980), 41–53; and 'Eliot's *Four Quartets* and French Symbolism', *English*, 29 (1980), 1–37.

Victorian poetry. There are obvious links backward from here to *The Waste Land*, more indeed than are explicit or are usually guessed at by critics. The most notorious murder of the period was the horrifying and pathetic Thompson-Bywaters case of 1922, in which the pitiable romantic Edith Bywaters encouraged her young lover to deal with her brutal older husband by taking a lesson from *Bella Donna*, the Robert Hitchens best-seller of a decade earlier, about a *femme fatale* who attempts to murder her innocent young husband by feeding him digitalis. Eliot was (in my view) perhaps remembering one or two striking moments from this in fact well-written and absorbing novel in his Thames-scapes in 'The Fire Sermon', as well as recalling the title in 'The Burial of the Dead' ('Here is Belladonna, The Lady of the Rocks, / The Lady of Situations'). This interest in a terrain that could be called peculiarly 'English' at that period – an elusive but strong-flavoured, haunting blend of the violent and the seedy, the aspiringly hopeless and the grubbily romantic – is certainly to be found again in *Sweeney Agonistes*, and gives an odd complex substance to its theoretical design.

And yet that Englishness is radically qualified. The speech-style of Doris and Dusty, at the opening, may consciously reproduce the Cockney, but all the same it is wholly unlike the loquacious aggressive drawl of Lil's friend in 'A Game of Chess'. The staccato machine-gun-fire exchanges of the two girls, as it might be a high-kicking chorus-line of two: this is something else again, something nervous and new. Where did Eliot get it from, this jazz-age or machine-gun-fire style that contributes so much to the force of his fragments? Despite its lower-class London sound, it is worth noticing that the girls' phrasing in fact blends perfectly with the diction of their American and Canadian visitors: which, like the predominant style of 'Fragment of an Agon' and indeed of Sweeney himself, is by no means mere English:

> I gotta use words when I talk to you
> But if you understand or if you don't
> That's nothing to me and nothing to you
> We all gotta do what we gotta do
> We're gona sit here and drink this booze
> We're gona sit here and have a tune
> We're gona stay and we're gona go
> And somebody's gotta pay the rent.

The idiom of both fragments is somewhat changeable, just as, in the second, routines from Broadway vaudeville are followed by a pastiche of W. S. Gilbert. All the same, hard listening to Sweeney's idiom added to the Irish connotations of his name hardly leave one in much doubt as to his transatlantic place of origin: a certainty which rapidly grows to positive suspicion that his friend –

> I knew a man once did a girl in.
> Any man might do a girl in

– was surely a Chicago gangster. The American gangsters of the 1920s tended to specialize in the distribution of liquor; and the need to take the drinks to Doris's flat (from which the action never moves, unless Sweeney is to scramble his eggs in that 'London pub') bespeaks the time and place of the speakeasy, the private club and party of the Prohibition period. Alan Jenkins (to stay within the field of sources quoted earlier) actually gives a list of the names of these leading Chicago gangsters: 'Orazio "the Scourge" Tropea, Murray "the Camel" Humphries, Spike O'Donnell, Sam "Golf Bag" Hunt, Dingbat O'Berta, Jake "Greasy Thumb" Guzik, Hymie "Loud Mouth" Levine, and Machine Jack McGurn' (p. 130). Among these, Sweeney 'the Poet' Agonistes would fit with no trouble at all.

It is this predominant Americanness which Eliot was clearly advertising in his first title, *Wanna Go Home, Baby?*; an Americanness which is more than a mere matter of diction – it affects the vision and substance of the whole:

DORIS: I don't care
DUSTY: You don't care!
            Who pays the rent?

This is not like Lil's friend; it is the speech of a different time, a different continent. Seneca may call it stichomythia, but America calls it the wisecrack pure and simple. Moreover, the girls are something new in Eliot's work: Doris and Dusty affront their fate with a blatant insolence that is almost a latterday innocence. The most appropriate critical reaction to the opening of *Sweeney Agonistes* would be the respectful acknowledgement that a learned, obscure, and inward poet had managed to invent the Dumb Blonde in literature: that T. S. Eliot had fathered Marilyn Monroe. For, given the peculiar intellectual and spiritual context that introduces

and entraps the two girls, Dumb Blondes are what they contras-
tingly define themselves as being. From Doris's marvellously
dogged dark mindlessness ('I'd like to know about that coffin') to
the bright limits of her more cheerfully competent friend Dusty
('Well I never! What did I tell you?'), this farcically blank and yet
diamond-hard address to life is, whether Balham or Bronx, the
speech of a quite new type, a caricature of the female that lasted for
more than a half-century, and is only now going into recession.

Eliot did not, of course, invent the Dumb Blonde. But *Sweeney
Agonistes* was put together at a time extremely close to her
invention, and I find it difficult to believe that he wrote in complete
ignorance of that event. In fact, I would suggest that it may have
been that very invention which helped the realization of an impulse
towards drama that, for lack of a proper style, was proving little
more than abortive; it found him a glittering new set of
conventions more seductive than anything his vague sense of
'furnished flat sort of people' could provide. Probably the most
significant event in the evolution of the Dumb Blonde occurred in
the year before Eliot published his fragments in *The Criterion*.
Through the spring and summer of 1925 a young writer brought
out, in six monthly episodes in the American *Harper's Bazaar*, a
series of little stories which met such enormous success that she was
able to publish them in book form in the late autumn of that year
(and English publication followed early in 1926). The book proved
one of the great best-sellers, not only of the 1920s, but of several
succeeding decades: William Empson put bits of it into a poem, and
Santayana cited it ('with a grin', so the flattered author says in her
autobiography) when asked to name the best philosophical work
by an American. The book in question (which is, of course,
Gentlemen Prefer Blondes, and the writer Anita Loos) is the self-told
success story of a cherubic-faced nail-hard amateur whore or
'gold-digger', Lorelei Lee of Little Rock, and her story opens:

> A gentleman friend and I were dining at the Ritz last evening and
> he said that if I took a pencil and a paper and put down all of my
> thoughts it would make a book . . . I mean I seem to be thinking
> practically all of the time . . . So this gentleman said a girl with
> brains ought to do something else with them besides think.

Accompanied by her much nicer, cleverer, but less successful friend
Dorothy, Lorelei gets herself educated, her tutors consisting

mainly of people like 'Gus Eisman, the Button King', and 'Sam
. . . who is a famous playwright who writes very, very famous
plays'; although it is always open to the reader to feel that if any
educating is done, it is Lorelei who does it: 'When I came out of it,
it seems that I had a revolver in my hand and it seems that the
revolver had shot Mr Jennings.'[1]

Gentlemen Prefer Blondes is a splendidly sustained if unrepeatable
joke about being a woman in a world usually run by men like Gus
and Sam. And most of its peculiar force and flavour comes from the
brilliant invention of its personal style. This structure of complex
crudities, the 'Lorelei style', is a pure urban-pastoral medium of the
1920s, capable of seeming to sum up in its cadences – with a
limpidity that hung in the air for decades – the whole difficulty of
maintaining innocence at this late point in human history. Thus,
sentences like 'Fun is fun but no girl wants to laugh all of the time'
(the one which haunted Empson) or the more famous 'Kissing your
hand may make you feel very very good but a diamond and safire
bracelet lasts forever' manage to absorb into themselves the whole
dissolution of Victorian romanticism in the anarchistic unillusioned
1920s (even Lorelei's shoddy-Wagnerian name packs its own
specific punch). But this potent and suggestive stylistic device
hardly started, strictly speaking, with Anita Loos, whose invention
was largely dependent on an acknowledged master, a writer far
more serious and accomplished than herself. This was the journalist
and humorist, Ring Lardner. Though he himself no doubt learned
from predecessors in the American tradition (Mark Twain offers
himself as the obvious forebear in the mimetic vernacular line),
Lardner was enough of an original genius to have had a real place in
the beginnings of *Sweeney Agonistes*. He deserves a moment's
consideration on this ground; for he helps, I think, to give quite as
sure a sense of what the poem's real background is as does a mere
word like 'Aristophanic'.

Beyond the world of the Ph.D. student (if there) Lardner hardly
seems to be remembered now, certainly not in England. And yet
by 1926, the year of the publication of the first fragment in *The
Criterion*, Lardner had become one of the 'ten best-known men' in
America. And the year before, writing in *The Saturday Review of
Literature*, Virginia Woolf (unlikely as it may seem) spoke of this

---

[1] Quoted from the English edition, pp. 11, 48.

baseball commentator and comic journalist as writing 'the best prose that has come our way' – a fact which brings Lardner closer to Eliot's world. But Lardner was in fact born within that world. He came from an educated, sophisticated, and highly literate milieu not much unlike Eliot's own, though one that had lost all its money. He was the friend of Scott Fitzgerald, and is said to be portrayed in Abe North of *Tender is the Night*: Abe, 'who was desperate and witty', and 'his achievement, fragmentary, suggestive and surpassed' (Fitzgerald's very description of his work brings him a little closer to *Sweeney*). Grover Smith has postulated, in fact, that *The Great Gatsby* is an important source for *Sweeney Agonistes*, partly on the ground that Eliot is known to have written in admiration to its author when the novel appeared in 1925, partly because the novel contains a list of grotesque names and a comic telephone conversation. But Fitzgerald's romantic novel seems to me extremely unlike Eliot's savagely funny play-poem; Fitzgerald's names and telephone conversations are naturalistically or sociologically used, Eliot's are highly conventionalized and edged towards black farce. But the connexion is interesting on quite other grounds. It was Lardner who read the proofs of *The Great Gatsby* for Fitzgerald, correcting its writer's always shaky grammar and spelling as he went along; and Grover Smith may well be (or so I would suggest) unconsciously remarking the evidences of Lardner's influence on both Fitzgerald and Eliot. For it is Lardner who is the original inventor, both of preposterous American names ('Mr Kloot', 'Rube de Groot', 'Mrs Garrison', 'Mr and Mrs Glucose') far closer to Eliot's own, and also of play and story titles ('Some Like Them Cold', 'What Of It?', 'How to Write Short Stories') that mix the nonsensical and the self-undercuttingly vernacular in a manner very like *Wanna Go Home, Baby?*, and *Sweeney Agonistes*. More importantly, it is the now forgotten Lardner who made a whole literary generation suddenly aware of how to use ironic, self-exposing conventions of vernacular speech and habit, such as the telephone monologue: several of his most brilliant stories involve persons who betray their innocently detestable personalities in letter-writing. It is possible, in short, to trace back to Ring Lardner, but certainly not much further, a startling number of the most potent literary inventions of the 1920s and 1930s (Hemingway's intensely idiosyncratic style, for instance, is as much indebted to Lardner as to Gertrude Stein: Hemingway was highly impressed by

Lardner when young, though he angrily rejected his influence later). This one man, baseball reporter and short-story writer, seems personally responsible for a surprising number of the conventions of the whole sophisticated, melancholy, nonsensical, and racy humour that develops in America in the 1920s, and of which both the Marx Brothers (or their scriptwriters) and some of the best *New Yorker* writers of the period were products.

Lardner like Eliot worked with success in the theatre, and produced through the 1920s revue-sketches, playlets, and musical numbers against which it makes some sense to see *Sweeney Agonistes*. His 1925 volume, *What Of It?*, for instance, includes three brief (three-page) 'plays', all of them (unlike many other parodies of modernism) marked by real wit, humour, and poetry. After an opening procedure as lengthy as Eliot's introductory apparatus, *I Gaspiri* (or 'The Upholsterers') goes on:

. . . *Two strangers to each other meet on the bath mat*
FIRST STRANGER:
Where was you born?
SECOND STRANGER:
Out of wedlock.
FIRST STRANGER:
That's a mighty pretty country around there.
SECOND STRANGER:
Are you married?
FIRST STRANGER:
I don't know. There's a woman living with me, but I can't place her.

(pp. 45–46)

This nonsensicality is not uncharacteristic of Lardner. But all the same, his very best work is a good deal tougher; and it is to be found outside his writing for the theatre. Lardner began life as a baseball reporter, and never entirely lost his connexion with baseball; what he clearly did lose, though, was his early capacity for focusing a kind of personal idealism on the game, for finding in it a quality of inarticulate myth. As Virginia Woolf observed, games are vital to Lardner's art, and 'the game' became in his writing, as disillusionment set in, an image of what we have learned to call the 'rat-race'. Long before Laing, he became expert in 'the games people play', a bitter expertise paralleled if not reflected in what Eliot has learned to do in the card-reading, the dance routines, the lovebird talk, and the story-telling of *Sweeney Agonistes*. In terms of the 'games they play', Lardner moved outward from his baseball players to portray a whole mean and crooked and complacent, small-town-minded, success-obsessed and money-hunting culture: the America of the pre-Slump 1910s and 1920s as he came to see it. There is an immense detailed realism in Lardner's laconically comic writing. His 'reporting' brings alive a whole continent of tiny self-contained worlds, self-defining egos: crooks, baseball players, smalltime business men, haircutters, Hollywood executives, middle-aged housewives, and 'Thurber' husbands (Thurber was influenced by Lardner too). But the talent that achieves this breadth is both specific and peculiar. It was a highly formalized gift for verbal mimesis. Everything in Lardner is ironic monologue (such as the rejected opening of *The Waste Land* tried and failed to be): his characters come alive and address us off the page, unintroduced and uncommented on, in their own purely individual speech or lingo; but they exist only within severe limits of the self-preserving ego, and with a serene self-possession never remotely impaired by the frightful, though usually comic, insights that their sometimes pathetic self-revelations precipitate.

This painfully funny, melancholy and often lethal talent is in no way easy to exemplify. It depends on a flawless art, controlled through the whole story, and on the impressive variety of verbal types Lardner can handle. One characteristic story, 'My Roomy', may be worth mentioning, though; because it is just conceivable that Eliot read this anecdote of a baseball Coriolanus (whose name is, oddly enough, Elliott) when it first appeared in *The Saturday Review of Literature* during the summer of 1914, while the young graduate Eliot was working on his philosophy thesis at Harvard and taking boxing lessons in his spare time. He certainly dated back Sweeney's real-life source to around this time; if he read it (as he might have, given his interest at all periods in the demotic) it left an image in his mind, which at one moment emerged as 'Sweeney Erect' and at another became the grander, more haunted Sweeney 'in conflict', 'in the game'. Elliott, whose story is told by a hard-headed senior player, is a lonely, half-mad, and heroic innocent, winning huge baseball victories simply to earn the money to marry the girl he probably knows all the time is already married anyway and whom in the end he near-murders with a baseball bat, before being taken off to an asylum:

> Another o' his habits was the thing that scared 'em, though. He'd brought a razor with him – in his pocket, I guess – and he used to do his shavin' in the middle o' the night. Instead o' doin' it in the bathroom he'd lather his face and then come out and stand in front o' the lookin'-glass on the dresser. Of course he'd have all the lights turned on, and that was bad enough when a feller wanted to sleep; but the worst of it was that he'd stop shavin' every little while and turn round and stare at the guy who was makin' a failure o' tryin' to sleep. Then he'd wave his razor round in the air and laugh, and begin shavin' again. You can imagine how comf'table his roomies felt![1]

It was in this same magazine, *The Saturday Review of Literature*, that just over a decade later, in August 1925, Virginia Woolf published her essay on 'American Fiction' from which I have already quoted. She says there that what most deeply impresses her about Lardner's work is the absolute self-sufficiency which both the writer himself and his characters manifest. 'He is not merely himself intent on his own game, but his characters are equally intent on theirs . . . Mr Lardner is not merely unaware that we differ; he is unaware that we exist'. Virginia Woolf profoundly admires this (as she takes it) pure Americanism, this calm uninterestedness in the European. It is in this spirit that men like Lardner are, she concludes, creating a new literature:

> All the expressive ugly vigorous slang which creeps into use among us first in talk, later in writing, comes from across the Atlantic. Nor does it need much foresight to predict that when words are being made, a literature will be made out of them. Already we hear the first jars and dissonances, the strangled difficult music of the prelude. As we shut our books and look out again upon the English fields a strident note rings in our ears.[2]

It is, it seems to me, this 'note' of the American that we hear in *Sweeney Agonistes*: a specific and new music Eliot is half inventing and half learning for his own purposes. The quality in Lardner that

---

[1]Reprinted in *How to Write Short Stories* (1926), pp. 181–216 (p. 188).
[2]*Collected Essays*, 4 vols (1966) II, 121.

Virginia Woolf sensed unerringly is surely that which attracted Eliot even more strongly: for 'self-sufficiency' is the attribute a would-be dramatist most needs to endow his characters with, and yet one too that is most difficult for an inward poet to learn. It may even be Lardner's supreme possession of it that inclined the poet towards attempting drama in prose, and made him also try to think like the American journalist in terms of a very specific social milieu in *Sweeney Agonistes*. He had already, in the rightly-rejected introductory monologue of *The Waste Land* ('First we had a couple of feelers down at Tom's place'), found out how alluring but how difficult was the colloquial American style perfected by Mark Twain and by Ring Lardner. If in his 'jazz-age' poem Eliot came strikingly nearer to Lardner's subtle and brilliant demotic speech, something that combined the fragmentary sophisticated farce of *I Gaspiri* with the dry pathetic violence of 'My Roomy', then the reason may have been that the task suddenly became easier. Through Lardner's chief pupil, Anita Loos, Lorelei Lee's electric-drilling sweetly-lethal note ('Fun is fun but no girl wants to laugh all of the time') brought the vernacular style straight into the demotic urban present of Prohibition, and gangsters, and Broadway vaudeville; and so offered the poet (always in any case more interested in the metropolitan than the provincial) precisely the medium he needed. Eliot recognized – so we may conjecture – a transcription of Lardner's achievement simple enough to catch the ear and strong enough to be imitated; for a helpless infectiousness is of the essence of this style. Fired, amused, and perhaps even moved, the poet at last 'saw' his prose sketches in 'jazz-age' verse, a highly Eliotic verse but 'after' Lardner and Loos. Some such background is, it seems to me, necessary to explain the peculiar achievement of the style of *Sweeney Agonistes*.

I have dwelt on the medium of *Sweeney Agonistes* and its apparent satirical antecedents because in ignoring this stylistic medium criticism has neglected what is most vital to the work. Drama came to Eliot from the beginning not as a dramaturgy but as an identifying speech, the self-defining language of the isolated. In all his verse the poet is perhaps the greatest literary stylist of the modern period, his inventions and experiments in the verbal medium always cognate with what is deepest in his meaning. This is more than ever so in the first of the dramas, for *Sweeney Agonistes*

is a work that *listens*: 'I gotta use words when I talk to you.' Anyone
can quote this line from Eliot, a fact that makes us realize that
Sweeney Agonistes is one of the most commonly quoted, the most
rememberable of all the poet's works. Its harsh utterances are
somehow conjunct with the ironical and yet normative speech of the
mind: it says what we need to say. Its way-out elements, from the
Choephoroi to Doris, seem to cancel each other out, to reduce each
other down to a fantastic metaphor for normalcy. In the process, the
limits of an impoverished speech act for Eliot, rather as Lardner's
'games' did for him, as an aesthetic discipline; a narrow vocabulary
in constant repetition moves towards an expressive music:

> There's an awful lot in the way you feel
> Sometimes they'll tell you nothing at all
> You've got to know what you want to ask them
> You've got to know what you want to know . . .
>
> I've been born, and once is enough.
> You don't remember, but I remember,
> Once is enough.

Sweeney Agonistes comes to have this effect because the work is
the first in Eliot's career which puts into the simplest practice that
principle of humility expressed morally in *Four Quartets*. Its
universe is a world of sound in which people share a single speech
style ('I gotta use words') which scarcely even distinguishes them
from the inanimate. The girls 'speak', but so does a telephone: *Ting
a ling ling, / Ting a ling ling*; the door says KNOCK KNOCK
KNOCK just like Wauchope and Co., the cards have a story to tell,
as Sweeney does. In 'A Game of Chess', rich woman and poor
were equal in the intensity of their egoism; *Sweeney Agonistes* goes
further and envisages the world (almost as in the Elizabethan
Orchestra) as one uttering and dancing and suffering comic
movement, a medium of universal even if degraded speech:

> We're all hearts. You can't be sure . . .
> What comes next? . . . What comes next . . .
> You cut for luck. You cut for luck.
> It might break the spell. You cut for luck.

The eloquence of *The Waste Land* lies in the way it turns fragments of
broken civilizations into metaphors of feeling. *Sweeney Agonistes*

goes in a direction almost opposite, and makes metaphors out of the *un*civilized. Its author has fallen in love with the expressive power of inarticulacy, with a brute and vulgar lingo of incommunication in which Tooting and Brooklyn meet and mix. Trashy phrases in the poem linger in the mind with a weight that is ironical, but that goes beyond irony into the dramatic; beyond the 'purposive', one might say, into the truly aesthetic: 'We're all hearts. You can't be sure.' The academic critic who demotes or disregards the 'farcical music-hall style', the 'improper vehicle for [a] serious theme', is neglecting plain aesthetic fact. For the two girls' agitated interest in the playing-cards (like the reader, they believe that they exist enough to have a fate) and Sweeney's painfully heavy-breathing and struggling anxiety become equally an expression of an almost vatic utterance freed from pretension or pomposity. Such characters are found a diction, an East Side or East End guttural half invented by the erudite and talented in two continents, that by its taciturn, even Tacitean, omissions achieves wit, even profundity, even a form of necessity. If Eliot did not 'finish' his play it is because he did not need to; it was completed when Sweeney and Doris were found a speech.

For the language of the play itself implies that action sought for in 'plot'. By its omissions and implications, by virtue of what is not quite said, it can imply whole dimensions of human relationship. This is an aspect of Eliot's art more explored by later writers like Beckett or (at a lower level) by Pinter; but in *Sweeney Agonistes* the potentialities are present. Thus, though the two fragments do not have a plot, they gesture towards a dramatic situation by the very nature of their duality, the one against the other. The first is given to Doris's and Dusty's party, the second to Sweeney's apprehension of aloneness. Together they suggest that Sweeney, who has fallen in love with Doris, tries to draw her away from her unindividuated role within the party, her degradedly social existence, to make her a person: to make her help him understand aloneness so they can be together. This implicit dramatic situation, which is perceived simply through 'the way they talk', is reflected in the repetition of two threadbare but enigmatically touching lines, Doris's miserable and silly 'A woman runs a terrible risk' answered by Snow's patient 'Let Mr Sweeney continue his story'. The two lines match, like an unrhymed couplet in bathetic heroic verse; and the situations rhyme too, Doris's second-rate company-seeking fear and dreariness silenced by Sweeney's dogged attempt to understand and hold by such truth as lies to hand. Or this situation will reverse itself: Sweeney's in any case sensational and melodramatic insights take on an essential weakness in the terrible tough absolute presence of Doris ('I'd be bored . . . I'd be bored'). And this failure, under her eyes, like an elephant's before a mouse, comes through the diminuendo of the ironic and pastiche pop-songs of love and death that dissolve into the mechanism of her unvarying negation:

> I don't like eggs; I never liked eggs . . .
> That's not life, that's no life.

There is an important difference between the characters of Sweeney and Doris in this work and those in 'Sweeney Among the Nightingales'. The earlier poem presents its persons with a flat contempt and disgust. But the personages of these fragments, within their curiously universalizing wild rhythms for which the cant term 'swinging' is totally appropriate though not yet invented in that sense – these persons are more like the characters in Eliot's cat poems; they may not be amiable but there is something to be said for them. When Doris here states flatly 'I'd be bored', it is not absolutely clear that there is no virtue in her point of view (as in Dusty's answer to the men's avowal that they 'like London fine': 'Why don't you come and live here then?'). We are, however obscurely, for the moment ready to concede that each has something to say. Eliot has in short achieved the self-sufficient embodiment of drama. Writing much later in life, he glanced back at his own *The Family Reunion* and remarked provocatively that the characters for whom he now felt sympathy were Amy and the chauffeur. The remark shows how much, when he achieved an actual embodying language, it could leave his persons free to alter despite his purpose, or what at least such things as plot–drafts induce us to call his purpose. The terrible Doris and Dusty are clearly meant to illustrate, morally and satirically, the human inability to be alone, which is 'to be' – and they do; but at the same time the force of what they say puts life into them. Doris's decisive 'I'd be bored' to Sweeney's fierce vision of existence has a kind of authorial amusement inside it: her touching idiocy is sometimes, out of mere self-interest, on the verge of being good sense. Similarly, her sombre 'I'd like to know about that coffin' hovers between the farcical and the troublingly sane, since despite all her self-important superstition she is right in her assumption that coffins are a question demanding sooner or later to be gone into.

Particularly in its relation of Sweeney and the girls the whole of the work has this intense humour that fades into pathos, and a final vision hesitating between farce and pain, with an effect of odd aesthetic beauty deriving from the exactness of their balance. The good-time girls in their rented flat sit waiting for 'gentlemen friends' whose apotheosis is Sweeney: hunted, haunted, brutish and out of touch, intersected by alarming and even nonsensical glimpses of love and death which he can neither wholly possess nor be possessed by, there is not much 'fun' for them here. None the less, the situation is in its poise dramatic. And it is made so by the discovery of a medium that embodies the speaking self by isolating it. The essential quality of the people in *Sweeney Agonistes* is that they are free-standing, unlike the figures of *The Waste Land*, who are always contained within the moral criterion of the presenter, Tiresias. The people in *Sweeney Agonistes* are what they are, despite all the diminution that the purpose of the play seems to impose upon them:

> He didn't know if he was alive
> and the girl was dead
> He didn't know if the girl was alive
> and he was dead
> He didn't know if they were both alive
> or both were dead . . .

It is striking that Sweeney's one action is to try to tell a story. Eliot's plays do maintain a real if ambiguous relation to story: the mind that created them clearly loved stories, but in process what it most seems to love is untelling them, turning them on their head or inside out, as *Four Quartets* does with chronology. Thus, Sweeney defends his own stasis:

> What did he do! What did he do?
> That don't apply.

In *The Cocktail Party*, which opens after the end of a 'story' that may have been well worth hearing but whose point is that 'there *were* no tigers', Julia takes this up with what Eliot may have seen as specifically female perspicuity, not unlike Doris's and Dusty's:

> Then what were you doing, up in a tree,
> You and the Maharajah?

Sweeney and Doris are clearly up in the same gum-tree, illogically planted in an action in which

> Nobody came
> And nobody went

and for which, consequently, there is no plot. But self-evidently something is (as we say) 'going on', something interpretable variously, perhaps a crime or perhaps just a metaphor. But at whatever level we choose to interpret these goings-on, they possess a *style*: the means by which we recognize that what is before us is not *The Cocktail Party* but *Sweeney Agonistes*.

It is for this reason that I have chosen to talk about Eliot's play, not as involving its Christian–classical context, not even as a 'game of moral philosophy' (relevant as these matters certainly are), but in terms of Eliot's capacity to learn from other writers very different in their ends how flexible, how sophisticated, and even at moments how deep a medium the tragi-comic vernacular could be. In the hands of its best exponents this demotic medium could do almost anything – anything except reach that poetic absoluteness of utterance that Eliot had to look elsewhere to find (primarily, in my view, in French Symbolist literature). To turn back to Lardner's stories from *Sweeney Agonistes* is to understand why Lardner himself, intelligent and aesthetic as he was, always condemned himself as a total failure. For his narrow, bitter, and accurate reports on experience are a journalist's triumph, but as works of art they are severely limited. Eliot took the style and used it to explore and embody states of mind considerably more inward and (if one wants) metaphysical:

> If he was alive then the milkman wasn't
> and the rent-collector wasn't
> And if they were alive then he was dead.

The effect of this borrowed style is certainly to give to *Sweeney Agonistes* that effect of limitation, even of sterility, which irritates many of its academic critics, who would compare it to its loss with the major poem it follows: the richly eloquent *Waste Land*. But it is precisely this diminishment which is the writer's first decisive step towards dramatic focus and precision. Moreover, the work's final quality is one that is dependent on this very limitation. An inarticulate medium – used as metaphor, and with flaws, dissonances, changes of key within its conventions – generates an odd, dreamy, pathetic, and comic detachment, as of a removed diffused tenderness, which extends and blurs the harshness of the 'story's' outlines. This is a quality summed up in the title Eliot invented for use elsewhere, 'Doris's Dream Songs'; neither Lardner's nor Anita Loos's characters really have the capacity to dream. Through these two fragments of drama by Eliot, injected in them perhaps by the dislocations of their given titles and sub-titles, the assonance between the epigraphs and what follows, there moves an irrational power of reverie: so that the swirling repetitions of the converse seem not merely the resource of empty mindlessness, but the probing hesitancies of uncertain thought; and brute platitude turns into a feeling for the basic such as no mere brute could articulate – rather, the feeling for 'the bottom' that a drowning man might helplessly engage in:

> . . . it might be you
> > Or it might be you
> We're all hearts. You can't be sure.
> It just depends on what comes next . . .
>
> I've been born, and once is enough . . .
>
> I tell you again it don't apply
> Death or life or life or death . . .
> KNOCK KNOCK KNOCK

In the French classical theatre the play starts with three knocks. Sweeney's fragment ends with a beginning, an awakening from the dream of the play. Until that moment, a girl runs a terrible risk; but let Mr Sweeney continue his story.

9

Auden Askew

There is an academic myth (vaguely Victorian in feeling but probably like most Victorian principles dating back a half-century earlier) that scholars study facts whereas critics make it all up out of their own heads. It afflicts English studies as it does most others, and had a recent airing in John Carey's inaugural lecture at Oxford which proposed that scholars handle texts whereas critics only vandalize them by reading them. This double and triple illusion usefully affords occasion for simple restatements: that, for instance, to read at all is in itself a creative and interpretative act, an evidence of mind which it dignifies human beings to perform; that scholars and critics alike read inventively, to some extent knowing what they are looking for and to some extent finding it; that there is no such thing as a 'text', and if there were it would degrade literature to be treated as it – and there was probably no such thing as a fact, either, until some human being invented it. The only difference is that some people are much better readers than others, whether of books or of reality, better in the sense of 'truer', more accurate and more revealing: and may well be helped to be so by being rid of the illusion that as 'scholars' they have some easy advantaged road to the truth.

This myth of scholarship seems extra liable to crop up where the lives of poets are concerned, and not necessarily because (or not only because) the biographer may suffer from its illusions, but because the very concept of the 'life' of a poet seems unavoidably to entail them, and the writing of the life to foster and promote them. It is partly that biographers are a species of historian, and historians are still – or so it appears – likely to console themselves with the thought that they are primary servants of Fact, and therefore engaged with truth. But also poets do seem to be exceptionally difficult subjects, because both they and many of the people they move among may well prove more expert – because more professional – realists of the imaginative life than even the biographer himself. A man who, to put it simply, has made a very great success in public of being a poet in private may, while retaining a capacity for the most scrupulous personal honesty, at the same time make it remarkably difficult to define what is, or is not, a 'fact' of his 'life'. If both Eliot and Auden, to name only two, showed a strong disinclination to have their lives written, the reason may not have been that they had secrets to hide or disliked public discussion of their work, so much as that they recognized that the biographer is, like the critic, as much a writer as themselves, and as writer a rival and competitor: one whose treatment or re-treatment of the poet's own materials of experience might prove considerably less expert than the poet's own, while also because of the nature of the market more likely to last. Moreover the poet will probably start with the handicap of being dead.

Humphrey Carpenter's excellent life of Auden has a nice turn of phrase in recounting the moment when Stephen Spender, arrived in an Oxford of the later 1920s which was pervaded by the legend of Auden, at last met his fellow-undergraduate and 'found the reality just as remarkable as that legend'. The story appears to have emanated from Spender, himself equipped with a vigorously romantic imagination and to that degree already much acquainted with legends; and it helps to show how much Carpenter's splendidly documented and always enjoyably told nearly five hundred-page life of Auden poses the problems of telling a life in which legends and reality were already peculiarly interfused. Nor is this an oblique way of impugning the biographer's accuracy. Carpenter seems thoroughly well documented; as well as having been able to rely as fully upon a wide circle of the poet's friends and acquaintances as if this were (as it is not) an official biography, Carpenter has evidently depended on or even worked fairly closely with Edward Mendelson, perhaps Auden's 'scholar-in-chief', his literary executor and the editor who worked directly according to his wishes. And yet legends afflict Mendelson's work as well. After his edition of the *Collected Poems*, which retains Auden's own order and chronology, Mendelson edited *The English Auden*, which offered most of the poet's pre-1939 work in its first published, unrevised form for those who (unlike the editor) preferred their

Auden neat; and in the useful scholarly Preface to that edition
Mendelson briefly referred to the period in the mid-1930s when
Auden worked with the GPO Film Unit, adding humorously that
'his colleagues may have hesitated to give him [great] responsibil-
ity: when he directed a brief shot of a railway guard, the guard
dropped dead a minute later'. Without mentioning Mendelson
Carpenter quietly corrects this in an illuminating footnote:

> According to Auden, 'We got a shot of a guard at Crewe, and he
> dropped dead about thirty seconds later'. This made a good
> story, but the truth, according to [Basil] Wright, is that the man
> was not a guard but a senior railway official, and it was not until
> some weeks later that he died.

The difficulties can be measured by saying that such scholars as
Carpenter in his new Life, and Mendelson himself in his recent
valuable study of the *Early Auden* – a critical essay devoted to the
period covered by *The English Auden* – are themselves good story
tellers, both the biography and the critical study being in their
different ways expert performances, the first highly readable, the
second formally elegant; and they are both involved with a person
or persons for whom the interaction of 'legend' and 'reality' was to
some large extent the stuff of human existence. Indeed, Mendel-
son's very theme is that interaction, and his book is highly
thematic, interpreting Auden's lived intellectual progress in terms
of the suggestive symbols thrown out by the poet's own work.
Thus, in a characteristic couple of sentences from Mendelson:

> Auden's maps were real, but he kept them tightly folded. Auden
> was training himself in a topography of the actual, but for the
> moment his landscape forbade him to participate in it . . .

There are moments when a reader can hardly help wondering
whether it can conceivably be safe or decorous to place such stress
on symbols derived from a poet whose chief doctrinal teaching
concerned the untrustworthiness of such poetic usages. Auden
himself, a great Lewis Carroll fan, would possibly have said that
Mendelson gets away with it by paying the images extra; and the
prose does have at moments a slightly expensive quality.
    Carpenter tends to run into the opposite problem: not so much
of overvaluing symbols as of underestimating the potency of their
makers. There are some splendid stories in his first two hundred

pages particularly, whose charm derives in part from their being presented as biographer's facts, from their cool randomness of occurrence: but it is again hard to believe that the 'facts' have not already been transmuted by letter and anecdote, that the odd black poetry of Auden's Thirties existence didn't take some of this quality from its being made so by its participants, who were after all some of the best writers of the period. It may not be easy to gauge the documents of an age that invented such brilliant documentaries, or whose novelists pretended to be a camera. Take one of Carpenter's best stories, Auden's marriage and more particularly its immediate aftermath. Thoman Mann's daughter Erika – who though once-married was not very likely to marry again – was a cabaret artiste whose heroically anti-Nazi material had lost her her German passport, and who therefore approached the nearest Englishman, Christopher Isherwood, and proposed that he should provide her with a substitute by marrying her. Isherwood backing down, Auden – who all his life seems to have retained and exercised his own very special form of gentle-manliness – had the buck passed on to him and accepted it with alacrity. Very soon after, his new wife's ex-colleague, a very large and formidable lady equally unconjugal in temperament, found herself in the same quandary, so Auden (exclaiming 'What else are buggers for?' in a perhaps only slightly complex tone) produced like a rabbit out of a hat a friend of E. M. Forster's, who happened to be slight in physical build, though surely large in moral stature. Carpenter describes the ceremony in cool flat prose, the huge bride and tiny groom, the splendid bouquet and the amazed registrar, and Auden buying everyone large brandies in a pub

> declaring 'It's on Thomas Mann'. He would have played the pub's piano to add some jollity to the occasion, but the instrument proved to be locked, and when R. D. Smith asked for the key he was told that the pub's landlord had just died and had been laid out on the billiard table in the bar next door . . .

It would be folly to challenge so capable an Auden scholar as Carpenter on the factual truth of this story, nor would one want to. But Carpenter begins his biography by stating flatly that it is *not* to be a work of literary criticism. It is clear that to him the life comes first: and yet he may be treating as 'life' what is already half literature, and therefore demands a different kind of reckoning. I suspect myself that in a life of a writer some literary criticism is unavoidable; and that this story of the second wedding – to take only one casual example in well over four hundred pages – is simply a little too good to be true, too shapely, too Thirties, too sour-sweet and sadly farcical. Its mocking image of Auden derives, one would have thought, in part from Auden himself and in part from the two witnesses at the marriage, R. D. Smith (later a distinguished BBC producer of drama and already clearly with a good eye for it) and Louis MacNeice, whose impassive fantastic wit lights up every one of the handful of pages on which he appears. It is MacNeice who remarks of his fellow-poet on their trip to Iceland together that 'everything he touches turns to cigarettes', and that Auden in his special Iceland gear of seven or eight layers of clothing looked amphibian – 'When he walks he moves like something that is more at home in the water.' In fact, this talent for deadpan farce in the protagonists may surely have affected another of Carpenter's calm factual accounts, the trip to Iceland itself, where Auden, MacNeice and a friend of Auden's slept

> the night at Reykjavik lunatic asylum as guests of the doctor in charge – who talked to them in Latin . . . [Later], Auden, MacNeice and Yates slept at the Salvation Army hostel, into which they managed to smuggle a bottle of Spanish brandy obtained from the British vice-consul . . .

In both these cases there is no question of suggesting that the accounts are untrue. It is merely worth pointing out that the very reason why they help to contribute to so enjoyable a biography is that they contain problematic dimensions within themselves: they are already to some extent literature, events and accounts already formed and worked upon interpretatively by their earlier recorders. They add to Carpenter's life an element of legend perhaps not sufficiently taken stock of. And what is true in a small way of these localized passages proves true also of the whole of these otherwise admirable and scholarly books. In the amassment, sorting and presentation of data relevant to Auden's work and life Carpenter's *W. H. Auden: A Biography* and Mendelson's critical study of *Early Auden* take their place at the centre of Auden studies, particularly when considered within that large-scale process of systematic tidying-up which has developed in the eight years since the poet died. They are both highly informative and dependable in that whole area of Auden's career that involves external relationships on which facts can be provided. Carpenter is excellent on the complicated genesis and evolution of such collaborative works as *The Dog Beneath the Skin*, and on the previous plays which survive digested within it; Mendelson offers some fascinating information about the poet's debts and sources, as for instance the phrases from a topographical description of England which can be made out clearly in the beautiful Chorus, 'The Summer holds . . .', from that same play. But at the same time, while he appreciates the virtues of these two informative studies, a reader may well finish them instructed but also aware that the biography and the critical essay are alike interpretative, an image of Auden that is not and cannot be complete and objective; and this is all the more true, the more both books follow a kind of ideal of impersonal high-powered scholarship – because it is this very un-self-questioning trust in 'impersonality' that proves most self-limiting, least flexible in practice. Perhaps no scholarly essay is safely embarked on without some belief in the indeterminacy principle, or the fact that a recorder by recording invariably alters what he sees.

One simple example may serve to show the way in which an innocent scholarly method may accidentally distort, or at any rate silently condition, readers' assumptions about the writer so dealt with. There are certain presuppositions which these two books share, and which can therefore be regarded as an incipiently 'established' and consequently powerful image of the poet in question; and one of the most important is reflected in the *form* of both books. Neither makes particular display of having a form, and both therefore escape the imputation to which they would be liable as works of art (rather than works of scholarship), that of having specific limits – of being coloured and conditioned in a certain way or towards a certain kind of meaning. None the less each does have a form, and in essence it is the same form, the more potent as it is more tacit.

Mendelson's critical study, *Early Auden*, covers precisely the area of his *English Auden*: that is to say, it takes us up to that moment early in 1939 when the poet left England for America. The bipartite division which dictated the structure of *The English Auden* (and will presumably dictate a volume on 'Later Auden') may be assumed to be partly prompted by Auden's own division of his poems into groups for his 1966 *Collected Poems*. In the two previous collected

editions of 1945 and 1950 Auden had of course arranged his verse in
achronological sequence, listing them only in the alphabetical order
of first-line initials; but for the 1966 volume Auden arranged his
poems in more or less chronological sequence, making breaks,
moreover, at what he called 'each new chapter of my life': 1932,
1938, 1947 and 1957 (where he terminated). It seems to make a
distinct psychological difference that this is therefore a 'retrospec-
tive' rather than truly collective volume: its author–editor, being
still alive and writing – and indeed under sixty at the time, with a
conceivable quarter-century of writing still ahead of him – could be
presumed free to rethink these patterns again, producing ideas as
different again as these were from the 1945 and 1950 sequences. It is
at all events a very different matter when a posthumous editor and
critic offers a volume as self-contained as *The English Auden*. This
most certainly implies no criticism of that beautifully edited and
presented volume: but its very excellence, taken together with
Early Auden, gives the two books together a potent force of
imposition not easy now to elude.

   This potency is made far greater by the substance of *Early Auden*.
Mendelson's essay has that sophisticated self-awareness, that self-
autonomy, characteristic of much recent American criticism. It
makes of the disjunction in Auden's career at the end of the decade,
not merely an accident but a means, and not merely a means but an
end: it internalizes it into the form of decision. Mendelson's
account of what constituted Auden's career is exceedingly shaped
and shapely, it is both purposive and – one would say if the word
were not so tendentious – tendentious: it tells intently and
insistently the story of how Auden came to decide, in seeking
steadily for some means of overcoming his own profound
isolation, that he must at last leave his 'island', England. And this
thesis the critic converts into an historical psychodrama making
consistent use of the poet's own images and symbols, and framing
each chapter into a microcosm of the whole, which in its turn
utilizes the profoundly Audenesque concept of Journey or Quest
across a territory at once inward and outward – thus: 'When the
vision faded Auden again found himself on the frontier . . .' And:
'The young poet-healer who made England his schoolroom . . .
had retired to give some new thought to the curriculum.'

   The effect of this self-defining, expressive if tacit pattern is to
give enormous importance to the imputed division in Auden's

career, and moreover to introvert that event into the poet's will and consciousness, as though the move to America were not only the most important thing that happened to him but as though it were important precisely because in some form it expressed his deepest wishes. And it is a striking fact that this same pattern is given an equivalent significance by Carpenter. In his Preface Carpenter modestly and amiably defends himself against Auden's proscription of biography, making it his apologia that he thinks of the poet as a 'man of action'. How he describes those actions, therefore, is a matter of some weight, particularly since most of his readers cannot help reading the life in order to see what light it throws on the poems: since Carpenter would hardly be writing the life if Auden had not distinguished himself as a poet. The single most immediately perceptible factor in the biography is its division into two rather more than half way through. Of this 450-page biography, the first section is entitled 'England', the second 'America – and Europe'. The first slightly longer section comes to a resounding close on page 249, with the boat train bearing off Auden and Isherwood, leaving E. M. Forster and a friend of Isherwood's waving on the platform:

'Well,' said Isherwood, 'we're off again'. 'Goody,' said Auden.

There we finish until, after blank pages to mark the crossing (rather as in *The Winter's Tale* or *To the Lighthouse*), we start again with Part II on page 253, accompanying the two poets into New York under heavily falling snow, and with the news announced that Barcelona has fallen at last – that the Republican cause is in effect defeated, and war therefore now unavoidable.

It is difficult to gauge from the rest of the Life whether the biographer really intended the full force of this boat-burning climax, which does tend to make of Auden and Isherwood not merely deserters but conscious deserters, abandoning their country in the full knowledge of coming war (other of Carpenter's references seem to suggest that Auden, who had a strong moral but fallible political sense, thought the war would not take place). If Carpenter had been that other kind of 'historian of fine consciences', the novelist, his intention at this point would be plainer. But later in his Life it is possible to feel very uncertain as to whether he can be aware of what is implicit in his own shaping of materials. From a larger point of view, this division into two encourages the

sense of how thin both Auden's active and creative life became once
he had moved to America. For Carpenter breaks at page 249, and of
these first pages some 70 are given to childhood and adolescence,
and then a whole 170 to Auden's first ten or twelve years as a
writer. The second section of the Life covers Auden's later thirty-
four writing years, and yet is given only 200 pages. Carpenter
himself explains that after the 1950s poetry did not play the 'central
and vital part' in Auden's life that it did during the 1920s and 1930s,
but was rather 'a series of footnotes to his life'. If those thirty-four
years of life have deserved only 200 pages, and the poetry is only a
'series of footnotes' to them, the poems must be thin indeed. And
yet in the closing paragraphs of his life Carpenter rebukes those (by
implication) 'less perceptive' critics who see in Auden's career a
decline. That decline Carpenter has himself figured for us. For if
poetry is *not* the most important thing in Auden's life, it is hard to
see why Carpenter should have given so large a section of his
biography to the poet's first most creative decade, granted that in
the next 'action'-packed thirty-four years the poetry has dwindled
to a 'series of footnotes'. If poetry *is* the most important thing in
Auden's life, it is hard to see why it is so wrong to impute some
degree of decline (in any case a natural human factor) to those long
later years, for which even the biographer can spare less than half
his space.

If there is confusion here, it derives perhaps from some central
uncertainty in the book as to what it is a biographer of a poet is
actually writing about – what constitutes the 'life'. What remains
clear is that Carpenter shares Mendelson's premise that Auden's life
and career and poetry divide into two distinct sections, the
'English' and the 'American', the 'early' and the 'late', the
'attractive' or 'exciting' and the 'honest' or 'true' – for these are the
moral categories in which Carpenter describes the posited change
in Auden's style. It must be said that all these divisions only follow
very obvious categorizing tendencies in Auden himself, whose
thought patterns make him one of the most dualistic poets who has
ever written; and that in this shaping of the poet's life as in so much
of the externally informative in what they offer, both biographer
and critic are acting in some accord with Auden's work. Similarly
this division of Auden's life into these two sections makes *some*
perfectly good sense at the literal or historical level, in that Auden
did leave England shortly before war was declared, and showed no

signs whatever of wanting or intending to return in the course of the war, unlike (say) Britten and Pears, who did so return after some three years in America: and it is an important fact, since it surely had immeasurable results, not limited to the simple dislike and disapproval lastingly felt by many who stayed on in a small and impoverished country that was to defend civilization more or less on its own until the third year of the war.

For Auden to leave England at that time had a kind of terrible gracelessness from which the poet's reputation has never really recovered. (It is suggestive that both these volumes have at moments a certain defensiveness which is perhaps their least pleasing quality: it rises at times to a sort of Anxiety of Establishment, a closing back-to-back to fight off any alien low interloping criticism of the poet, which surely Auden himself – who hated Maestrodom – would not at all have cared for.) At all events, it is reasonable for Carpenter to devote careful and lengthy consideration to this much-discussed action. Not finding a single motive for it, he impartially lists a number of motives proposed both by Auden himself and by friends and acquaintances, and leaves the reader to decide or let the issue stand as it does. And yet this gesture on Carpenter's part is not quite as impartial as it seems, for it excludes one possibility: and it is precisely that possibility which it may be most important to allow for, in considering Auden's work. 'Significance' may lie in effect or in cause, and they are not the same thing. What neither Carpenter nor Mendelson leaves quite enough room for is the possibility that Auden (who at the end of his life wore dark glasses, 'for no apparent reason' as Carpenter says, but perhaps to ward off the sight of things) decided nothing at all, or simply did not know why he acted as he did: that in the general pattern of his life the crossing of the Atlantic was a significant non-event. Poe's famous story of the Purloined Letter tells of an object that was 'hidden' only by being exposed beyond certain habitual expectations: Auden's departure may be an event that in the same way does not demand the search for hidden motives. Both Carpenter and Mendelson are at least conceivably hindered by a wrong hypothesis concerning 'action'. The right question is not 'Why exactly did Auden leave England?', but 'When did Auden ever stay anywhere for long?' The poet was clearly possessed by that restlessness of the depressive temperament which Dr Johnson once summed up in an ashamed letter to Boswell:

I was glad to go abroad, and, perhaps, glad to come home; which
is, in other words, I was, I am afraid, weary of being at home,
and weary of being abroad. Is not this the state of life?

Certainly Auden wrote in a comparable letter in 1939, 'I never
wish to see England again', but he unsaid it later. His relationship
with places was clearly the same as that with the people around
him, which Carpenter's documentation throws so much light on
in the Life. Auden approaches everyone with real and great and
even innocent warmth ('I can't tell you what a pleasure it is to
collaborate with you', 'one of the greatest men I've ever met',
'really extremely nice'; he seems rarely out of love; even the mar-
riage to Erika Mann he took very seriously, 'swiftly came to
admire her', tried to maintain relations). And yet, as Spender
narrates, friendships broke down, people drifted away, Auden
'ended rather isolated'. The poet seems to have turned to the idea
of each new place with delight, and yet his life there became so
depressing despite all his attempts that he could rarely, it appears,
stand more than a decade in any one place: or perhaps it could not
stand him. In 1948, after nine years of to-ing and fro-ing within
America and between America and Europe, he began to rent his
house in Ischia and half settled in there; in 1958 he left Ischia
('Never never will I go back there again') and purchased his
much-loved house in Kirchstetten, Austria; in 1972 he sold his
flat in New York, where he had always maintained a foothold,
and returned to Oxford, which he evidently saw as a place to die
happily in – though he was not, in fact, happy there, and died a
year later in a hotel in Vienna. Carpenter narrates all these changes
with great lucidity, and Mendelson, too, brings out the fact that
even the 'early Auden' was really at home nowhere, much though
he longed for a home, but existed always 'on the frontier'. Thus,
though when Auden after a few months in America used in a
public statement the phrase 'We in England', Carpenter calls it
'surprising in the circumstances', a re-definition of the circum-
stances would not find it surprising. Auden always in some sense
stayed at home: a friend he met after his translation to America,
James Stern, later described him as 'the most unalterably English,
the most unlikely expatriate', and Nicholas Nabokov similarly
spoke with affection of Auden's 'clumsy laughter, his assertive
way of telling not quite exportable (English parsondom's) jokes'.

The poet himself, when asked about his nationality, would say: 'I'm a New Yorker.'

Both Carpenter and Mendelson allow their (perhaps not entirely conscious) imposition of form to be conditioned by their silent interpretation of Auden's whole life, in which they see this one action, the crossing from England to America, as a wholly significant factor. If it was significant, it certainly needs to be seen clearly: for evidently much depended on it then and much depends now on the interpretation of it. But to see it clearly need not be to see it as important in the fabric of Auden's real life, and any importance it has need not be the importance of decision. Mendelson quotes a journal entry made by Auden during the early 1930s and concerned with Freud, which says: 'the real "life-wish" is the desire for separation.' And the critic himself charts out the conflicts of this 'life-wish' with splendid fullness and interest. It drove Auden, by a series of mixed impulses and half-awarenesses, half-decisions, into a departure from his country after a decade's serious and in some sense impassioned identification with it. Of the possible ways of looking at this event, in Auden's case that of 'motive' seems least fruitful. Since the poet seems to have believed, like many other people in England at that time, that war was not going to take place, the most striking aspect of the event is the bad luck of its bad timing, which left Auden framed for ever afterwards in an imputation of cowardice and disloyalty. And yet bad timing and bad luck are not, as it happens, wholly external factors: 'accident' is not random when we talk of the accident-prone. Auden is surely a person who seems to attract the words 'lucky' and 'unlucky' about his fortunes, even as they are certainly important in his poetry; and they perhaps reflect a certain quality of the out-of-control about this clever and talented man. In the wealth of personal reminiscence that has appeared since the poet's death (Osborne's biography as well as Carpenter's, Spender's collection of salutes from friends and acquaintances) there are frequent recollections of Auden's peculiar physical clumsiness. Nicholas Nabokov's striking phrase extends this to the poet's 'clumsy laughter', and perhaps one ought to extend it even further, and see a kind of large generic clumsiness in the whole conduct of Auden's life, a helpless gracelessness or unluck that often spoiled what he intended. It was bad luck (one might say) that war came so soon, unreckoned on; bad luck that no sooner had Auden reached America than he fell wildly in love with what appeared to be the first wholly reciprocating person he had ever met, an action that certainly made any intentions of return that he might have formed go for nothing. But the feeling for Kallman was perhaps a more essential, a more characteristic gesture, on Auden's part, than any sheerly rational decision to change continents could have been. For love, like Auden's affiliation to 'luck' and 'unluck', went with everything in his life that was irrational, out of his control. All the symbols of decision in Auden's poetry, and all his proclamations of the importance of choice, have the excitement and beauty of the things which it is not natural for us in ordinary life to achieve.

The division of Auden's career into two halves which in Carpenter and Mendelson is near to becoming 'authoritative' or 'established' is regrettable not simply because it places extreme emphasis on this one action of Auden's. If the event may have been to some degree a non-event, the action an inaction, then the emphasis serves to conceal both this fact and the corresponding importance of that species of non-event or inaction in Auden's actual writing. In making the life seem different from what it may have been, it distorts the sense of the work. This is merely a matter of stress, and one would not want to ignore the amount of ordinary good sense in this more conventional account of the poet's life and actions. It does all the same neglect qualities which to my mind become extremely important in the poetry, however much overlooked or underestimated they are there. Isherwood once described Auden's poems as 'like rabbits produced from a hat – they couldn't be talked about before they appeared'. This element of profound irrationality, a kind of creative inaction, is something which Auden's own descriptions of the writing process lay much stress on, (and which appears perhaps in the poems in the strong affection for animals, all the 'ears' that 'poise before decision, scenting danger') but which critical accounts of his work rarely pay much attention to. It must be presumed that this is one of the losses which has accompanied gains on other fronts in our approach to the arts during the last century. Moving away from the Victorian notion of poetry as 'magic', we have learned to respect the intelligence of poets: unfortunately we seem also to have unlearned how to recognize intelligence.

Mendelson's persuasive, well-supported and self-consistent thesis gains its strength and coherence largely from the degree to which it 'rationalizes' Auden – converts the act of making in him into a peculiarly willed and deliberative process, marked out at every stage by a system of *choice*. And it is the critic's very respect for his subject that urges him to write in this way: he sees Auden as that respect-worthy object, an out-and-out all-round top-level success, who

> became the most inclusive poet of the twentieth century, its most technically skilled, and its most truthful . . .

a man who, in Mendelson's eyes, achieved his whole career as would a general his most famous campaign, one who

> rejecting the romantic premise that individual vision is the true source of poetry, willingly submerged his personality in colla-boration with others.

And Mendelson finds that beautiful, lazy and ardent poem 'A Summer Night' an action like Caesar's crossing of the Rubicon:

> a prodigious step, made in opposition to the reigning assump-tions of almost two centuries of philosophy, psychology and art.

There is a real sense in which these statements are probably true (although it is interesting that Auden himself found Brecht, the literary figure with whom Mendelson links and compares him, 'a horrible man'). It is when the critic gets nearer to the actual writing process that he helps one to define the sense in which something has none the less gone wrong here:

> The unstable tone is one of the barriers Auden uses to isolate himself from his readers, or at least to keep his relation with them radically problematic . . .
> Auden in his early poems treats the separation of language from the world as the ultimate subject to which all writing refers . . .
> [Auden] now tried replacing his first theory with its exact opposite.

It is this last sentence that at last encourages a reader to sit up suddenly and find the terms of his *No*. If Auden's thought was any good, it was not arrived at like this; and if it was arrived at like this, it does not deserve to have a book written about it. Mendelson is

lured into a theory about thinking, about writing and even about
living itself, which is worth protesting against because it is so very
prevalent in sophisticated criticism. And if this is what he assumes
to be Auden's theory rather than his own, then he has the problem
of explaining how Auden ever wrote any good poetry by it.

Strikingly, this is an image of Auden's character which seems to
be at least in part shared by his biographer, for early in his life of the
poet Carpenter firmly concludes his brief description of Auden's
childhood with this summary:

> The chief characteristic of his childhood was security, a security
> that gave him the immense unshakable self-confidence that was
> his overriding attribute.

If this 'self-confidence' was 'unshakable', it is presumably Carpen-
ter's conclusion that Auden retained it all his life. And yet it is a part
of the value of this biography that it offers such full evidence that
seems simply to contradict the conclusion he maintains: or at least
to qualify and complicate it. It seems as if the poet could hardly
frame a memory of the past that was not loaded with anxiety,
melancholy, even terror. On the page facing the reference to
'unshakable self-confidence' is quoted Auden's earliest memory, of
an occasion when he was five years old and his parents went to a
party in travesty – in clothes they had exchanged with each other: 'I
was terrified'. This primal scene is succeeded by his prep-school,
populated solely with 'hairy monsters with terrifying voices and
eccentric habits': and the prep-school recollections of insult and
humiliation, though classic and archetypal, are too many to quote
here. As the years passed, at home Auden's mother (or so a visiting
friend of the boy's felt, or was told by Auden) 'disapproved of
almost anything Wystan said or did'. At Oxford, 'I was more
unhappy than I have ever been before or since' (and the third-class
degree earned by this first-class intellect was one of the worst pieces
of unluck in his life). So it goes on through the Thirties; even
Iceland, before the kind and uproarious MacNeice arrives, is
misery ('You can't imagine any of them behaving like the people in
the sagas, saying "That was an ill word" and shooting the other
man dead'). On a slow boat to China with Isherwood, Auden wept
and said 'no one would ever love him'. And the withdrawal a
few years later of Kallman from any very close relationship seems
more or less to have finished Auden off. When this large-scale

literary figure bought, at fifty, his little house in Austria, he 'sometimes . . . stood in the garden with tears of gratitude and surprise that he possessed a home of his own'.

Auden was clearly sometimes capable of high spirits too. More importantly, he inherited from his parents an ideal of public service, of social behaviour, and above all of self-control, that made it extremely unlikely that he would ever reveal his deeper feelings to casual acquaintances; and he was obviously in a simple way publicly shy all his life. Auden developed in fact a standard of 'shop-front' which led to a real schism in public and private behaviour, a division in what he seemed and really felt. And this was a characteristic consistent from his earliest schooldays –

> to his school-fellows he may have seemed self-assured, but in his own eyes he was largely a failure . . . he felt himself (he said) to be 'grubby and inferior and dull . . . doomed to a life of failure and envy'

right up to the moment many years later when what he had hoped was a 'marriage' with Kallman broke down:

> His loyalty to Chester meant that very few friends were aware that there had been a change in the relationship between them . . . Only occasionally did his deeper feelings become apparent.

The subject of Carpenter's life cannot have been characterized by 'immense unshakable self-confidence', and is unlikely to have written the kind of verse displaying the qualities of purposive decision which Mendelson's technique implies. In his own eyes, in fact, Auden was a man 'whose mind works . . . not slowly but weakly, passively, impotently'; who could often feel he had 'even less character and intellect than I thought'; a man who believed that he needed his steady ritual, once in America, of boosting and tranquillizing drugs because he was 'fundamentally a weak character', only enabled to act at all by virtue of the will-power supplied by drugs. Carpenter tends to some extent having recounted all this to brush it aside, as he does also the question of neurosis in Auden – choosing to give little space to the subject of the poet's parents, and his relation with them. These choices are Carpenter's own, and are perhaps made in the fear of spoiling the poet's public image: or perhaps the biographer himself is impatient with such evidences of the more private self.

There can be little doubt that Auden was either born with problems or suffered real damage in his earliest years from his loving but highly masculine and domineering mother. To ignore this fact would be to fail to understand how a child of such large talents, one so intensely clever and lively, became a person for whom certain kinds of decision and action were evidently impossible. Auden grew up a person of 'surface' and 'depths': on the surface was an extreme aggressive ebullience, an energetic dogmatic strength perhaps only accentuated almost to the point of caricature by the sense always of weakness, even of void, beneath. And this is surely the curious complex quality or character that comes through directly in the poems: a huge vitality of surface outgoingness, of intellectual life and energy, that is (precisely) of the surface, because powered only by a sense of internal void, of weakness, of failure, almost non-existence. Whether or not this is neurotic, in his poetry Auden managed to correlate surface and depth as he could almost never in life; he wrote a poetry in which the 'unluck' of his life became the 'luck' of his verse. And by virtue of this capacity it achieved, perhaps, that normative quality which is the opposite of neurosis. It is Auden's sense of failure which is the true success of his poetry. He found a manner and a depth that could make a reader feel what Johnson said in his letter to Boswell: 'Is not this the state of life?'

The side of Auden's poetry that speaks of experience rather than communicating information of one sort or another is, as John Bayley has said in his elegant and persuasive essay on the poet, often rather neglected by Auden criticism, which tends (Bayley suggests) rather to describe a poem's views or contents than to say how it works. Bayley's own answer to this question is that Auden was a certain kind of symbolist, but one who leans very lightly on what he is doing:

> Auden is very much a new type of aesthete, who sees art not as religion but as a game, to be played with as skilful and individual a touch as possible . . .

and he stresses that at Auden's most characteristic 'we find it almost impossible to take him seriously'. Carpenter clearly shares this reading of the poet, speaking of *The Orators* as 'fundamentally largely a joke', and of Auden a little later as 'still flirting with the Lawrentian Fascism with which he had amused himself in *The Orators*'.

Yet it is Carpenter who also quotes Spender's impression (apparently from a letter from the poet) that *The Orators* was composed 'in sweat and blood'. There is surely something in Auden, as a poet and not as a teacher or preacher or any kind of purveyor of wisdom, that *is* to be taken seriously. And perhaps Bayley's 'game' and 'playing' (however closely they follow Auden's own theorizing) err as much as Carpenter and Mendelson in their stress on the predominance of will, the superiority of detachment. The essence of the *game* is its choice of limits, which is what differentiates it from most of human life, where the limits are not chosen but there from the beginning. Both John Bayley and Humphrey Carpenter see very much the same Auden, and it is a seeing and not a hearing: for what they leave out of their account is the sound, as it were, of Auden's human voice, which governs and controls the 'playful' images. The interesting thing is that the poetic voice is not itself playful. Nor does this voice have quite the qualities which Bayley ascribes to the verse, as Carpenter to the man – 'rhetorical, self-confident to the point of arrogance, intent on securing the advantages of an immediate effect': it is rather the sound of a man who – however complicatedly – knows that he sounds like this, assents to sounding like this, but is not like this ('To his school-fellows he may have seemed self-assured, but in his own eyes he was largely a failure'). The unchanging sound of Auden's verse, through all its changes and its brilliances and its nonsenses, is the sound of someone putting up a shop-front, or putting on a turn, or playing to the gallery: the sound, precisely, of a kind of comic heroic despair, as of one who knows exactly what junk he is selling but has to keep on with it because there is nothing whatever else to do.

The relation of the poet's 'voice' to his materials is not unlike that of Prospero to Ariel – though it was Caliban, as Carpenter tells us, that Auden saw as his part in life and chose to play at school. Of the several ambitious long poems which Auden wrote in the decade after he settled in America, probably the most enjoyable is 'The Sea and the Mirror', a kind of poetic footnote or cast-list or final bow by the characters of Shakespeare's *Tempest* fitted into that ambiguous moment before the curtain has quite come down; and of all these 'Epilogues' the best is the last and only prose one, that delivered by Caliban. This enormous monologue is delivered by Caliban in the most unlikely and indecorous or 'Ariel' style possible, the beautiful mannered orotundities of late Henry James; it is essentially about the impossibility of Art; and it comes to a climax in a wonderful long period detailing absolute ridiculous theatrical failure: 'Our performance – for Ariel and I are, you know this now, just as deeply involved as any of you – which we were obliged, all of us, to go on with and sit right through to the final dissonant chord, has been so indescribably inexcusably awful . . .'

This fifty-line apologia (at the end of the monologue) for sheer rock-bottom failure, which is only forgivable because it knows, devoutly, just how terrible it is, is a triumph which initiates that late phase in which it amused Auden to adapt to Christian truths a high theatrical camp surely learned from the opera-loving New Yorker Kallman. But the passage is in any case only a late virtuoso form of what every poem of Auden's says in some way, and the saying constitutes the poet's seriousness beyond that 'mystery and charm' which Bayley rightly praises. Carpenter quotes a splendid description of Auden (as Caliban again, perhaps) in the mid-Thirties by Harry Watt, who directed *Night Mail* with Basil Wright:

> He looked exactly like a half-witted Swedish deckhand; his jacket was far too short in the sleeves, and he had huge, bony red hands and big, lumpy wrists and dirty old flannel trousers and an old sports jacket and this blond towhead, and then the rather plummy, frightfully good accent, which was very surprising coming out of him . . . There, on that old Post Office table, he wrote the most beautiful verse. He kept bringing it, and – the cheek of us, in a way – we turned down so much. He'd say, 'All right, that's quite all right. Just roll it up and throw it away.'

In a way, every poem that Auden wrote carries a device saying 'Just roll it up and throw it away' – a device which is essentially that fugitive tone of comic despair never quite localizable but always recognizable as the Audenesque. It is embodied, for one thing, in the richness and bulk of a career – nearly fifty years of good writing – that at the same time was peculiarly involved with the expendable, with the collaborative and the commissioned, with a politics and a theology each of which demotes poetry to the second-best, with momentary tasks and purchasable needs. If the early verse is engaged with a love that will certainly pass, the later exists in a 'suburb of dissent': what they have in common, beyond their alteration from the 'attractive' to the 'honest' or the 'exciting' to the 'true', is a shared understanding that existence is always askew from where it ought to be or might be, as the personnel in Auden's poems are always cut off from Eden and doubtful about Heaven, or as a 'dear one is mine as mirrors are lonely'.

This sense of the askew, of inhabiting a moment that gains definition only from the degree to which it lacks the absolute, pervades Auden's verse from first to last. This is why it is a poetry of fragments and splinters, always changing styles and doxologies. We recognize the Audenesque by the way things don't fit: epithets together ('tolerant, enchanted', 'warm and lucky') or objects with their figures of speech ('the winter holds them like the Opera') or style with substance (camp with Christian, Horatian with Ischian, mediaeval alliterative verse with lost souls in a New York bar, haikus with home truths). The revisions Auden made to his earlier poems are mistakes, and are indefensible, because he tried to improve something whose character it is to be unimprovable – 'wrong from the start'; he tried to polish poems whose art it is to voice, with the most exquisite accuracy, that 'clumsiness' which so many friends record in anecdote, whose authenticity is a fractured syntax and a melodramatic language of gesture. One of the saddest, most characteristic stories Carpenter tells describes how Auden double-sold *The Double Man*, offering it to Lehmann for the Hogarth Press while still contracted to Faber & Faber, where Eliot promptly published it as *New Year Letter*. Auden answered Lehmann's angry letter with no more than a telegram saying: 'I am incapable of dealing with this.' The poet's life, like most people's, was clearly full of things which he was 'incapable of dealing with': but it was his gift to harness that incapacity, his talent to ride the nightmare:

> And all sway forward on the dangerous flood
> Of history, that never sleeps or dies,
> And, held one moment, burns the hand.

It is this particular sense of the 'dangerous flood', of History as something that over-rides, which humanizes Auden's poetry most often; and it is this that militates, too, against that deliberative, purposive and successful quality which Carpenter and Mendelson tend to endow it with. 'Today', Auden says, 'the makeshift consolations': he is the genius of the makeshift, the virtuoso of contingency, and to perfect his achievement is to endanger his essential character. There is really no 'Auden story' to tell, either in biography or criticism, because his life clearly got nowhere, and his art was not of the kind that develops steadily and out of itself. He was, rather, like Dryden, a professional poet, endlessly generously responsive to the demands and challenges of the moment. His career has no real pattern as his life has no real form: there are only the enormous number of good poems which he wrote, all of them highly vulnerable to criticism for one thing or another. Why not?

10

Philip Larkin: After Symbolism

When Philip Larkin's *The Less Deceived* first appeared in 1955 the *Times Educational Supplement* called it a 'triumph of clarity after the formless mystifications of the last twenty years.' Now after two decades of steadily increasing success, Larkin has come to be thought of by many as not only the best English poet but one of the best in Europe. By an odd reversal, however, his most recent volume, *High Windows* (1974), seems to have struck a number of reviewers as – for all its excellence – a triumph of obscurity. Over the last few years, charges of obscurity have cropped up with a frequency that is odd if one recalls how short a time it is since Larkin's almost painfully courteous lucidity and conscientious narrowing-down of range first laid him open to attack for effects quite other than that: for being '*naif*' or '*faux-naif*' or 'genteel' or 'suburban' or 'parochial' or 'provincial' or downright Philistine – for heading a general selling-out of modernistic culture. Moreover, Larkin himself has provoked such attacks: his rather rare pieces of literary-critical journalism have often been sceptical about modernism, and the Introduction to a collection of jazz reviews which Larkin published in 1970 went so far as to allege that the 'obscurantism' of modern art has sacrificed a vital relationship with its audience to a mere sterile involvement with its own working materials. In such a context, it is interesting to watch Richard Murphy contemplating *High Windows* in *The New York Review of Books* (May, 1975) and sagging at the sight of

> a bewildering triptych called 'Livings', which Clive James has deciphered in a penetrating essay: it juxtaposes three separate lives in far-off periods and places, each full of its own comforting certainties that seem faintly threatened in mysterious ways, the implication being that they are on the verge of catastrophe.

'Bewildering', 'deciphered', 'juxtaposes', 'seem', 'mysterious', 'implication' – these are new (but also familiar) words in the criticism of a poetry that has always seemed to many to have the virtue of not requiring 'penetration'. The 'decipherment' to which Murphy alludes took place in Clive James's *Encounter* review of *High Windows* (June, 1974); and it is equally striking that this highly appreciative account of Larkin's verse refers to the second part of 'Livings' – as also to another poem in this volume, 'Sympathy in White Major' – as being distractingly *obscure*: 'While wanting to be just the reverse, Larkin can on occasion be a difficult poet.' Difficulty is in itself, like obscurity, a difficult subject, but Clive James's remark helps to throw some light on it by the way it begins with what Larkin 'wants'. An effect of poetic failure is not at all general in Larkin's work: his idiosyncrasy is the flawless success of the art with which he records the life *manqué*. So unvarying is this efficiency that he has even been accused of unambitiousness: of doing what clearly comes too easily. Clive James is therefore to some extent deriving, from critical pronouncements or from the persona of the poet 'behind' the poems, someone who is capable of 'wanting' anything, other than what the poems are capable of showing him getting. 'Wanting' and 'getting', like the whole concept of poetic *intention*, are inread criteria: not necessarily untrue or unhelpful in reading poetry, but more relative to the reader than to the poet. And the usual partner of 'intention' is 'difficulty' or 'obscurity', which really means our inability to see the poet communicating what we see him as wanting to say.

The problem with all these terms is that they overstress the side of poetry concerned with the communication of statements ('Is that clear?') and understress the side which is a more private, less communicative perpetuation of experience, deriving as much from a universe of *things* as from a language of concepts. They do this unavoidably, because they are philosophical terms abstracted from discourse, and discourse is fully public as poetry is not; to debate about poetry at all is partly to falsify what often takes its strength from inarticulated intelligence; and it is from these necessary falsifications that there proceed the endless and equally necessary infightings of criticism. *High Windows* is both 'clearer' *and* 'more obscure' than *The Less Deceived*; just as Larkin's new style of ferocious lucidity tends often now to the four-letter-word, a linguistic prop which one may, as one wishes, find 'easy' *or* 'difficult', emerging as it does from the writer whom Alvarez once called (not wholly without reason) the Poet of Gentility:

> My wife and I have asked a crowd of craps
> To come and waste their time and ours: perhaps
> You'd care to join us? In a pig's arse, friend . . .

This is the opening of 'Vers de Société', one of the poems from *High Windows*. Its subject is the terms on which the isolated individual may become socially available; and it displays most aspects of the style in which the later Larkin is available to the reader. 'Livings' and 'Sympathy in White Major' do not differ strikingly from it as poems. If, therefore, they can be found *obscure*, this is not from a lack of plainness of language or from the use of esoteric concepts. It is rather from some failure, for this or that given reader, in the *availability* of the poem, some breakdown in specific relationship with the reader, such as Larkin himself has spoken of as characteristic of modernism. With the new Larkin, a reader may see what the words 'say', but not what they 'mean' or 'amount to': ('a bewildering triptych . . . it juxtaposes . . . each full of its own . . . the implication being . . .'). John Bayley has praised Larkin – in a *Times Literary Supplement* review expanded in his *Uses of Division* (1976) – above all for the creation of a new, totally sympathetic poetic personality or 'self' which constitutes a relationship with the reader approximating even to 'the intimacy . . . of the lounge bar'. What Larkin's most recent volume shows, perhaps, is some degree of retraction or withdrawal of that poetic personality; or, to put the matter more precisely, *High Windows* shows more explicitly a side of Larkin's work present from the beginning – a poetic *im*personality. That impersonality cannot, I think, be properly considered except in relation to the 'modernism' which Larkin himself has often and sharply criticized, with the sharpness (perhaps) which a person may reserve for the concerns which most tempt or involve him. It is, in fact, the obscurities of *High Windows* – though they are also its lucidities – which throw light on an aspect of Larkin's verse that has surely always been there. His poems appear to have profited from a kind of heroic struggle *not* to be modernistic, not to be mere derivative footnotes to a Symbolism as much disapproved of as admired; they have wished to be, not merely after, but *well* after Eliot.

This general impression can be made specific by considering for a moment one of the two poems which Clive James found very obscure. 'Sympathy in White Major' is a linguistically fairly simple, almost monosyllabic poem, whose three stanzas describe a man (the poet, or 'I') who pours himself out a large drink and hears as from a toastmaster his social virtues celebrated in warm clichés. The style is mostly commonplace, the situation being downrightly imagined: the drink fills a stanza, elaborately detailed, and the clichés of praise load every rift with ore. If the poem strikes a reader as obscure, the reason must lie not in the area of paraphrasable meaning but in 'how to take it' – the absence of a sense of why the man and the drink and the fantasies of praise frankly matter at all. The answer to this does not lie in paraphrasable content, as we might expect it to, given some current descriptions of Larkin's poetry, but in the ordonnance of the whole. Rather than offering a strong logic of statements whose syntax follows what we like to think of as normal colloquial usage, the poem works by an interaction (or 'juxtaposition') of striking images. It misses out rational connections between these. Primarily, it refuses to allocate statements, so that all speeches in what is nominally a social situation in fact dissolve into one solitary monologue. It also leaves unexplained connections between the drink, for instance, and the italicized laudations, like '*He devoted his life to others*'; between the apparently sober statements of the second stanza, 'It didn't work for them or me', and the complacent or unbothered éclat of the last, '*A decent chap, a real good sort*'. We never properly know whether the drink is because the praise did not work, or the praise is because the drink did not work, or whether both work or do not work. On the other hand, 'proper knowledge' is not what the poem is about. It exists as a fuddled and yet marvellously clear (clear as ice and gin and tonic are clear, clear as whiteness is blank) tangle of intoxications and illusions; it is a poem about the conditions of a 'sparkling' success in art or life in general, and about the fantasizing but commonplace vanities or emptinesses which may be latently present in such success.

If 'Sympathy in White Major' is as readable or available as it is, this is partly because it uses pointers and directions that start us off without difficulty in the right direction. Those who find the poem obscure have happened to miss, or happen to be unable to use, the pointers given. In part this is a matter of what one likes to call 'purely aesthetic' dispositions: the exquisite tonal artistry lavished on a gin and tonic, the 'music' of clichés of praise. But these ridiculous felicities of technique are not self-supporting – they relate backwards to an origin. 'Sympathy in White Major' could actually be called a learned poem, even an esoteric one, precisely in the way in which we expect a modernistic poem to be. And by what can hardly be considered coincidence, the learning in question happens to be something in the nature of a 'history of Symbolism'. It would be radically untrue to say that anything in this poem absolutely depends on a knowledge of this or that fact outside it; all of it except perhaps the title can clearly be understood by any ordinary person with common sense, some intelligence about loneliness and vanity and fantasy-making, and no knowledge whatever of Symbolist poetry. None the less, it remains a fact that this lucid and comical and inarticulate poem reminds one in flashes, as one reads, of a remarkably wide area of aesthetic history – an area that can be evoked by half a line of verse but that takes a disproportionate amount of discourse to sketch in. It can be said that though Larkin's poem does not appear to need or benefit from extraneous information, none the less there *is* extraneous information which can lead a reader to find it even cleverer and funnier (or possibly sadder) than at first strikes one; and which in some sense consolidates both its almost imagistic procedure and its argument concerning Vanity in both art and moral life.

This context of information begins where Larkin begins, with the title – the carefully 'gauche', spoofing or horseplaying, spuriously-cultural, abstractly inartistic if synaesthetic half-sentence, 'Sympathy in White Major'. 'Symphonie en blanc majeure', or 'Symphony in White Major' (which Larkin's title parodies with conscious discord) is the title of a poem written in about 1850 by the French Parnassian poet Théophile Gautier: a series of extremely fine, chillily erotic quatrains sensuously detailing the whiteness of a female swan. Some fifteen years earlier Gautier had prefaced his 'shocking' novel of bisexuality, *Mademoiselle de Maupin*, with a defiant statement of Art for Art's Sake, declaring war on the useful and the ugly – on bourgeois civilization, in short; thus, it was probably with some conscious reference to Gautier's Art-for-Art's-Sakeism that a decade after the poem, in the 1860s, a French art critic borrowed from Gautier's title the phrase 'symphonie en blanc' to describe the effect of the work of a different artist, a painting that was on exhibition in Paris. That painting was a study of a young woman in a white dress, Whistler's *White Girl*; and Whistler, who fairly certainly knew Gautier's poem anyway, and who was to become the first conscious exponent of Art for Art's Sake in England, as well as serving as a kind of medium for – and reciprocal influence on – French Symbolism, liked the critic's use of the phrase so much that he promptly re-christened his picture 'Symphony in White No 1' and went on to do three more paintings on the same theme and with the same titling. The second of these, 'Symphony in White No 2', shows an exquisite young woman in white framed against a mirror into which she is not quite looking. This now famous image had enormous contemporary success: Swinburne, for instance, wrote a poem based on it, called 'Before the Mirror', in which a beautiful young woman contemplates her image – 'But one thing knows the flower; the flower is fair' – and wonders which is the real person, and which the ghost, as between 'the white sister' and herself.

This chain of Anglo-American-French images appears to enter Larkin's poem with the title 'Sympathy in White Major': the lines which follow are a sympathetic 'symphony in white' as aesthetically clever as Gautier's own; its speaker is framed against an image of himself, as 'the whitest man I know', like Whistler's subject, and hesitates between illusions as Swinburne's beauty does. But Larkin's speaker is not merely 'before the mirror' of self-contemplation; he is actually (if perhaps ironically) toasting himself there. The gesture of this drunken and yet abstaining 'private pledge', which is Larkin's phrase for it, takes us further into Symbolism. For, though not a Symbolist himself, Gautier's purity of aims and extreme technical skill earned him the respect of poetic contemporaries and successors who were: it was to him that Baudelaire dedicated *Les Fleurs du Mal*; and later Mallarmé in his turn – the finest, and most obscure, of the Symbolist poets – wrote 'funeral poems' for both Gautier and Baudelaire. One of Baudelaire's best and best-known prose-poems ironically but seriously exhorts us to 'Get drunk! . . . With wine, with poetry or with virtue as you please. But get drunk!' Baudelaire's classic *topos* must have been in Mallarmé's mind (he re-casts many Baudelairean themes) when in 1893 he composed the lines called 'Salut' (Greeting) which Larkin's 'Sympathy in White Major' seems closely related to. This 'Salut', which Mallarmé afterwards used as Preface to his published *Poésies*, was first delivered with champagne-glass in hand, in precisely the gesture which Larkin recalls – 'I lift the lot in private pledge'. For Mallarmé, in many ways the most reticent of men, was asked to act as toastmaster to a banquet given by the review, *La Plume*: and on that occasion first read his brief, oblique and playfully obscure poem. In it, the bubble-filled glass of champagne becomes a symbol of that great Symbolist Nothingness of things which poetry both represents and redeems. The poem opens: 'Rien, cette écume, vierge vers/A ne désigner la coupe' (Nothing, this foam, virgin verse/Defining only the cup); and as the poet speaks the lines, calling the poem into being as he goes, the rhythm assumes the pitch and toss of intoxication, and the whole becomes a small craft rocking on a sea of wine towards arrival or wreck – whatever end awaits the drunk, the sailor and the poet alike: 'Solitude, récif, étoile/À n'importe ce qui valut/Le blanc souci de notre étoile' (Solitude, reef, star,/Whatever merited/The white care of our sail).

Mallarmé's 'Salut' is not one of his best poems, but it illustrates well enough an art that one might think of as possible in late nineteenth-century France but *not* in the England of the late 1970s. Larkin's poem is by contrast obdurately modern, of the last twenty years, and intensely English, even Little-English: as 'English' in its clichés as other poems in this volume are 'modern' in their obscenities. All the same, 'Sympathy in White Major', with all its appealingly artless, gruff and simple manner, its near-monosyllabic rhythms and its absence of 'images', is in its way as brilliant and as learned a fragment of translation as one is likely to find: a fragment, rather, of that art of Imitation which the Augustans deployed, a form of translation which fully recognizes that change of times and styles makes literalism inappropriate. Larkin's first stanza is a remarkably clever game, an exact conversion of Mallarmé's now deeply dated 'champagne and Poesy' conceit into a precise modern and English equivalent which simultaneously records, as a scholar would, its sources of information. For Larkin's cinema-screen-advertisement-large, lights-in-Piccadilly-Circus-high, icily-musically 'chiming' glass of gin-and-tonic that 'voids' (*void* being the key Symbolist concept for the cosmic Nothingness to be confronted and embodied and so, in theory, overcome by Art), this fantasia derisively picks up the lingo of a whole tradition; and then makes something new out of it.

It is Larkin's *use* of the symbols of this tradition in his first stanza for purposes of his own that at once arouses some scepticism at the proud claim of the second stanza, that as artist the speaker is morally blameless to the point of sainthood, in his withdrawal from the common human condition of *use* of others: 'Other people wore like clothes/The human beings in their days . . .'. This scepticism is already in fact aesthetically implanted, like a form of self-knowledge, in the graces of the first stanza, where we see the vast greedy drink 'void'

> In foaming gulps until it smothers
> Everything else . . .

An art which turns aside from what it conceives of, harshly or cheerfully, as the gross Philistine materialism and spiritual emptiness of its own social civilization, will sooner or later lay itself open to certain moral and intellectual charges. It will become self-obsessed, cold, empty of matter: a ghost staring into a mirror. These dangers or vulnerabilities have probably always been even clearer to those who have at various times pursued purism in the arts (or in morals) than to their adversaries. Gautier's original poem, for instance, ends with a cool ironic turn, 'Cette implacable blancheur' (This ruthless whiteness) which Larkin's closing 'White is not my favourite colour' possibly echoes in fact as well as in effect. There is a critique in all Mallarmé's symbols of reflective imprisonment, of which the best-known is the swan trapped in ice; and there is similarly a force of moral irony in the use of the figure of Narcissus in the work of the last true French Symbolist, Valéry. But such awareness is peripheral in true Symbolism. It moves to the forefront only in a work of late Symbolism or even 'post-Symbolism', Eliot's *Four Quartets*: poems which continually wrestle to justify morally the aesthetic purism which their author inherits, distrusts and loves, just as his early Ode half celebrates and half detests its titular hero, 'Saint Narcissus', the virtuous starer in the mirror. As critic, too, Eliot made an especial point of objecting to the Narcissism or Vanity latent in the approach of those poets, Mallarmé and Valéry, whom he loved, was indebted to, and in so many ways resembled. In a manner that is almost a brilliant postscript to Eliot, Larkin brings Saint Narcissus into the 1970s. The style is balder, more simply self-mickeying, more seriously involved with commonplace and cliché morality: '*He devoted his life to others* . . . It didn't work for them or me'; '*Here's to the whitest man I know/* – Though white is not my favourite colour.' An elegy on Symbolism is delivered in an age of TV commercial; and in its style.

In a *London Magazine* interview published in 1964, Larkin was asked by Ian Hamilton whether he ever read French poetry, and answered: '*Foreign* poetry? *No!*'. Larkin's writings often suggests a man of scrupulous honesty, even to the point of some literalness. This exchange therefore opens up some interesting possibilities. Literature is a medium that can seem wonderfully simple in effect, but to produce that effect involves endless complexities. Perhaps the poet simply felt that a joke is a joke, and that one is not on oath in public interviews. Or perhaps he had not read much French verse at that stage, or much contemporary French verse, or had ceased to read it, or to remember it, or had sometimes read it in such excellent translations as C. F. MacIntyre's of Symbolist poetry, without which, a non-bilingualist can hardly feel sure he is really reading this very difficult verse; or perhaps the poet's obvious modesty, like that of scrupulous scholars who say that they have not read something, but only 'looked at it', made him deny reading much foreign poetry. The statement would tie in with the hatred of cultural pretentiousness that Larkin shows elsewhere: a dislike of an abstract and unreal talk of 'poetry' or 'literature' or 'culture' at large which in fact destroys or renders sterile this book, this poem, this line. '*Foreign* poetry', *No*; but yes, (perhaps) to an image or two experienced once intensely enough to make it survive for a good many years and then re-emerge with enough life in it for another man's poem.

It is hard, at any rate, to manage without conjecturing such survivals. For it is not only 'Sympathy in White Major' which suggests a poet knowledgeably interested in French verse, as in Symbolist art in general. In Larkin's first successful volume, *The Less Deceived* (which on coming out in 1955 was saluted by the *TES* reviewer as a blow dealt to modernism) the poem called 'Arrivals, Departures' reads like a beautiful imitation, in the same technical sense, of Baudelaire's prose-poem 'Le Port'. Larkin's wonderfully English 'Toads', in that same volume, have a strong resemblance to the Chimeras carried on the shoulders of men in Baudelaire's prose-poem 'Chacun sa Chimère'. And the title of another in that collection, Larkin's 'Poetry of Departures', refers to a whole phase of French Symbolist verse with the kind of ironic casualness that is liable in Larkin's case to be the detritus of more knowledge than he cares to display. (As in Eliot's case also, any accidental discovery by a reader of the poet's 'sources' usually reveals not less but much more learning than superficially appears). *The Whitsun Weddings* is not a 'French' volume: Larkin seems there to be intent on developing the easy, colloquial and if one likes traditionally 'English' persona that strengthens his mature poetry. But in *High Windows*, published nearly a decade later again (1974), what are conceivably early and original tastes and interests re-assert themselves; for it shows a consistent but perhaps more boldly individual use of French Symbolist poetry, a use that makes new poems, rather than merely 'alluding' or imitating.

Thus, the title poem, 'High Windows', meditates on the human pursuit of happiness in a style that at first displays an abysmal, rock-bottom four-letter-word 'modernity', the tone of the present day: but this colloquial brutality quietly modulates towards the refined and extreme contradictory intensity of the end:

> And beyond it, the deep blue air, that shows
> Nothing, and is nowhere, and is endless.

The radiant colour and the 'nothingness' are too Mallarméan to be only coincidentally similar. '*L'azur*' (the blue) is Mallarmé's most consistent and philosophical symbol, delineating both the necessity and the absence of the ideal, an ideal which we imprint on the void sky by the intensity of our longing; his poetry is full of '*De l'éternel azur la sereine ironie*' (the calm irony of the endless blue). The poem by Mallarmé in which this image becomes most definitive is '*Les Fenêtres*' (The Windows), which compares the state of the poet, sickened by existence and enduring the perpetual life-giving suffering of an always despairing and then re-purified idealism, to that of an old man dying in a dreary hospital, his face wistfully pressed to the windows, longing for the blue sky outside. Larkin's 'thought of high windows' is close enough to Mallarmé's poem to be worth contrasting with it: as it is, in addition, with an earlier treatment of the topic perhaps larger, tougher and more classic than Mallarmé's, and one to which the later French poet must in his turn have been indebted. Mallarmé's 'Les Fenêtres' is presumably dependent on two superb prose-poems by Baudelaire, one of them the very well-known lines with the English title 'Any Where Out of the World', and beginning '*Cette vie est un hôpital où chaque malade est possédé du désir de changer de lit'* (This life is a hospital in which every patient is consumed with the desire to change his bed), and the other similarly titled 'Les Fenêtres' and opening, *'Celui qui regarde du dehors à travers une fenêtre ouverte, ne voit jamais autant de choses que celui qui regarde une fenêtre fermée'* (The man who looks in from outside through an open window never sees as much as the man who looks at a window that is closed).

Most poets have been highly literate, resourceful scholars of language. There is more than one way of being the kind of 'Little-Englander' or even 'suburbanite' that Larkin has sometimes been accused of being (the language-teacher Mallarmé lived an obdurately 'suburban' and domestic existence). Such accusations can in fact never be very sensible when directed at a poet so evidently intelligent and knowledgeable, so aesthetically original and verbally adept. The familiarity with poets like Baudelaire and Mallarmé which his work seems to reveal – though not to display – is not, therefore, primarily interesting: it is only what could be expected. What may be more worth notice is the specific and critical use which Larkin seems to make of Symbolist imagery, or of kinds of thought and feeling which come close to its idealisms. *'High* Windows' is not the same as *'The* Windows', in Baudelaire or Mallarmé, and *'Sympathy* in White Major' is obviously derisive in a way in which Gautier's 'Symphony' is not. In both cases, Larkin is evidently humanizing and moralizing. His 'Sympathy' (which is, as it happens, another Baudelairean and Mallarméan concept – the later French poet ends one poem by cursing himself for possessing so much of that fluid, irritating and aesthetic quality) is, however, probably the most direct and ordinary moral and emotional equivalent of aesthetic sensibility, 'tea and sympathy' being what one might call the English translation of French 'champagne and poesy'.

Similarly, to make the windows 'High' gives them a certain metaphysical or even ecclesiastical status that distances them romantically but unsatisfactorily from the real human condition. Symbolism is being used negatively, in a post- or even anti-Symbolist fashion. But it has been rightly said that all negatives in poetry, once stated, become a special kind of poetic positive. Larkin's Symbolist imagery is a disrelation with the idealizing originals more than a relationship with them; but the context is one in which disrelations are relations, too. In the poem immediately facing 'High Windows', called 'Forget What Did' (and Larkin's poems do seem to be printed so that they relate to each other in ways like these) the poet describes a diary which had stopped short because the writer wanted to forget, not to record 'Such words, such actions/As bleakened waking'; but the peculiar effect of this remarkable poem is to resurrect and sustain those unendurable half-memories, the uncited words and actions, just as its end devotes the diary's still blank pages to hypothetical 'Celestial recurrences,/The day the flowers come,/And when the birds go.' Larkin often seems to write like this – as a man experiencing and surviving the exact end of something vital, 'out on the end of an event': as one 'stopping the diary . . . a blank starting'. And this transitional effect can also be described in a purely literary or technical way. It could be said that Larkin's position as a writer is difficult to chart exactly because of what appears to be a highly ambiguous relationship with an important tradition of aesthetic values. He makes use of, and very consistent use of, that species of literary idealism which Symbolism implies, *only* in order to record its unavailability. Thus, 'Sympathy in White Major' is not a '*Symphony* in White Major' – its title implies parody; having translated the original aesthetic intensity into a moral quality, it then finds in this transposed aestheticism only a kind of *naïveté*, a species of weakness: 'White is not my favourite colour.' Similarly, 'High Windows' is 'Les Fenêtres' Englished and brought up to date: but that entails the violent random flatness with which the new poem modishly opens, with a savage but hardly explicit irony:

> When I see a couple of kids
> And guess he's fucking her and she's
> Taking pills or wearing a diaphragm,
> I know this is paradise . . .

The conscious baldness of the writing, leaving rhythmic effects naked, makes the repeated dactyls stand out, as though 'fucking her' and 'diaphragm' were each a gross ironic half-rhyme with 'paradise'; the three words jangle together, in the void of their blank unstated relationship, with a disharmony like a verbal headache. This sexy disharmony is broadened by the parallel with the equally pathetic hopeful illusions of the past, the hope felt by some two generations back that a priestless theology-less freedom might descend on to children grown blissfully into '*free bloody birds.'* It is perhaps the memory of birds driving themselves against closed windows which provides the logic which closes the poem: in the Symbolist image of blue-containing windows which finally embodies and resolves all its impossibilities.

Any attempt to describe 'High Windows' would have to account for not merely what it says but the tension and extremity of its style: that violent flatness of its opening which modulates into the exaltation of the close. It would also have to point out that this loftiness of the close is altered by its context into something peculiarly hypothetical, unavailable. Symbolism remains a resource like those 'Observed/Celestial recurrences' which might one day fill with images of flowers and birds the remaining pages of a diary left blank years ago: but never precisely with propriety, or within reason. It offers a dead language, like the discretions of Latin, for illuminating human illusions without contempt or condemnation, and in a form more luminous than satire or parody. For some of the poems in *High Windows* achieve this tacit or ironic or contradictory symbolism with extraordinary finesse and depth. Few poems could be more unpretentious, more obdurately turned away from the coerciveness of Symbolism, than the mild and sociological 'Friday Night in the Royal Station Hotel'. It evokes the hushed cosy unnerving meaninglessness that tends to descend at late evening in a hotel, the sense of waiting for something to happen or the feeling that something just has; and it creates this sensation of uninhabited void by describing sequences of human gestures first divested of import and then located in interior bric-à-brac: 'Light spreads darkly downwards . . .', 'Empty chairs/. . . face each other, coloured differently', there is 'loneliness of knives and glass', someone reads 'an unsold evening paper', departure is through 'shoeless corridors'. The image of the Grand Hotel is very Thirties, and the writing here has much of Auden's conceitful wit, but Larkin's poem is more concentratedly suggestive, its furniture *broods* more intently. Mallarmé wrote a number of poems, all of them among his most interesting and obscure, featuring late nineteenth-century household interiors: in them, mana emanates from a fluttering net curtain, a swollen vase or a massive sideboard. Larkin, by comparison (so his poem makes us feel) writes from a place and time from which to recreate such presences would be mere heartless obscurantist antiquarianism, and where furniture is only datable junk: where 'Home' itself becomes the 'Royal Station

Hotel', the place where 'Hours pass'. Therefore his poetic objects – the empty chairs, the corridors, the ash-trays – which could hardly be perceived with more intensity if they *were* symbols, have a complex burden to bear: that of not even being capable of symbolizing the absence which they happen to remind one of. For Symbolism necessitates and is arrogant; the humbler literature which follows it inherits only the randomness an ebbing symbolism leaves behind, like 'letters of exile' . . . '(If home existed)'.

It can often be hard to explain why poems as wilfully modest as Larkin's are, are also as good as they are: as peculiarly potent. There can be few other major poets who have been as often and as reasonably called 'minor' as Larkin has. The power of a poem like 'Friday Night . . .' tends to be locked up in the self-denying ordinances of Larkin's special non-symbolic symbols. The laws of this after-symbolism are maintained also, or so it appears, in most of the poet's utterances on aesthetics outside his actual poems. A characteristic moment occurs, for instance, in the *London Magazine* interview from which I have already quoted: where Ian Hamilton refers, very justly, to the poet's consistent habit of turning and shaping his poems by giving them a sharp self-undercutting close, and Larkin sharply undercuts any merit that might be supposed to derive from any such habit by answering ruminatively

> It's a very interesting question and I hadn't realized I did that sort of thing. I suppose I always try to write the truth and I wouldn't want to write a poem which suggested I was different from what I am . . . I think that one of the great criticisms of poets of the past is that they said one thing and did another, a false relation between art and life. I always try to avoid this . . .

Larkin seems to be positing here a modern ethic of poetic sincerity which is – like his *'Foreign* poetry? *No!'* – not without its own inward complexities. The problem is nicely voiced by the peculiar and even comical lucidity of the prose style used. The poet's presumably quite unironical 'I hadn't realized I did that sort of thing' has an echo of the way in which (for instance) the all too understanding Wittgenstein would tell intellectual opponents that he didn't understand them. Larkin's mind frequently reveals itself in both poems and critical statements as capable of considerable intellectual complexity: 'Sympathy in White Major' is not precisely the diary of a simple man. And the simplicity of the conversational style recorded in this interview makes the impression of being related to a courteous but also combative *simplesse*, its nearest parallel or indeed even source being that *imbécile-de-génie* manner with which William Empson has always used the playful infantilism of the 1920s to communicate his most difficult ideas.

If such considerations underlie Larkin's simple sentences, then it may be allowed that his criterion of 'sincerity' is not in itself a simple one, either: a 'true relation' of art and life is not an identity of the two. It is sometimes assumed, and Larkin himself occasionally writes as if he were assuming, that the two are in his work identical, and that 'sincerity' and 'truth' are one; that Larkin is a 'simple', in fact a 'clear' poet. But this is the precise assumption that can lead to finding the poems obscure: which is to say, incomprehensible because withdrawn from simple statement in a way that the given reader had not counted on. There is, in short, a continual complexity in Larkin's verse which his treatment of Symbolist images in the poems I have mentioned serves to represent, and which is not summarized with entire justice by terms like 'saying one thing and doing (or not doing) another': for Larkin's poems do not *say one thing*, whether or not he does the same thing in life. In the very funny and characteristically modest introduction Larkin added to the later (1964) edition of his early novel *Jill*, he tells how when he and his friend Kingsley Amis were undergraduates together at Oxford in the early years of the war, the Labour Club magazine, then edited by Amis, accepted one of Larkin's poems for publication, "but a second, much less ambiguously ambiguous, was denounced by the Committee as "morbid and unhealthy" '. A fair way of describing Larkin's after-Symbolist developments would be to say that he is getting much less ambiguously ambiguous.

Larkin's Edens

Philip Larkin has gone down in print as saying that his poems are too simple to profit from criticism. It is true that to be chewed over in critical prose is a fate that no poem deserves. But to believe without reservations in the simplicity of Larkin's work is another matter – except in so far as any artistry is a simplification of life, an abnormally clear noticing of human conditions that come to the rest of us fogged with the general imprecisions of the usual. To this degree, all good writing is magnificently simple. But it is unsafe for anyone other than its writer to say so. For the simple gets confused with quite different things – with the literal; with the crude; with the artless and sociological. Larkin is quite often read as a simple observer of contemporary English society, a realistic reporter whose detachment from what he sees (for even the most literal reader can see that there is *some* difference between 'Here' and a British Railways timetable) is explained as the writer's disaffiliation of mood: for as poet, Larkin is almost universally described as 'depressed', his writing melancholy, his scenes a dreary summary of an England to which principle attaches him but which he cannot bring himself much to like. It seems therefore worth while to set down a different impression. Larkin's great art is to appear to achieve the literal while in fact doing something altogether other; his three volumes of major verse are the odd reticent triumph of a self-undercutting artist whose skills make him a 'secret poet' as some men are secret agents or secret drinkers. And the results in Larkin's case are so far from the sociological, and so other than the dreary, that the poet might be described as creating the most potent contemporary images of Eden.

His 'literalism' needs tackling first. Larkin's deviation from the literal is apparent in, for instance, 'The Building' (from *High Windows*), the big central set-piece which holds the same position in its volume, that of the public, representative statement, as did 'Church Going' in *The Less Deceived*. The 'Building' (in itself) may be assumed to be a hospital, one of the huge new-built or extended concrete-and-glass edifices towering on the outskirts of most large provincial English cities; and the poem may be described as a brilliantly accurate evocation of a visit, *qua* patient, to just such a modern medical establishment. But the interesting thing is that the word 'hospital' never occurs, and whenever it or its associates seem about to crop up the poem slews mockingly away. 'What keep drawing up/At the entrance are not taxis' – ambulances, reduced to an unnerving negative rune or verbal kenning: the reception area 'like an airport lounge' is then uneasily focused as 'more like a local bus'; the looming shadow who comes and goes fetching and bringing back patients, almost like a psychopomp from the underworld, is called '*a kind of* nurse'. As the plot thickens and the pace speeds with the third and fourth stanzas patients huddle together in the waiting area as 'Humans, caught/On ground curiously neutral' – and the narrative voice of the poem explains their forlorn postures with a sympathetic irony that proves decidedly suggestive:

> all
> Here to confess that something has gone wrong.
> It must be error of a serious sort,
> For see how many floors it needs, how tall
> It's grown by now, and how much money goes
> In trying to correct it.

There is a fine appropriateness of social tone here to the occasion. One would have to be gravely ill to talk gravely in a hospital; anxiety communicates itself in an edgy flippancy, as doctors unbend to the idiot patients with a terrible jokey banality. The poem's figures of speech, that is, have a dramatic decorum. Because of this dramatic decorum the literal level comes into play, exact and satisfying: this is precisely how one feels and how they sound in a hospital. But the figures of speech here – the meioses, the conceits, above all the sustained ironies – have a second and larger function, just as colloquialism always serves Larkin for force more than for imprecision. An uneasily vagrant fancy in the Out-Patients opens up corridors of imagination:

> For past these doors are rooms, and rooms past those,

And more rooms yet, each one further off

And harder to return from; and who knows
Which he will see, and when?

The colloquial use earlier of words like 'confess', 'error', 'serious' prepares the way for this Kafkaesque terrain, one too vivid to seem a merely ironic metaphor: it is a metaphysical hinterland that reaches back verbally in that 'harder to return from' to underworlds faintly Dantesque, even Virgilian. This largeness of allusion is hardly incongruous given that before the poem ends the very wards are called

> The unseen congregations whose white rows
> Lie set apart above – women, men;
> Old, young . . .

– where the orderliness of image is positively graveyardish, and the invisible 'congregations' are given cadences straight out of the Litany. The poem's undertones of allusion are so ecclesiastical or metaphysical that, even at the literal level, 'The Building' could almost as easily be a church as a hospital – and, as the end of the poem lets fall, the latter does tend to replace the former in human experience in a secular age. The result of this context of reference is that the final 'All know they are going to die' leaves room within a modern monosyllabic trenchancy for a classic and monumental timelessness of statement.

An earlier poem by Larkin, 'Mr Bleaney', locates its hero at 'the Bodies' before he moves into the 'one hired box' of his present lodgings. Spoken English had before its current depressing lapse into fuzzy abstraction a tradition of peculiar sometimes comic concreteness. Since 'box' is in this case a contemptuous colloquial metaphor, it must be presumed similarly that 'the Bodies' is merely a fairly commonplace name in some Midlands locale: but this concretion of name neatly allows it also to mean 'in the body', as contrasted with the (literally) 'hired box' of the coffin. Mr Bleaney's limited life-scale is therefore more interesting and more representative than one might think. Comparably, certain kinds of blocks of mansion flats built in England upwards of a century ago were and are known as 'The [Something] Buildings', or – abbreviated – 'The Buildings': a fact which gives to the title of 'The Building' and then to the rest of the poem an easy exactitude of

contemporary realism. But there is a further realism by which the
name foreshadows that anxious euphemism concerning illness and
death which the rest of the poem – I have earlier suggested –
imitates: 'the building' is to 'the hospital' as 'passing on' is to
'death'. But at this stage of meaning literalism begins to implode
into its opposite. It is as if human beings themselves are far less
merely literal than they think, simply cannot bear or endure to live
on surfaces. Thus the poem, like its title, is about the pathetic and
yet perhaps heroic aversion of the eyes from death, the human will
not to see or to name; the apprehension in short of life itself as a
'wasteful, weak propitiatory flower', and as a thing that we can't
help meaning to keep that way. And this is an apprehension
reaching out further and deeper than any mere hospital building: so
much so that we might say rather that the poem itself is 'built' or
architectonicked according to the strength of that experience. For
all its realism, the poem grows towards and into something as little
of time and place as any symbol is, a noble metaphysical construct
built out of the present's concrete-and-glass.

Larkin's poems seem to contain equal measures of quite opposed
qualities: a strong, highly 'literal' realism, *and* an idealism the more
intense for its bodilessness. The continual transitions between the
two and the unresting conflict between them gave his verse a
strength and energy sometimes hidden by the temperate calm of its
surface. But the dynamic movement is always there, one term
necessitating the other – as is proved by the fact that the supposed
'mere literalism' of a Larkin poem can sometimes be *dis*proved,
shown to be a fallacy. One insignificant example must suffice here.
'Livings III' (in *High Windows*) is more or less invariably referred to
as a poem 'about Oxford'. This luminous evocation of collegiate
life two or three centuries ago may, if we want, be said to feel
Oxfordish, but it cannot be *about* Oxford. For the 'Snape' its first
verse mentions happens to be a village some fifty miles east of
Cambridge on the way to the North Sea coast (nowhere near
Oxford); just as the 'sizar' of the third verse is a form of bursaried
scholar once to be found in Cambridge, but never in Oxford. If the
poem still feels more Oxfordish than Cambridgey ('Tonight we
dine without the Master,/Nocturnal vapours do not please') it must
surely be said simply that the poet has blended images from both –
perhaps from several – ancient universities, and from reading as
from lived experience, to produce that quite untopographical and

timeless actuality that the poem is. In one sense 'Livings III' has a superlative feeling for place and time – but the exactitude lies in the feeling, not in the place and time; just as the poem's realism has a depth and glow, a form and colour and shadowy resonance –

> The candleflames grow thin, then broaden . . .
> The bells discuss the hour's gradations

– that are metamorphoses of the felt and of the imagined, not just of the seen. In short, just as 'The Building' both is and is *not* about a hospital, so is 'Livings III' both about and *not* about an Oxbridge College. Both poems are built on a special quality of apprehension, in all its strength and all its fragility, such as one might properly locate in (say) a modern hospital or (say) an ancient learned foundation: but it is the experience that is important, not the location. 'Nothing, like something, happens anywhere'.

A 'quality of apprehension' is probably all that even the very greatest art has to offer. It is also true, however, that so far as one knows no *other* form of human truth has a greater claim on our attention: the intelligence does what it can, in whatever field may be proper to it. At their most conscious and least merely literal level, at the points where they are most explicitly reflective, Larkin's poems have from the beginning seemed to try to be as clear as is humanly possible about the exact laws by which this 'quality of apprehension' works: to define, if one likes, his own special simplicity. The poem which opened Larkin's first successful volume, *The Less Deceived*, took pains to be very precise about the way in which a love-poem (and love, and a poem) might be said to be both like and *un*like a photograph: the photograph, one might say, representing that literalism or realism which Larkin's art evidently hungers for and respects but also sees around – 'But o, photography! as no art is,/Faithful and disappointing!' Faithfulness is of course not a virtue to be sneezed at. At the end, the poem holds the beloved object addressed in security for ever, 'Calm and dry,/It holds you like a heaven': *it* being here partly the past, but partly also a loving memory, and partly too the poem, since the first two can only achieve their own faithfulness through the third. But the witty comparison of poem with photograph makes tenderly plain that what they have in common is their capacity to *focus*, which means to make one see the limits of any human experience, the edges of the dating even if unfading snapshot image: growing 'Smaller and clearer as the years go by'.

All Larkin's poems, however violent or ugly in detail (as some of the later ones are) pursue a faithfulness that will make them in some sense 'like a heaven': but this heaven is essentially a fallen Eden, a dwindling Paradise glimpsed always from the outside and through a vision of limits. Matching the opening poem, *The Less Deceived* closes with the most flawless lines the poet had written up to that point, 'At Grass': which out of the image of retired racehorses, itself culled from the monotone irrealism of a newsreel, creates a figure for human innocence within the terms a civilized existence offers. The horses are perceived – 'The eye can hardly pick them out' – at the distant heart of that long quiet afternoon which lies both before and after the dream of human history, here diminished with beautiful wit to an Epsom or an Aintree shadowily evoked in 'fable', 'artificed', 'inlay', 'faded', 'classic', 'silks', 'memories', 'almanacked', 'the long cry', 'stop press'. The very precision of the wit, whose condition is the detachment of the observer, forms the limiting frame of this in fact highly sophisticated image of Edenic innocence – a wit almost as ironic as Swift's use of his Houyhnhnms, and as formal as the Scriptural image of meadow grass to summarize life's brevity; and this consciousness sounds most in the tacitness with which the end arrives:

> Only the groom, and the groom's boy,
> With bridles in the evening come.

Poems finish, and the long afternoon wanes.

All Larkin's Edens have these 'bridles', framing enclosures of the thing looked-back-on, like a dream awoken-from. In fact, that peculiar formal excellence in the poet's work which all his critics agree on – but sometimes so as to imply a smallness of scope in it – needs to be seen as in itself, paradoxically, a conditioning law and element of their intense if individual romaticism, their idealism. In terms of myth we know Eden by the closed gate and the sword of the angel. The formal proprieties of Larkin's poems have force (as they might not in another man's work) because of the opposing strength of what they form and control. Hence what an early poem called, reflecting on the fences around prairie steers, the '*electric* limits to their widest senses'. These 'electric limits' appear invariably in Larkin's verse, either as positive forms like the edges of windows (or posters or snapshots or even playing-cards: or in one case even a small Dutch genre painting, filled to the brim with a 'secret, bestial peace') – forms such as one might look in-through or out-of, all the things that at once permit and limit vision; or negatively in the acknowledged blanks and voids of the seen, where 'sun destroys/The interest of what's happening in the shade', all the things about which the voice of the poet says levelly, 'I don't know', 'Have no idea why', 'Or lied'. Almost every poem by Larkin has an essential 'framing' which – as the word by suggestion may imply – is a matter of internal lineaments as much as of external boundaries, a matter which may start as formal technical device but certainly does not stop there: poetic form in any good poet unites technique to metaphysics. At the beginning of a Larkin poem a door 'thuds shut', or experience starts divergently 'Swerving east' towards light and loneliness, or the *miniature* gaiety of togetherness on a seaside holiday is 'To step over the low wall that divides' – but the wall goes on dividing: holidays are not everyday. Matching all these intransigent beginnings are the conclusive (in all senses) endings, where reason and morality bring their iron bridges: 'Out of reach', 'Nothing to be said', 'Could not now', 'That vase', 'Endlessly', 'Truth' – all the barriers that enclose Eden or declare it lost.

Moreover, Larkin's poems, which are as it were 'framed' experiences, themselves sometimes contain small insets which are again seen through a frame or across a barrier – intensifying their inaccessibility. Thus, if 'Livings III' has to be said to be *not* an 'Oxford poem', then perhaps 'Dockery and Son' might be called just that: for three lines in it frame wonderfully a human dream about the 'dreaming spires', the 'city of lost causes', the place where the constrained mathematics don, Lewis Carroll, wrote about the magic garden that the innocent could never lastingly get into:

> I try the door of where I used to live:
>
> Locked. The lawn spreads dazzlingly wide.
> A known bell chimes. I catch my train, ignored.

Between 'locked' and 'ignored' something known once dazzles, chimes. Whether this ironic, self-conscious and brilliant insetting makes the poems more or less 'real', more or less literal is a difficult question to answer. It adds to them a dimension, as of 'rooms, and rooms past those', which further builds up the sense of how peculiarly explicit and secret at once Larkin's art is. At all events, this sense of the limiting conditions which are the price of a certain kind of intensity of seeing figures largely in two other major poems in *The Whitsun Weddings*, the title-poem and 'Here'. The first has a great human directness, and Larkin has himself spoken of its autobiographical origins; and the second is usually praised as what it certainly is, a superlative piece of landscape poetry, a vista of the north-east corner of modern England, centring on the coastal city Hull. And yet there is room to add to these accounts something about the form of each, the way each is 'framed', that helps to explain their power, and perhaps complicates their meaning. 'The Whitsun Weddings' is about these ceremonies first as seen through a train window and then as invading the actual train the observer travels in; and the poem's central four stanzas like his carriage are crammed with a dense social comedy of these events, a novel-type realism of contemporary manners and styles that affectionately caricatures

> the perms,
> The nylon gloves and jewellery substitutes . . .
> And banquet-halls up yards, and bunting-dressed
> Coach-party annexes.

But it is worth noticing that the most *intense* part of this poem (and the best written too) is not in this substantive centre at all but out at its frame: particularly in the rapt quiet beginning, where the narrator starts late on his heavenly work-free holiday, the train taking on his silent secret blissful release as it ran

> Behind the backs of houses, crossed a street
> Of blinding windscreens, smelt the fish-dock; thence
> The river's level drifting breadth began,
> Where sky and Lincolnshire and water meet . . .

In this description of the flat airy country south of Hull there is another 'wedding' too, in the lying together of those natural powers – sky, land, water – whose simple beauty and strength the human beings emerging from a modern urban society cannot help so comically and pathetically lacking. But the condition of attendance at this other wedding is the solitude of the observer: who is permitted a vision of how things come together only by virtue of seeing precisely how they glitter apart ('a hothouse flashed uniquely'). This 'unique' perception is indissociable from the understanding of human loneliness; and it ushers in with its sympathy the central stanzas of community and togetherness so hopefully attempted, as it also foreshadows the dying-fall sadness of the poem's gathered-in ending. Rain begins; London arrives; the journey is over; Eden closes. That the even finer 'Here' is similarly no simple landscape poem may be suggested by the technical, but in effect highly potent, detail of its being framed as one enormous driving twenty-eight-line syntactical unit, a single sentence, followed by brief coda-like additions ('Here leaves unnoticed thicken,/Hidden weeds flower . . .'). This great sentence unifies what might be seen from a train window into a figure of insistent will and energy ('Swerving . . . swerving') parallel to those desires of the human 'cut-price crowd' that throngs the busy city with the flat brilliant images that fill the central stanzas of 'Here'. But it is a profound irony of the poem, usually described as being 'about' the city in question, that this unrelenting steady sentence takes the traveller in fact from solitude to solitude, from silence to silence: from the beginning in the 'solitude of skies and scarecrows' to the moment at the end where the train stops, and the land stops, and the poem stops, and life begins: 'Facing the sun, untalkative, out of reach'. As topographical poem, 'Here' creates a magnificent new image that re-sites the busy city at its apparent heart, between the intense aloneness of natural life and the golden edge of the void itself: experience located within a field of being not found in most atlases or gazetteers.

Poems like 'Here' and 'The Whitsun Weddings' have – as their titles suggest – a perfectly clear 'literal' sense, an allusion to time and place, that may be a little ironical but that is a part of their meaning. To propose a further meaning is merely to extend the levels on which we read. The poems in *High Windows*, Larkin's most recent volume, may not be 'extended' in this way; for in them the literal and the metaphorical approach an absolute identification. The volume is the 'simplest' on the poet's own terms, governed by an art far more tacit and intrinsic than that of the earlier volumes, and each clear poem bears resemblances to a symbol that are

remarkably difficult to define articulately. In short, Larkin's Edens
are here most absolute. This volume, which is surely by far the
poet's best – with a great strength and subtlety and originality – at
the same time foxes and repels criticism as does no other recent
poetry, certainly none that possesses Larkin's lucid and courteous
rationality. So deeply is meaning embodied in form and style that
quotation is far easier than commentary; but so coherent and self-
consistent is the work that quotation damages the aesthetic object
to a surprising degree.

This very difficulty however is in itself of interest: it carries its
own meaning, directing the attention as it does to the 'simple', the
self-contained, the way a thing 'shows' its own meaning: 'by their
fruits ye shall know them'. 'Cut Grass' sculpts out the form and
image of summer according to the slow fading and sweet-scented
brevity of summer's own cut grass: a decline so intrinsic and so
beautiful as to make the white June flowers that fill the poem's
twelve short lines seem incomparably solid ghosts of themselves, as
transient as

> cloud
> Moving at summer's pace.

And all the Edens in the volume are both intense and yet also
cloudy or ghostly or shadowy in this way: a kind of soul of sense.
The soul of sense reverses, in a near-miracle of half-ironic style,
into a sense of soul in the volume's last (as it were 'Victorian')
poem, 'The Explosion', which tells of a group of young miners
killed in a pit disaster; one, as they made their way to work that
brilliant morning, finding a nest of lark's eggs, and after the
explosion seeming to the survivors as if returning, walking out of
the sun, and 'showing the eggs unbroken.'

This imaginative tactility, eggshell fine and hollowed out by
unbelief, is the architecture of *High Windows*: a series of poetic
makings or showings whose unlikelihood is their solidity and their
completeness. 'Show Saturday', a poem about the kind of local fête
that contains displays of work, builds up a dazzling image of a
universe that has nothing, so to speak, to show for itself *but* shows,
being an explosive randomness that the living regularly transform
into amazing cornucopias of patient faithful making, 'All worthy,
all well done,/But less than the honeycombs'. The virtue of the
poem is its impassive, interested, packed inventiveness (as of

'Mugfaced middleaged wives/Glaring at jellies') rendered in a dense semi-monosyllabic style distantly related to Old English alliterative verse: by its nature not a style easy to quote from representatively; easier (significantly) is a moment of intermission, as

> Folk sit about on bales
> Like great straw dice. For each scene is linked by spaces
> Not given to anything much, where kids scrap, freed,
> While their owners stare different ways, with incurious faces.
> The wrestling starts, late; a wide ring of people; then cars;
> Then trees; then pale sky . . .

Within a world void of any reassuring concept, the world of sense takes on the semblance of innocence, an extraordinary steady gravity, a weighty floating-free in time and space: as the 'folk' endlessly poise on their random straw dice, and the wrestling match shines for ever against the empty sky.

A very minor part of the reason for this convincingness is the fact that poetic form embodies sense in a specific technical way: the poem contributes to a tradition, if not timeless at least very long-lasting, by envisioning the 'folk' in roughly the style and metre in which Langland envisaged *his* 'field of folk' (similarly, the vision of the young nineteenth-century miners is cast into the metre of *Hiawatha*). This is only one of the ways in which the poems of *High Windows* build up an imaginative universe, which is so self-consistent that one can, as it were, get in and wander around in it: but precisely this element of self-consistency in fact differentiates it from the real, which does not in this way 'hang together'. The very *unreality* of this poetic world, its beautiful hollowness and the severe limits to the kind of reassurance it can give, are really the solid terms which give poet and readers a meeting-place, like the 'great straw dice' on which 'folk sit'.

This tacit agreement certainly functions in the volume's opening poem, 'To the Sea', which celebrates the still not quite dead English tradition of the family seaside holiday; but it affords too its own holiday or Eden-like pleasure, which is to find existence simplified to the ravishingly pragmatic, to a world of sense-experience where time and space are simultaneously comprehensible as Here and Now, and memories of the past and apprehensions of the future become as clear as water and as soft as sand:

> The small hushed waves' repeated fresh collapse
> Up the warm yellow sand, and further off
> A white steamer stuck in the afternoon . . .

> The same clear water over smoothed pebbles,
> The distant bathers' weak protesting trebles
> Down at its edge . . .

'To the Sea' is a world in which 'collapse' can mean advance, and 'protesting' seems to have something to do with happiness. This may be because time has turned into space, and space into a poem. A poem, like a memory, is a place where one generation after another can meet on the same shelving remembering beach one afternoon; where 'farther back' in time means only 'further off' in space; and space itself becomes uniquely tactile, apprehensible, so that an afternoon holds a steamer 'stuck' firm, a 'treble' voice is strong enough to tie 'down-there' to 'up here', and we only know that the day is dying by the fact that 'like breathed-on glass/The sunlight has turned *milky*' – light solidifying into a liquid ghost of itself, but a ghost innocent, white, goodly: only in Larkin's Eden could sunlight do just this. For this space-pervaded, hollow and yet touchingly resonant world of sense is a world of 'sense' in another sense: it has its own clear laws. The aesthetic geometry that holds it together in consistency has form – has limits; the 'low wall that divides' may be stepped over but does not fall down; the last word of the poem is *ought*. Persons in their prime here care for those at the limits, the very old and the very young. The noise of the surf and of the transistors is crossed by odd cadences from Handel's *Messiah*, and the Good Shepherd comes hand in hand with infants in plastic knickers:

> gently up and down
> Lead the uncertain children, frilled in white,
> And grasping at enormous air.

'Enormous air' gives something of its scale to the persons in these poems, where being small in a random world oddly does not make people trivial. The title of, for instance, the three-part-poem 'Livings' suggests by its colloquialism the randomness of the little lives it surveys. The three men who speak in it are nameless – are as far as is conceivable from fame, from success. History surrounds them in the form of monotonies; life is a great 'elsewhere';

existence is to be 'shelved'. Each man is merely, at different points in time and different places in England, having his dinner of an evening – that most modest, most 'literal' of occurrences. And yet the manner in which each does so is so unappalled, so orderly, as to have the effect of minutely setting back chaos. In I, somewhere between the Great War and the Great Slump a businessman of roughly our father's generation is carrying on *his* father's business with the same simple unaffected straightforwardness, 'business-likeness', with which he works through his meal 'from soup to stewed pears', then chats, then takes a walk. In II, serenely out-of-date within some permanent present moment, a lighthouse-keeper affectionately relishes his fierce universe of sea-creatures and sets out his own small meal decently, under the great light overhead that serves only to light the path of the products of a mad technology heading always west into decline. In III, two or three centuries back, at the end of a Renaissance culture that we inherit and can no longer understand, a don dines wittily, knowing that all his learning will one day seem as distant and as merely black-magical as did the arts of the Chaldeans to Old Testament Jews: as distant as the stars seemed to him then and do to us now.

In each of these three men the same intellectual consciousness takes quiet stock of its world, though in each case in a form and style appropriate to the person, as the form and style of each poem differs: each speaks to us – half to us, half to himself – with a light gravity, as 'smoke hangs under the light', or 'snow swerves', or stars 'sparkle over crowded roofs'. It is the odd, luminous weightiness of this stock-taking, this 'cherishing' of the given, that suggests another reason why the poet chose the word 'Livings'. A 'living' is the precise term for the proper ground of a rector, the owned land where he lives. Examples of the random as these poems are, they are also images of rectitude. Each man is an occasion of fidelity, of faithfulness in a calling, and it is this steadiness that in each poem seems to set back the darkness of night for a little while: as the businessman takes his evening stroll under a 'big sky . . . like the bed of a golden river', and the lighthouse-keeper muses under the guarding 'brilliance' of the lantern, and the don talks by the candleflames and firelight of Hall. A poet who has praised the 'faithfulness' of photographs in their re-creation of lost time surely himself exceeds it in these three superlative poems.

Poetry and Soda

The Penguin Book of Unrespectable Verse.
Edited by Geoffrey Grigson, 1980

The Penguin Book of Light Verse.
Edited by Gavin Ewart, 1980

Anthologies are coming from the publishers with the speed of Verey lights from a sinking ship. What could be better: six hundred pages of other men's flowers, offering relief from what Henry James is supposed on his death-bed to have attributed his wearing-out to – 'the labour of discrimination'? But the recent profusion does leave room to reflect that some anthologies are better than other anthologies, and that some subjects are better suited than other subjects to anthologies, and that some subjects are not good subjects anyway – just as anthologies are not necessarily the best form of book-making. Poems have as obstinate a life of their own as hamsters or baby pythons, and may profit as little from being gift-wrapped. Whoever edits, say, a gathering of Satirical Verse is going to have to fight the fact that *Absalom and Achitophel* or the *Dunciad* don't get better by being bound up with a few hundred other satires; and since they need the authority of their full length as well as demanding circumambient space, excerpted bits don't read at all well. Similarly, a collection devoted to that delightful and now very fashionable subject, English topography (or 'Poems and Places'), has to confront the fact that because poems are mental events, remarkably few are really topographical at all: once past 'Tintern Abbey', the anthologist will have trouble finding other good poems he likes that could truthfully be said to do more than *mention* localities.

Gavin Ewart is a very good and very readable writer of verse which, if not 'light', is not heavy either. If, therefore, his *Penguin Book of Light Verse* is less wholly pleasurable, even less admirable, than Geoffrey Grigson's now nearly ten-years-old but newly reprinted *Unrespectable Verse*, then part of the reason may be (given that the two volumes share a number of poems) that Grigson has had either the wisdom or the good fortune not to get saddled with a category as terrible as Light Verse. The concept is insensitive even if used, as most anthologists have used it, in a party-game do-it-yourself spirit like Auden's 'Alice and Mabel', by which almost anything can be made for fun to fit into one of two categories: for any anthologist worth going along with finds himself wanting to include poems that don't fit his definition, as Ewart insists on including Rochester's savage farce, the 'Ramble in St James's Park', in a collection he defines as 'playful', without 'strong emotion'. A book that was really all Light Verse would be like a ton of candyfloss. For Light Verse is not a term like 'good poetry' that can be argued about and played with at will, a useful mechanism for the release of the anthologist's talents. It is something much more like a fixed historical manifestation, something angular and actual that happened at a given place and time: the place, England (and apparently nowhere else), and the time, principally the nineteenth century.

It is noticeable that all or almost all the poems liable to provoke argument concerning their 'lightness' occur in roughly the first, or pre-1800, half of Ewart's collection. There are objections to be made, perhaps, about this or that offering in the later part of the book, but these nineteenth-century-and-after poems provoke a different kind of objection. Thus, a reader might point out that some of the second half are not *poems* in any way: Ewart's modern Rugger Song could, I suppose, just survive its sadistic obscenity, but its sheer crassness probably finishes it off as poetry. There are others, rather a lot of others, in the book's latter three hundred pages whose technical finesse makes them probably qualify as poems, but which are liable to make a reader find them not very good poems. There are, on the other hand, plenty of good poems in the first three hundred pages: they simply happen not to be *light*. This first section admirably fulfils the general function of anthologies, which is to introduce a reader to new poems or give him the pleasure of meeting old poems, looking new, in a context created by a taste and judgement both different from his own and distinctive and good in itself. Thus we have the 'Ramble in St James's Park', a fiercely comic glimpse of Restoration London by night as seen by a highly civilized but obscene, unhappy and half-mad lover –

> Much wine had passed, with grave discourse
> Of who fucks who and who does worse

– immediately followed by an anonymous love-poem in thieves'
or beggars' slang, 'The Maunder's Praise of his Strowling Mort' –

> Doxy, oh! thy glaziers shine
> As glimmars by the Salomon!

– and that, by William Walsh's namby-pamby pseudo-pastoral,
'The Despairing Lover':

> Distracted with care
> For Phillis the fair,
> Since nothing could move her,
> Poor Damon the lover . . .

The three together liven each other up splendidly, and give a real
sense of the possibilities (and impossibilities) of the period. But
once one has said this, it has to be added that neither they nor one's
sense of critical categories seem to gain anything from calling all
these 'light verse'.

The fact is, surely, that if we do call all these 'light', we merely
point to a quality inherent in the aesthetic. For (as Eliot more or less
said) *no* verse is light for the man who wants to do a good job; and
all verse is light compared to some of the things unliterary people
want to make it into. It seems probable that what we all vaguely
recognize as 'light verse' is a specific form that emerges late in the
eighteenth century as one of the effects of industrial society; and it
contained within itself an actual antipathy to the aesthetic – or, if
not an antipathy, at least an adulteration of it. The notion of
adulteration comes to mind because so much early nineteenth-
century verse has something in common with that characteristic
drink of the Regency buck, hock-and-soda-water; and light verse
thrives throughout the Victorian and Edwardian periods as, to alter
the class of the drink a little, a sort of aesthetic shandy, poetry for
people who don't really like poetry, or at least can't take it neat. It
has to have something added, like its jingling rhymes, or its jokes
and jocularities, or its knowing social references, to make it
palatable, or perhaps to make it 'true' to some new and unalterably
art-less world. It is this watered-down quality, sometimes so oddly
touching and nostalgic in its own right, as of a kind of new poetry

of the semi-poetic (or the unpoetic, even the anti-poetic), that is
strong in Gavin Ewart's nineteenth-century section, from Hood
and Praed and Calverley through Lear and Carroll and then W. S.
Gilbert on to Belloc and Chesterton. Indeed, almost all of the
book's second half is shandy, exceedingly good of its kind – but
that kind is essentially different from the real thing in the first half.
And the mixing of the two causes restlessness in the reader, for the
enforcement of the later 'lightness' back on to the earlier poetry is
an act that does not particularly harm the poems but may
boomerang back on the anthologist.

Worse: since philistinism, as it used to be called, was one of the
by-products of the industrial world that created the need for 'light
verse', the insistence that unlight poetry is light can't help but seem
philistine too, as though the anthologist were simply a tired
businessman. It has to be said that up to about 1660 or 1700 no
verse is really light because no verse is heavy: it is only when the
effects of the mid-seventeenth-century revolution and its reaction
begin to make for a wary hardening of imaginative arteries, and
moral pretension begins to grow both in answer to and as voicing
the emergence of a business ethos, that Heavy Art becomes feasible
(Romantic) and Light Art develops with it (Regency). Before this
stage, the earliest critic I can think of who holds forth about Light
and Heavy is the meddling politician Polonius. 'Tragedy, comedy,
history, pastoral, pastoral–comical, historical–pastoral, tragical–
historical, tragical–comical–historical–pastoral, scene individable
or poem unlimited; Seneca cannot be too heavy, nor Plautus too
light . . .' This tends to remove Light and Heavy, very properly,
from literature into the nonsense of power-politicians and business-
men. It is interesting that the first seventeenth-century poem that I
would concede could be called 'light', Butler's *Hudibras*, has
something distinctly Polonian about it; and this morose, mean-
spirited but energetic poem gets what aesthetic life it has only by a
kind of moonglow reflection from that anarchic 'fantastick'
Metaphysical enthusiasm which it makes it its job to destroy.

Certainly not many others among Gavin Ewart's pre-1700 or
even pre-1800 verses really ask or deserve to be called light. He
begins with some Anglo-Saxon riddles, presumably feeling that,
being both riddles and rude, these must qualify. They fit into his
admirably strong and sensible taste and it is good to have them. But
the probability is that though it may suggest 'lightness' to us now,

this riddling quality was an essential part of Anglo-Saxon poetry and merely manifested the learned ingenuity of a verse written by monks for monks. Similarly, to call medieval poems like 'Adam lay y-bounden' and Skelton's 'Merry Margaret' light is to seem to suggest that this all-too-sophisticated, even decadent culture must be, because distant, something like quaint – that Merry Margaret lived in Merrie England. And if this is true of Skelton, how much more so of Jonson's wonderfully judged, poised and (as Leavis used to say) even self-consciously 'central' poem, 'Tonight, grave sir, both my poor house and I . . .'; and of Herrick's 'A sweet disorder in the dress . . .' and 'Whenas in silks my Julia goes . . .', and of Marvell's 'Ye living lamps, by whose dear light', and even of Suckling's 'Out upon it, I have loved'. And if these are light, it is hard to know what possible definition could serve both for them and – later in the volume – also for *The Rape of the Lock* and Blake's 'The Nurse's Song', two of the century's most distinguished *serious* poems: here presumably called 'light' because one treats of women and sylphs, the other of women and children. To call all these objects of ravishing balance and proportion 'light' and so to class them with the Rugger Song is not exactly to sell the pass, but it does risk converting it to a motorway.

Once the Industrial Revolution has taken over, the anthology comes into its own. The big names of Light Verse over a hundred and fifty years or so give not merely the sense of a consistent genre, but of a surviving though nearly vanished world. One's sense of 'Englishness' hardly goes back further than the nineteenth century; and this obstinate artlessness that is sometimes antagonism to art, this often brilliantly talented and intelligent philistinism, is a vital part of it. Hence the nostalgia Praed and Lear and Chesterton can arouse for the memory of an earlier England, pre-Modernistic, unAmericanized, authentically *there*. The odd thing is that Ewart's collection reminds a reader again how very dreary that world could be, too: for much of this light verse, this semi-poetry, is profoundly and characteristically melancholy. Possibly all entertainment literature acquires this frightful dreariness if preserved long after the need it served has died; perhaps nothing will seem more doleful fifty years from now than the succulent fiction that perfectly fills a Saturday evening. Certainly if one tries to remove that remorseless and pitiable purpose to amuse that makes 'light verse' out of these poems, some of the depressingness goes away:

Carroll's 'In winter, when the fields are white' (whose desolation
gave me nightmares when I read it as a young child) just turns into
premature Wallace Stevens, as Praed's beautiful 'Goodnight to the
Season' is Regency Philip Larkin. But all Victorian and later light
verse has, I think, this pragmatic tilt to the depressing, perhaps in
this case from the absence of what Nabokov called 'aesthetic bliss',
the resolute turning-away from a wild Romanticism found neither
feasible nor desirable, yet much parodied and cold-shouldered: a
whole Continent cut off by fog.

If praise for Ewart's in fact meaty and interesting collection tends
to the grudging, the fault is Grigson's. For Geoffrey Grigson is of
course the best anthologist in the country. C. S. Lewis once
referred to himself as 'Old Western Man': by that token, Grigson
must be Old Western Man of Letters, and there can't be going to be
many more of him. The catalogue of the Bodleian Library lists 106
items under his name; and though I can't myself pretend to have
read all of these essays, poems, anthologies, editions, books on
botany, landscape and painting, even an autobiography, I have read
none the less a good many of them, of which not one is anything
but good, and some are superlative. Grigson's anthology *Before the
Romantics* (1946) probably taught me more about eighteenth-
century literature than any critical study. The more recent
anthologies, the Oxford *Satirical Verse* and the Faber *Poems and
Places*, suffer a little, perhaps, from justifiable fatigue. But
Unrespectable Verse is from the period when Grigson still brought
incomparable powers of taste and judgement, clearly matured over
thirty or forty years of always widening reading, to bear on the job
in hand: and its subject, the 'unrespectable' face of the poet, was
surely highly congenial to a writer himself about as independent as
they come. It probably says something about the success of
Unrespectable Verse that, whereas Ewart sticks (as he was possibly
asked to do) to the Oxfordish trudge through chronological
sequence, and thereby makes a reader expect of him a historical
insight he may or may not have, Grigson – who probably does
have this historical sense of literature – creates his own grouping
throughout, moving from Stevie Smith to Baudelaire to Cavafy to
Cummings to Archipoeta to Langland to Auden to Larkin to
Rochester, and never puts a foot wrong: because the anthologist
has that rare thing, an absolute sense of what a good poem is,
wherever it occurs. Again, unfair as the comparison is, it is notable

that where Ewart wrongly calls Rochester's 'Ramble in St James's Park' light, Grigson takes from this poet instead two poems that really *are* light (if anything is), 'Love a woman, you're an ass!' and 'Tell me no more of constancy' – the first a tease, meant to make a girl's hackles rise, the second social verse – and calls them both, not light, but merely unrespectable, and undermining of shallow hypocrisies. It is notable, too, that where Gavin Ewart relies – quite permissibly – on erotic or obscene verse to give shocks, Grigson knows at least ten other ways of making the hair rise – from Stevie Smith's flawless deep needlings of God and Mother to Whitman's oceanic immodesties. The result is not only a collection of beautiful poems but a book full of quite lastingly disturbing life.